W9-CRA-927

Youth Violence

Other Books in the Current Controversies Series:

The Abortion Controversy
Alcoholism
Assisted Suicide
Computers and Society
Crime
The Disabled
Drug Trafficking
Ethics
Europe
Family Violence
Free Speech
Gambling
Garbage and Waste
Gay Rights
Genetics and Intelligence
Gun Control
Hate Crimes
Hunger
Illegal Drugs
Illegal Immigration
The Information Highway
Interventionism
Iraq
Marriage and Divorce
Minorities
Nationalism and Ethnic Conflict
Native American Rights
Police Brutality
Politicians and Ethics
Pollution
Racism
Reproductive Technologies
Sexual Harassment
Smoking
Teen Addiction
Urban Terrorism
Violence Against Women
Violence in the Media
Women in the Military

Youth Violence

David Bender, *Publisher*
Bruno Leone, *Executive Editor*

Bonnie Szumski, *Editorial Director*
Brenda Stalcup, *Managing Editor*
Scott Barbour, *Senior Editor*

Henny H. Kim, *Book Editor*

CURRENT CONTROVERSIES

Cover Photo: Magnum Photos/© 1993 Bruce Davidson

Library of Congress Cataloging-in-Publication Data

Youth violence / Henny H. Kim, book editor.
    p. cm. — (Current controversies)
    Includes bibliographical references and index.
    ISBN 1-56510-811-6 (lib. : alk. paper).—ISBN 1-56510-810-8
(pbk. : alk. paper)
    1. Juvenile delinquency—United States. 2. Violent crimes—
United States. 3. Problem youth—United States. I. Kim, Henny H.,
1968–   . II. Series.
HV9104.Y6856   1998
364.36'0973—dc21   98-5784
                                                                      CIP

© 1998 by Greenhaven Press, Inc., PO Box 289009, San Diego, CA 92198-9009
Printed in the U.S.A.

Contents

Foreword   11

Introduction   13

Chapter 1: Is Youth Violence a Serious Problem?

Chapter Preface   16

Yes: Youth Violence Is a Serious Problem

Youth Violence Is Increasing *by The Public Agenda*   17
Although violent crime rates have declined or leveled off in the past
few years, rates of juvenile crime and violence have continued to rise.
The very young age of some offenders is also a matter of concern.
Moreover, juvenile violence adversely affects youths who are not
themselves involved in crime.

Young Offenders Are Committing Increasingly Brutal Crimes   20
by Cindy Loose and Pierre Thomas
Violent juvenile crime is increasing with a degree of viciousness
never before seen in American history. Many young offenders who
commit senseless and chilling acts of violence seem to feel no
remorse for the harm they do to others.

The Problem of Younger Violators Is Increasing *by Bettianne Levine*   26
Vicious acts of violence are being committed by increasingly younger
perpetrators. The legal system faces the dilemma of trying and
sentencing young people for crimes that in the past were only
committed by hardened adults. Furthermore, experts are unsure what
factors have caused the increase in youth violence and what steps
should be taken to reduce the problem.

Girls Are Becoming More Violent *by Patricia Chisholm*   33
Until recently, violence among adolescents was thought to occur
mostly among boys. However, increasing numbers of teenage girls are
committing vicious acts, including murder. These young women turn
to violence in part because of societal pressures and low self-esteem.

Weapon-Carrying in Schools Is a Growing Problem   40
by Jennifer C. Friday
As youth violence has become more prevalent, a growing number of
students are carrying weapons to school. The majority of students
who bring weapons into the classroom do so for self-protection, but
the sheer presence of these weapons appears to increase the likelihood
of violent incidents in or near schools.

No: Youth Violence Is Not a Serious Problem

Youth Violence Is Not Increasing *by the Children's Defense Fund* 49
Politicians and the media have mistakenly focused on a purported future
crisis of youth violence. In actuality, youth violence has not increased
during the past few years, and children still are far more likely to be the
victims rather than the perpetrators of crime. Concentrating on
preventing both youth victimization and juvenile crime is the most
effective way of moving toward a less violent and safer future.

The Problem of Youth Violence Is Exaggerated *by Eric R. Lotke* 54
Politicians have exaggerated the seriousness of youth violence,
creating unnecessary fear and sustaining a lack of perspective about
the current juvenile crime situation. A careful examination of
statistics reveals that youth homicides actually occur much less
frequently than the general public believes. Most crimes committed
by juveniles are nonviolent offenses.

Teens Are Unjustly Blamed for an Increase in Violence 59
by Mike Males
Fears of a surge of youth violence are based less on fact than on the
need to target one group to blame for society's ills. Just as, in the past,
various immigrant groups were labeled as potential dangers to
American society, so are teenagers now being blamed for a troubling
problem that in reality is linked to poverty and racism.

The Extent of Youth Violence Has Been Distorted *by Barry Krisberg* 65
Americans have increasingly grown afraid that the nation is in the
midst of a crime epidemic, including a rise in the number of violent
crimes committed by youths. In actuality, juvenile arrests for violent
crimes have not significantly increased, and violent crimes account
for only a small percentage of juvenile crimes. Media hysteria over
the alleged crisis has distorted the truth about the extent of youth
violence.

Chapter 2: What Causes Youth Violence?

The Causes of Youth Violence: An Overview *by Richard A. Mendel* 70
The studies of criminologists, psychologists, and sociologists have
shown that a number of different factors can contribute to a child's
propensity for delinquent behavior. Youth violence has been linked
both to environmental factors, such as dysfunctional families and
poverty, and to physiological problems, including hyperactivity.

A Lack of Moral Values Causes Youth Violence *by Don Feder* 75
Society's failure to teach children personal responsibility and a sense
of right and wrong is a major cause of the juvenile crime problem.
Compared to previous decades, today's moral climate is lax and
inconsistent, deemphasizing personal responsibility and self-restraint.
Without strong moral guidance, young people have become
increasingly violent and ruthless.

Illegitimacy Contributes to Youth Violence *by Allan C. Brownfeld*   78
  The rapid growth of the illegitimacy rate has resulted in an increase in
  single-parent families. Children in such families do not receive the
  attention and guidance they need for healthy emotional growth,
  making it more likely that they will turn to crime and other forms of
  morally degenerate behavior.

The Lack of a Structured Family Life Causes Youth Violence   81
  by Emilio Viano
  The family serves as a small but essential community that teaches children
  how to interact socially and face personal challenges. If a child's family
  life lacks a strong emphasis on structured community values, the child will
  not learn about cooperation and personal responsibility and will therefore
  be more likely to engage in deviant or criminal behavior.

Gangs Perpetuate Youth Violence *by Nina George Hacker*   87
  Many young people join gangs because they want a sense of belonging
  and protection. However, gang culture often leads members to commit
  violent acts in the name of gang loyalty. Youth gangs emphasize illegal
  money-making activities, which also frequently result in violence.

Television Violence May Cause Youth Violence   91
  by Mary A. Hepburn
  Studies conducted both by television production companies and by
  independent researchers have revealed strong evidence that a connection
  exists between viewing television violence and committing violent acts.
  Moreover, increases in a region's violence rates appear to correspond to
  the introduction of television to that area.

Many Factors Can Cause Youth Violence *by Randi Henderson*   95
  No single factor has been designated as being the main cause of youth
  violence. Instead, a variety of problems, often interconnected,
  contribute to the increase in violent offenses by children and teens.
  Some of the possible negative influences that need careful
  examination are the disintegration of family structure, drug abuse, the
  availability of guns, poverty, child abuse, and media violence.

Chapter 3: How Can Youth Violence Be Reduced?

Reducing Youth Violence: An Overview *by Craig Donegan*   106
  Prevention and punishment play roles in a variety of measures
  designed to reduce youth violence. The current trend in juvenile
  justice favors punishments such as harsher sentencing for juvenile
  criminals, but less stringent preventive measures include curfews for
  young people, school uniforms, conflict resolution programs, and
  enforcing parental accountability.

Rehabilitation Programs Can Reduce Youth Violence   115
  by Mary Dallao
  Juvenile rehabilitation programs, such as Colorado's Youth Offender
  System (YOS), attempt to rehabilitate violent youth offenders through
  military-style boot-camp orientations, academic development, and

personal growth. Although still in the early stages, these programs already have been effective for at least a few young offenders who seemed resistant to other types of preventative programs.

Reforming the Juvenile Justice System Can Reduce Youth Violence   119
by Nick Gillespie

The current juvenile justice system does not effectively prevent youth violence and crime. Measures designed to protect young offenders, such as sealing juvenile records, actually send the message that youth crime is not a serious matter. The juvenile justice system should take a stricter approach with juvenile offenders in order to impress on them the consequences of their acts. The system should also stress preventive measures and help youths learn socially responsible behavior.

Training in Conflict Resolution Can Reduce Youth Violence   122
by Kim Nauer

In a violence-ridden culture, children often learn to use violence to resolve conflicts. However, programs that teach peaceful means of conflict resolution can help young people to choose more constructive methods of dealing with anger and social tensions.

A Grassroots Peace Movement Is Reducing Youth Violence   131
by John Brown Childs

A grassroots peace movement, centered around young people, is developing constructive means for reducing youth violence. The movement focuses on peaceful solutions and critical thinking as effective replacements for punishment and repression. Furthermore, its emphasis on youth potential instead of on potential threats empowers the entire community.

Organized Youth Activities Can Prevent Violence *by Bob Herbert*   136

Lack of public school funding results in a dearth of organized after-school activities. Such programs are sorely needed, especially in the inner cities. Organized activities could keep students out of trouble after school and provide them with the supervision and support they often do not receive at home.

Giving Teachers More Control Can Reduce Youth Violence   138
by Stephen Goode

The prevalence of violence in the schools creates difficulties for students who want to learn and teachers who try to provide an education. Giving teachers more options in dealing with violent and disruptive students and holding the students accountable for destructive actions will help to reduce youth violence.

Outreach Programs Can Reduce Youth Violence *by Robert Coles*   142

Outreach programs can effectively change the lives of troubled children and teens. This far-reaching approach includes working with gang members and school dropouts, conducting home visits, tutoring, and establishing medical and legal assistance programs. Such outreach efforts reduce youth violence and crime by helping young people to visualize and prepare for a successful future.

Church-Based Programs Can Reduce Youth Violence 146
by Jean Sindab
Many churches have made a commitment to working toward the
reduction of youth violence by helping young people who are
oppressed by economic and social disadvantages. By forming a
rapport with people on the street, inviting youth to study and practice
Christianity, and establishing alternative programs to help young
people achieve educational and economic success, churches can make
a difference in the lives of troubled youth.

Chapter 4: Should Violent Youths Receive Harsh Punishment?

Harsh Punishment for Violent Youths: An Overview 154
by Fox Butterfield
In recent years, most states have changed their laws to meet the
general public's demand for harsher punishment for violent youths.
For instance, some states have passed laws increasing the number of
juvenile offenses for which youths can be tried as adults. Proponents
of such laws claim that harsher punishment is the only workable
strategy left to combat an increasingly violent juvenile population.
Critics, however, warn that punitive measures will not solve the
juvenile violence problem and may actually make it worse.

Yes: Violent Youths Should Be Punished Harshly

Juvenile Justice Needs to Be Tougher by Ed Koch 158
The increase in violent crimes committed by youth offenders must be
met with appropriate legal actions, not outdated juvenile laws. Unless
society gets tough with these serious criminals, young offenders will
not cease committing brutal acts and youth violence will continue to
be a growing threat.

Violent Youths Should Be Punished as Adults by Robert L. Sexton 161
Youths in their mid-teens are old enough to be held accountable for
their actions, yet the current juvenile justice system is overly lenient
with young people who commit violent crimes. Such offenders should
receive punishment appropriate for the seriousness of their crimes.
Trying and sentencing these young criminals as adults would send a
clear message that society will not tolerate ruthless acts of violence.

Authorities Should Have Increased Access to the Records of 166
Violent Youths by James Wootton
Juveniles' criminal records can help authorities to identify chronic
violent offenders. Access to these records is often limited, however,
and expungement laws require that juvenile records be permanently
sealed once youths reach the age of majority. Both of these factors
make it difficult for authorities to distinguish first-time offenders from
habitual criminals. To successfully combat the growing problem of
youth violence, law enforcement and judicial authorities should be
given full access to juvenile records.

No: Violent Youths Should Not Be Punished Harshly

Harsh Punishment Will Not Help Violent Youths *by Lane Nelson*   175
  Harsh laws designed to send juvenile offenders to adult prisons are
  becoming increasingly popular. Violent youth offenders, some as
  young as fourteen, are being transferred to adult prisons, where they
  are vulnerable to victimization by adult inmates. In addition, young
  people who serve time in adult prisons rather than in juvenile facilities
  are less likely to be rehabilitated and more likely to commit worse
  crimes upon their release.

Violent Youths Should Not Be Tried as Adults *by James A. Gondles Jr.* 182
  Despite the recent increase in youth violence, there is no justification
  for trying young offenders as adults. Children's violent acts indicate
  little about their own ability to make conscious choices between right
  and wrong. Instead, such acts are the outcome of society's neglect of
  its youth.

Society Should Focus on Prevention, Not Punishment *by John Allen*   185
  The prevailing belief that juvenile violence is widespread has led to
  calls for harsher punishment. However, punitive measures will do
  little to affect the societal problems that foster youth violence.
  Although stricter laws may seem to be an easier solution, the more
  effective approach would be to step up prevention measures. Society
  should make a stronger effort to give children the attention they need
  to develop into nonviolent, productive adults.

Bibliography   191
Organizations to Contact   194
Index   198

Foreword

By definition, controversies are "discussions of questions in which opposing opinions clash" (Webster's Twentieth Century Dictionary Unabridged). Few would deny that controversies are a pervasive part of the human condition and exist on virtually every level of human enterprise. Controversies transpire between individuals and among groups, within nations and between nations. Controversies supply the grist necessary for progress by providing challenges and challengers to the status quo. They also create atmospheres where strife and warfare can flourish. A world without controversies would be a peaceful world; but it also would be, by and large, static and prosaic.

The Series' Purpose

The purpose of the Current Controversies series is to explore many of the social, political, and economic controversies dominating the national and international scenes today. Titles selected for inclusion in the series are highly focused and specific. For example, from the larger category of criminal justice, Current Controversies deals with specific topics such as police brutality, gun control, white collar crime, and others. The debates in Current Controversies also are presented in a useful, timeless fashion. Articles and book excerpts included in each title are selected if they contribute valuable, long-range ideas to the overall debate. And wherever possible, current information is enhanced with historical documents and other relevant materials. Thus, while individual titles are current in focus, every effort is made to ensure that they will not become quickly outdated. Books in the Current Controversies series will remain important resources for librarians, teachers, and students for many years.

In addition to keeping the titles focused and specific, great care is taken in the editorial format of each book in the series. Book introductions and chapter prefaces are offered to provide background material for readers. Chapters are organized around several key questions that are answered with diverse opinions representing all points on the political spectrum. Materials in each chapter include opinions in which authors clearly disagree as well as alternative opinions in which authors may agree on a broader issue but disagree on the possible solutions. In this way, the content of each volume in Current Controversies mirrors the mosaic of opinions encountered in society. Readers will quickly realize that there are many viable answers to these complex issues. By questioning each author's conclusions, students and casual readers can begin to develop the critical thinking skills so important to evaluating opinionated material.

Current Controversies is also ideal for controlled research. Each anthology in the series is composed of primary sources taken from a wide gamut of informational categories including periodicals, newspapers, books, United States and foreign government documents, and the publications of private and public organizations. Readers will find factual support for reports, debates, and research papers covering all areas of important issues. In addition, an annotated table of contents, an index, a book and periodical bibliography, and a list of organizations to contact are included in each book to expedite further research.

Perhaps more than ever before in history, people are confronted with diverse and contradictory information. During the Persian Gulf War, for example, the public was not only treated to minute-to-minute coverage of the war, it was also inundated with critiques of the coverage and countless analyses of the factors motivating U.S. involvement. Being able to sort through the plethora of opinions accompanying today's major issues, and to draw one's own conclusions, can be a complicated and frustrating struggle. It is the editors' hope that Current Controversies will help readers with this struggle.

Greenhaven Press anthologies primarily consist of previously published material taken from a variety of sources, including periodicals, books, scholarly journals, newspapers, government documents, and position papers from private and public organizations. These original sources are often edited for length and to ensure their accessibility for a young adult audience. The anthology editors also change the original titles of these works in order to clearly present the main thesis of each viewpoint and to explicitly indicate the opinion presented in the viewpoint. These alterations are made in consideration of both the reading and comprehension levels of a young adult audience. Every effort is made to ensure that Greenhaven Press accurately reflects the original intent of the authors included in this anthology.

Introduction

In the past few years, shockingly violent acts perpetrated by young people have figured prominently in newspaper headlines. On the morning of May 9, 1995, a homeless man in New York City was burned alive by five youths, ranging in age from twelve to nineteen. Shortly thereafter, a three-year-old in Los Angeles was accidentally killed by gunfire when the car she was riding in with her older brother was ambushed by a gang of juveniles. The same year, a five-year-old in Chicago was thrown out of a fourteen-story building after the youngster refused to steal candy for his twelve-year-old murderers.

Such stories have added to the general public's growing fear of a rising tide of violence among today's youth. Many experts argue that statistics on teen violence lend credence to this fear. According to James Alan Fox, a researcher in demographic criminology, while the rate of murders committed by adults over age twenty-four fell 10 percent from 1990 to 1993, the rate among young adults (ages eighteen to twenty-four) rose 14 percent and the rate for teenagers jumped 26 percent. Furthermore, Fox maintains that the problem of youth violence will continue to increase. "Complacency and myopia in preparing for the coming crisis of youth crime will almost certainly guarantee a future blood bath," he warns.

Alarming statistics and heinous crimes involving young offenders have created public outcry, which in turn has driven a trend toward tougher punishment for juvenile offenders. In January 1997, President Bill Clinton addressed the public regarding the need for "keeping our children safe and attacking the scourge of juvenile crime and gangs." The president's call for "every police officer, prosecutor and citizen in America [to work] together to keep our young people safe and young criminals off the streets" reflected the vigorous push in almost all fifty states to control juvenile crime through laws never before enforced on underaged offenders. These new laws have allowed juveniles as young as fourteen to be tried in adult courts, opened juvenile hearings to the public, and given authorities access to the records of young criminals. Many consider these tough new laws to be the last recourse in stemming the tide of vicious young predators.

Others, however, argue that this emphasis on punishment over prevention is misguided and clearly not in the best interest of young people. Prevention advocates insist that the most effective means to combat youth violence is early intervention for at-risk children and teens. They propose a number of strategies, including government-funded activities after school hours and outreach to gang members. Punishment, these critics assert, is an ineffective deterrent for most young people. They cite recent research that shows that juveniles who serve time in adult prisons are just as likely to return to crime as those detained in juvenile facilities. Some commentators maintain that society favors harsh punishment out of laziness. By locking these youths away, they argue, society can avoid the hard work necessary to prevent juvenile violence or to rehabilitate young offenders. Henry Giroux, author of *Fugitive Cultures: Race, Violence, and Youth*, contends that the trend toward harsher punishment stems from "degrading [media] depictions of youth as criminal, sexually decadent, drug crazed, and illiterate." As a result, says Giroux, young people have been scapegoated and unfairly characterized as a growing threat to the public order. In reality, many critics assert, the problem of youth violence is far less prevalent and severe than the general public has been led to believe.

The debate over the most effective response to youth violence is far from resolved. Moreover, it is only one of several controversies that figure prominently in the discussion over youth violence. The following chapters of *Youth Violence: Current Controversies* examine different aspects of this ongoing debate, including the seriousness of the phenomenon, root causes of violent behavior, methods of prevention, types of intervention programs, and modes of punishment.

Chapter 1

Is Youth Violence a Serious Problem?

Chapter Preface

In April 1996, an infant was thrown out of his bassinet and beaten and kicked into a coma. The tragic fact that this baby became permanently brain damaged was overshadowed by the horrifying discovery that the perpetrator of the vicious act was a six-year-old boy. This incident greatly perplexed prosecutors, defense attorneys, and judges faced with trying such a young suspect. It also heightened the public's growing fear that violent crime is increasing at the hands of younger and more vicious predators.

Many commentators point to such troubling incidents as proof that youth violence is becoming a serious problem. For instance, the Council on Crime in America, a bipartisan commission on violent crime, has warned of a "coming storm of juvenile crime." Pointing to demographic trends that indicate that the number of fourteen- to seventeen-year-old males will increase by 23 percent by the year 2005, the council warns that "each generation of crime-prone boys is several times more dangerous than the one before it." In the logic of many concerned observers, as this population grows, the prevalence of youth violence will also rise.

While such predictions are alarming, not everyone believes that they signal a serious increase in juvenile violence. Some researchers feel that the extent of youth violence has been exaggerated. They maintain that the media and opportunistic politicians have unfairly blamed the violent crime problem on young people from economically and politically disadvantaged communities. Furthermore, they argue, recent studies have revealed that juvenile crime is actually on the decline and that the number of violent crimes among juveniles is low compared to those committed by adults. For example, the FBI reported that in 1995, the number of juvenile homicides decreased by 18 percent from the previous year. In addition, a 1997 report from the U.S. Department of Justice found that violent crime by juveniles under age fifteen had decreased significantly. Noting statistics such as these, cultural scholar Mike Males contends, "The 'crime storm' is here, but most of it is adult and much of it occurs in the home."

As different studies report varying statistics, the debate over whether youth violence is a serious problem continues. In the following chapter, authors present their opinions on this controversial issue.

Youth Violence Is Increasing

by The Public Agenda

About the author: *The Public Agenda is a nonprofit organization devoted to research and education about public issues.*

In the United States, which has long had the dubious distinction of being the most violent and crime-ridden industrial nation in the world, fear of crime is a constant concern. But even by American standards, current worries about crime are remarkable. By early 1994, polls showed that crime had risen to the top of the list of the nation's most serious problems, replacing that hardy perennial, concern about the economy.

"More than any other issue," writes Pulitzer Prize–winning journalist Haynes Johnson in his recent book *Divided We Fall*, "the growing specter of violence leads people to think that something fundamental has been broken in America. This is as true among blacks as among whites, among Asians as Latinos, among liberals as conservatives. The degree to which crime has spread comes over strongly wherever you travel in the United States. Though the core of the problem still lies in our inner cities, it is most striking—because it is not expected—in areas far removed from big city ghettos."

Wherever they live, Americans are convinced that violence is more common and more pervasive today than it was a few years ago. Consequently, they feel more vulnerable and are demanding action. In a recent NBC/*Wall Street Journal* poll, the public sent a message to elected officials: 93 percent of respondents said the first priority for Congress and the President must be to pass effective anti-crime measures.

Concern over Violent Crime

In the November 1993 elections, the public's concern about violent crime and its insistence on doing something about it was clear. In New York City, Detroit, and even Minneapolis, mayoral candidates who ran law-and-order campaigns

Excerpted from *Kids Who Commit Crimes*, a publication prepared by The Public Agenda Foundation for the National Issues Forums. Reprinted with permission.

did well at the polls. Virginia Governor George F. Allen attributed his victory primarily to his tough stance on crime.

Judging by governors' 1994 state of the state messages, many are prepared to take new measures to fight crime. California Governor Pete Wilson said, "Our streets are being stained by the blood of our children, and it's going to stop." New York Governor Mario Cuomo declared crime his top legislative priority. "Governors are sounding like tough-talking sheriffs," wrote *New York Times* reporter Richard Berke, "Again and again, they talk about cracking down on juvenile criminals."

An Increase in Juvenile Crime

There is no question that public concern about crime is driven by fear and that media accounts of sensational crimes are fanning those fears. Still, Americans have reason to be concerned. Compared to our own past and to other nations, America's crime problem is very serious. To say that the U.S. homicide rate is the highest in the world does not begin to suggest the extent of the problem or how much worse it has become. By 1992, America's crime rate was five times higher than in 1960.

Nonetheless, recent crime statistics contain some good news about American crime rates overall. In 1993, violent crime rates declined

"By early 1994, polls showed that crime had risen to the top of the list of the nation's most serious problems."

slightly. Though some two dozen cities set record high murder rates in 1993, the nation's homicide rate is slightly lower now than it was a few years ago. According to one index of crime, the Justice Department's National Crime Victimization Survey, 23 percent of American households were victimized by crime in 1992—the lowest figure since the survey began in 1975.

While the overall crime rate has leveled off, the number of serious and violent crimes committed by juveniles has increased substantially over the past few years. "Youth violence," said Attorney General Janet Reno, "is the greatest single crime problem in America today."

Startling Statistics

Wanton violence among young people is nothing new. What is startling, however, is that violent crime has become so common among juveniles. A report by Northeastern University's National Crime Analysis Program indicates that during the 6-year period from 1985 to 1991, the number of arrests for murder by 13- to 17-year-old males rose by more than 100 percent.

It is particularly disturbing that serious juvenile offenders are often very young. In 1982, 390 young teens (age 13 to 15) were arrested for murder. A decade later, the figure had increased to 740. Geoffrey Alpert, professor of criminology at the University of South Carolina, observes, "Where many young people used to start their criminal careers with minor and property crimes, we're seeing them become more violent very, very quickly." The Justice Department estimates that nearly a million young people age 12 to 19 are raped, robbed, or assaulted each year, most often by their peers.

"The only thing more remarkable than these statistics," comments Bob Herbert, "is that the violent deaths of so many young people could occur without a frenzied national outcry. Perhaps that is occurring now."

Violence Far and Wide

If you travel around the country and talk to people about crime, you hear stories, not statistics. Throughout the United States, TV news shows often begin with live coverage from a crime scene—a brutal assault, a stabbing in a local high school, a store owner robbed at gunpoint by three teenage boys. When kids commit serious crimes, it is especially newsworthy.

Not surprisingly, the high youth crime rate has brought crime into the schools. According to the U.S. Department of Education, one in five high school students recently reported carrying a weapon to school at least once in the previous month, and 16 percent said they have been threatened at school by someone carrying a weapon. Even in medium-sized cities such as Indianapolis, public school students in the sixth to twelfth grades are greeted at the door by security guards using handheld metal detectors.

The toll of juvenile violence goes far beyond those who are caught in the line of fire, however. It undermines the ability of the schools to educate students in a secure environment. As Secretary of Education Richard Riley told a national forum on juvenile violence in July 1993, "Violence in schools or among school-age youth not only destroys our country's most precious natural resource, our youth, it also creates an environment in which children cannot learn, teachers cannot teach, and parents are reluctant to send their children to school."

What is happening in the schools is part of a larger problem: the lack of safety in public spaces such as parks, playgrounds, and streets. For a decade, millions of Americans have responded to the threat of crime by installing sophisticated home security systems, organizing neighborhood "crime watch" patrols, or hiring private guards. Judging by the urgency many Americans now attach to dealing with juvenile crime, it appears many have concluded we must deal with the problem itself, not just its symptoms.

Young Offenders Are Committing Increasingly Brutal Crimes

by Cindy Loose and Pierre Thomas

About the author: *Cindy Loose and Pierre Thomas are staff writers for the* Washington Post.

Six-year-old Talonda Lanier, of Silver Spring, was curled up, sleeping, on the back seat of her mother's car when a white Ford Escort passed. Six shots rang out, echoing off a concrete underpass on Interstate 40 in North Carolina. Talonda made a whining sound and in a small sleepy voice said, "Mommy."

In the pre-dawn gloom, Saidat Lanier turned to comfort her daughter, saying, "It's okay, baby." A moment later, she glanced back again. Blood was streaming down the vinyl seat.

Talonda and the 16-year-old who passed by and shot at the car for no apparent reason suddenly had become part of what the Justice Department calls "a crisis of violence by and against juveniles."

The trend has been developing over the last decade nationally and locally, and it is now crystal clear: More children are involved in violent acts; they are killing and being killed in record numbers.

Another Casualty

Nationally, violence took the lives of 2,428 children in 1992, an increase of 67 percent in just six years. In the Washington area, 76 children were homicide victims by the last week of November 1993—55 percent more than six years earlier.

Many more young people, like Talonda, live on, although forever changed.

Talonda spent the holidays learning to walk again at the Hospital for Sick Children in Northeast Washington. The left side of her body is partially paralyzed, and she has trouble concentrating and remembering. In six months in two hospitals, she has had three brain surgeries, her head shaved each time.

She doesn't think she is pretty anymore, and she worries that she isn't smart.

"If I could put all our pain and suffering into words, it would fill a book," said Saidat Lanier, 21, an operating room technician at Walter Reed Army Medical Center in the District. "The only thing we can't change is Mother Nature, and yet we let this go on. Why? Why are we all sitting here suffering?"

The year 1993 was one in which the overall crime rate dropped, but the decade-long surge in juvenile violence continued across the nation,

> *"The children being arrested these days are 'far more damaged.'"*

challenging the very notion of childhood as a time of innocence and security.

Most of the carnage has been in neighborhoods already plagued by crime. Locally, for example, most of the deaths and homicide arrests involving juveniles have been in largely black neighborhoods of the District and Prince George's County.

Damaged Offenders

But in city neighborhoods and suburban enclaves, something is drawing youths into crime, and workers in the juvenile justice system say they are being overwhelmed by the sheer numbers. Perhaps worse, they add, the crimes show an unprecedented level of viciousness and callousness.

The children being arrested these days are "far more damaged," said Vincent Picciano, director of juvenile court services in Fairfax County.

"The victims of homicides are getting younger and younger. A larger percentage of the homicide suspects are juveniles. This is happening even as the juvenile population continues to decrease. . . . It's scary," said Michael Rand, a statistician with the Bureau of Justice Statistics.

Local and national specialists say juvenile crime started a major upswing in the mid-1980s. Available metropolitan area statistics show that since 1981, homicide arrests of juveniles have tripled. Arrests for aggravated assault have jumped 45 percent. In the last six years, there have been year-to-year fluctuations locally in juvenile arrests for homicide and aggravated assault, but the numbers have remained high.

Moreover, arrests show an incomplete picture, since some criminals elude arrest. In the District, for example, no one is arrested in four of every 10 homicides.

Juveniles were charged with 112,409 violent crimes nationwide in 1992, an increase of 47 percent in 10 years. The increase among younger children has been even more dramatic.

In 1992, 1,521 children 9 and younger were charged with murder, rape, robbery or assault, an increase of 50 percent.

More than 7,600 children 10 to 12 were charged with at least one of those violent crimes that same year—an increase of 71 percent. Among teenagers 13 and 14, the figure was 25,034, a jump of 74 percent.

Chilling Crimes

Perhaps more chilling than the numbers are some of the crimes they represent:

- On Christmas Eve in 1993, a 10-year-old boy in Chicago, left alone with eight younger children, allegedly kicked to death a year-old girl to stop her crying.
- In the District in July 1993, an 8-year-old boy was accused of killing a 12-week-old boy by swinging him against a wall and banging his head against the floor to stop his crying.
- In Virginia's rural Shenandoah Valley in September 1993, 12- and 14-year-old sisters, with the help of a 15-year-old boyfriend, killed their mother as she slept, clubbing her and then stabbing her at least 19 times. The sisters didn't want to go to the military school their mother had chosen.
- In Springfield, four teenagers in July 1993 were ordered to lie on the ground. They were kicked and beaten by five other males, some of them juveniles. One of the attackers told them to shut up and stop crying, then gave the order: "Shoot them all." A 17-year-old died, and two friends were beaten and shot. The fourth youth was severely beaten.
- A month earlier, a carload of young people were cruising the Capital Beltway, looking for a car to steal. The 17-year-old driver, spotting a Mazda RX-7, allegedly said, "That's the one I like." They followed the driver to a cul-de-sac in Fairfax County, fatally shot him in the head and drove away in his car.

A Generation Lost

To those who regularly deal with youngsters involved in violence, it often feels as if an entire generation is hopelessly lost. The frustration is heard in the voices of those who jail juveniles and of those who treat their wounds.

"I've been here only four months, and I'm tired of it already," said surgical resident John Bilello, who works at the MedStar trauma unit of Washington Hospital Center. "I just can't stand the cruelty.

"To those who regularly deal with youngsters involved in violence, it often feels as if an entire generation is hopelessly lost."

"You take their X-rays to look at a new wound and you see another bullet from an earlier shooting. You patch them up and send them home, and they come back to the clinic for follow-up care wearing their beepers."

MedStar's youngest patients tend to be 15 or 16. At Children's Hospital, where a study found 132 children had been treated for gunshot wounds between mid-1991 and mid-1992, the youngest was 2 months old. Some children were shot or stabbed more than once.

"I get so upset seeing a familiar face," said Joseph Wright, a doctor at Children's Hospital. "I wonder how many times I can see this teen come back before he comes in dead."

When Wright was a resident at Children's Hospital, in the mid-1980s, he hardly ever saw a gunshot patient. But from 1985 to 1990, the numbers increased 800 percent.

Other Numbers

Indicators less dramatic than death also tell a story: School suspensions and expulsions are soaring, as are the number of weapons confiscated in schools. Well before Christmas 1993, for example, Fairfax had 87 expulsion recommendations on record, compared with 14 in the entire 1986-87 school year.

In Prince George's County, 246 weapons were confiscated by the middle of the 1992–93 school year, double the number of the previous year. In the first four months of the current [1993–94] school year, last year's record was broken.

Meanwhile, courts have seen a huge jump in requests to charge teenagers as adults, and detention centers are overcrowded.

The District is under court order to reduce overcrowding. In Fairfax, young people are sleeping on mattresses and extra beds are shoved into rooms built for one. In the Prince George's County jail, "we've recently had 12 to 15 kids who weren't even old enough to shave yet," State's Attorney Alex Williams said.

At the bottom of all this, people in every section of the juvenile system say, is a critical lack of parenting.

"Six or seven years ago, we were almost always able to get a hold of a parent when a child was arrested," said a D.C. probation officer. "Now, we often can't reach a parent or any responsible relative, and if we do reach them, they refuse to show up in court."

> *"Specialists say many of the children involved in violence have been failed by their families, their schools and other institutions entrusted with their protection."*

William M. Jackson, a judge in the Family Division of D.C. Superior Court, said many of the children he sees "have been bounced from family member to family member, without the love and discipline and guidance that children need. They have no anchor or security. They are literally children who are raising themselves."

Federal officials estimate that 70 percent of children in juvenile court are from single-parent households. In the last 30 years, the proportion of single mothers has grown from one in 20 to one in four.

Failed Institutions

The rise in violence is mirrored by a jump in child neglect and abuse cases, which are serious risk factors for delinquency, according to John J. Wilson, acting administrator of the federal Office of Juvenile Justice and Delinquency Prevention.

Nationwide, 2.7 million children were reported to be abused or neglected in 1991. In the District, a record 2,488 new cases of child abuse were referred to court in the last 22 months—each case representing at least one child with burns or bruises, broken limbs or empty bellies.

Specialists say many of the children involved in violence have been failed by their families, their schools and other institutions entrusted with their protection. What's more, they are furious about this failure, consumed with what Lloyd Murphy, who works with juveniles, calls "overwhelming anger."

"These kids are so depressed. They are so sad. They spend so much time camouflaging, putting up a big front," said Murphy, a District contractor who houses juveniles awaiting trial. "But back that kid into a corner, and he'll kill you."

Historically, juvenile crimes are opportunistic, impulsive, reactive. The easy availability of guns has made them deadly. "You'd think that for a juvenile to kill someone there would have to be some kind of bizarre circumstances," Jackson said. "But kids kill because someone looked at them the wrong way or someone told them to shoot and they did."

A gun is often the difference between a bloody nose and a gruesome injury or death. Specialists say guns go a long way to explain the jump during the last decade in both national and local statistics for juvenile homicides and aggravated assaults, the crime category that includes shootings.

Virginia in 1994 became the first state to make it a crime for a juvenile to possess a handgun or assault weapon. In a study of convicted juveniles in the state, 70 percent of those surveyed said they had possessed a firearm at some time.

The killing and maiming of thousands of young people each year challenges hospitals, which spend an average of $14,434 for each child shot, according to research by the National Association of Children's Hospitals.

Talonda's mother doesn't have to consult bills to recount the cost of her child's care: $93,000 for the hospital in Winston-Salem; $23,000 for doctors there; $545 for a leg brace; $1,045 for the anesthesiologist; an as yet unknown amount for a more than three-month stay at the Hospital for Sick Children.

"Just one bill—$93,000" Saidat Lanier said. "Can you believe it? That's a house and a pool and a white picket fence and a yard and a dog, and I could probably even get myself a husband out of that."

Possible Solutions

The response to the carnage includes ideas for prevention and punishment. Gun control is a common theme.

Jerome Paulson, a pediatrician and associate professor at George Washington School of Medicine, said his colleagues nationwide are organizing to fight for gun control.

"Our ancestors hunted saber-toothed tigers with spears," Paulson said. "It's absurd to say humans need automatic weapons to hunt rabbits and deer and squirrels."

Other prevention advocates say the solutions lie in solving the larger social ills of unemployment, teenage pregnancy and poverty. In the meantime they urge the creation of more after-school programs and classes in parenting and conflict resolution.

Wright, of Children's Hospital, and other doctors are urging that emergency rooms be used as a "capture point for intervention." Hospitals wouldn't think of patching up suicide victims and sending them home. Likewise, some doctors say, there should be a means of addressing the symptoms that lie behind injuries caused by violent crime.

Get-tough measures also are being debated or adopted by cities across the country. In the District, Mayor Sharon Pratt Kelly has proposed allowing offenders as young as 14 to be transferred to adult court for some violent offenses. The mayor also wants to make it easier to charge older juveniles as adults.

In Maryland, murder suspects 15 and older are routinely tried in adult courts. Some prosecutors are seeking such provisions for other offenses, arguing that juvenile courts were conceived to deal with shoplifting and rock throwing, not shootings and rapes.

> *"Historically, juvenile crimes are opportunistic, impulsive, reactive. The easy availability of guns has made them deadly."*

Congress, meanwhile, is considering allowing children as young as 13 to be tried as adults if they use guns during the commission of a crime.

The two teenagers charged in Talonda's shooting last summer [1993], both of whom had prior criminal records, were charged as adults and sentenced to 15 years in prison. They will be eligible for parole in 22 months.

That makes Saidat Lanier angry, "Even in 15 years, my child will still be handicapped," she said.

Lanier said no one can imagine how hard it is to work all day, come home to care for a 4-year-old daughter and also respond to the needs of Talonda in the hospital.

"Only my love of Jesus and of my children gets me through," she said.

On the day the two teenagers responsible for her daughter's injuries were sentenced, Lanier addressed them in the courtroom.

She told them about the moments after the shooting, when she frantically drove unfamiliar streets, looking for a hospital, as her 12-year-old sister, Adrienne, crawled from the front into the back seat, taking off her shirt and holding it to Talonda's head to try to stop the bleeding.

"I told them how it must have felt for a 12-year-old to see her niece bleeding half to death," Lanier said. "I told them I had to watch my child in a coma, with breathing tubes, and doctors telling me they didn't know whether she'd live or not.

"I told them that every day, my daughter was fighting to regain her life, and I was fighting every day to keep my sanity."

The teenagers, she said, "just sat there and looked at me." She saw no sign of remorse. "I would have felt better if I'd seen a tear," Lanier said. "That, at least, would have been something."

The Problem of Younger Violators Is Increasing

by Bettianne Levine

About the author: *Bettianne Levine is a staff writer for the* Los Angeles Times.

Four 15- and 16-year-olds were arrested in September 1995 in Lake Tahoe for what police call the "thrill shooting" of a 59-year-old man who was on a morning stroll when the youths, "looking for someone to scare," pumped four bullets into him.

A 14-year-old checked into a Costa Mesa motel in August 1995 with his girlfriend, also 14, after the boy allegedly murdered a 63-year-old retiree so he could steal his 1987 Dodge.

A 12-year-old and two other youths are charged with kidnapping a 57-year-old Pomona man and shooting him to death in August 1995, after taking a joy ride in his Toyota while he pleaded for his life.

Two girls, ages 13 and 15, are charged with beating a 32-year-old woman to the ground on Crescent Heights Boulevard in West Hollywood, then trying to steal her purse and her Mercedes on July 31, 1995.

A 15-year-old from Thousand Oaks is accused of murdering the 16-year-old son of a Los Angeles police detective in a suburban back-yard attack in May 1995.

Five Tustin youths, ages 15 to 17, have been charged in the May 1995 slaying of a 14-year-old who tried to reclaim the $2,500 stereo system his grandfather had given him.

That's just a few weeks' worth of juvenile crime stories noted in the *Los Angeles Times*. It is far from a complete list—and it is not just a Southern California phenomenon.

An Increase in Kiddie Crime

All around the country, tales of what might be called kiddie crime seem to take more and more space that was once filled with stories of more adult felons—that is, anyone over the age of 18.

It is not a media mirage: Statistics confirm that more horrendous crimes are being committed by increasingly younger children.

Although nonviolent crime committed by juveniles has dropped reassuringly in the past 10 years, the number of murders, robberies, rapes, kidnapings and other violent acts committed by juveniles has risen to new highs.

Between 1984 and 1992, the number of homicide suspects *under the age of 15* increased by 50%, according to the FBI.

An analysis of data in California cities showed that homicide arrest rates for juveniles were increasing faster than for any other age group. Between 1980 and 1990, the homicide arrest rate for youngsters ages 10 through 17 increased 65%.

Causes Are Difficult to Pinpoint

Even criminal experts do not agree on the causes of this increased mayhem— or on how to reverse the tide.

Poverty, crime-ridden neighborhoods, ineffective schools, parents addicted to drugs or alcohol are the traditional supposed causes of juvenile crime in the inner cities. But those causes do not explain the increasingly violent crimes committed by youths in more privileged areas, where people have more money and families are presumably a bit more intact.

"It used to be that you expected crime in some places and in other places you felt safe. Now it's quite similar everywhere," says Peter Greenwood, head of the Criminal Justice program at the Rand Corp. and a member of the state's juvenile justice task force.

"It's increasingly clear that everyone's kids are at risk—not just the kids of South-Central."

While academics still debate the

> *"Statistics confirm that more horrendous crimes are being committed by increasingly younger children."*

causes of juvenile crime and how to rehabilitate those who commit it, law enforcement officials and angry citizens are faced with more urgent immediate concerns: How should the legal system treat children who commit acts that, until very recently, were committed only by hard-core criminal adults?

Juvenile Justice Is Changing

Increasingly, the national urge is to remove the young felons from society for as long as possible, to mete out adult-style punishment for adult-style crimes.

Juvenile offenders have traditionally been tried in juvenile courts, where the emphasis is on rehabilitation rather than punishment and the court considers the "best interests of the minor" above all else.

That is changing rapidly. Many states have already reduced the age at which juveniles can be tried as adults.

Colorado, for example, recently passed a law that permits 14- to 17-year-olds to be tried as adults in cases of violent crime.

In January 1995, California followed suit. It lowered the age at which juveniles can be tried as adults from 16 to 14, if accused of any of 29 violent crimes—a list to which the Legislature keeps adding.

Harsher Punishment

Although youths under 18 still cannot receive the death penalty in California, those as young as 14 can now be sentenced to a lifetime in prison without possibility of parole.

Juvenile crime prosecutors have clamored for this.

"One function of a prosecutor is to protect the public and prevent law-abiding citizens from becoming victims," says Laura Priver, deputy district attorney in charge of the Sylmar juvenile division. "The other concern is to rehabilitate juveniles who commit crimes. Both concerns have to be balanced."

But if a juvenile commits a violent crime such as robbery with a hand gun, Priver says, then "there is nothing the juvenile justice system can offer him; we need to protect society by treating the offender as an adult."

"How should the legal system treat children who commit acts that, until very recently, were committed only by hard-core criminal adults?"

Tom Higgins, head of the District Attorney's juvenile division for the southern part of Los Angeles County, says he tends to "agree with state legislators" that youths who commit serious crimes should not be given lenient treatment just because they are young.

"The victim is just as dead, even if a 15-year-old killed him. The family feels the loss exactly the same. The age of the perpetrator doesn't change the nature of the crime."

Or, increasingly, the nature of the punishment.

If there were a proven method of rehabilitating young offenders, it might be easier to argue against imprisonment. But after decades of trial and error, there is still no agreement on either the causes or the cures of juvenile crime.

Many experts point out that we are talking here about a very small percentage of the juvenile population, that the great majority of youngsters never commit a serious crime—although about half of all juveniles have at least one brush with the law in their teen-age years.

Once Is Enough

Studies show that 30% to 40% of all boys growing up in urban areas of the United States are arrested before their 18th birthday. Most of those will never be arrested again.

Higgins refers to an Orange County study that shows 70% of all juveniles who've had one arrest are not arrested again. About another 20% of those commit two or three crimes and do not get rearrested.

These figures seem to be true nationwide, the experts say—and there are interesting ramifications to the findings.

Says Higgins: "This means that up to 80% to 90% of all kids who are arrested and must appear in court say to themselves, 'Whoa, I'm not going to go through that again.' Not because they got any kind of rehabilitation from the court, but because the experience was life-changing for them.

"On the other hand, there is about 8% to 10% of kids who seem to be unreachable, at least once they've embarked upon serious crime."

The Nature of Juvenile Crime Evolves

But Higgins and other experts have some less calming observations as well. Over the last two decades, the nature of juvenile crime has changed.

Whereas the prime source of illegal income for minors used to be stealing, now it is selling drugs.

And whereas illegal firearms were not easily available to 12-year-olds just a few years back, guns can now be obtained in any neighborhood by almost any youngster who has a yen for one.

And with juvenile crime increasingly violent and widespread—in urban, suburban, poor and middle-class neighborhoods—it seems possible that the low percentage of juvenile repeat offenders may rise.

"The victim is just as dead, even if a 15-year-old killed him. The family feels the loss exactly the same."

There are those who say this whole emphasis on punishment and pragmatism is a doomed venture, almost guaranteed to cause us more trouble from our children in the future.

How many juvenile boot camps and detention facilities can we build, they ask?

How many young lives can we throw away because we believe that, after committing one major crime, a 14-year-old must be sent away for life?

Young People Can Be Salvaged

"I deeply feel that there are very few 12- or 14-year-olds who are unsalvageable," says Clyde Crohnkhite, former police chief of Santa Ana, deputy chief of the Los Angeles Police Department, director of the Center for the Administration of Justice at the University of Southern California (USC), and now chairman of the department of law enforcement and justice at Western Illinois University in Macomb, Ill.

"I have found again and again that adults who commit serious, habitual, violent crimes cannot be changed easily if at all. But young people, in varying degrees, can definitely be changed. They are in a learning mode."

Unless they are sociopaths, Crohnkhite says, youngsters have the ability to rearrange their priorities and goals.

"Sociopaths—which constitute less than 1% of the population—don't feel remorse, aren't concerned if they hurt others and live only for today," he says.

Children Without Purpose

"I once did a study to find common denominators between children who commit crimes from well-to-do and from socially deprived homes," Crohnkhite says.

"All children from both sets of homes felt they had no purpose in society, felt they weren't important to their parents, had no strong parental supervision. They had low self-esteem.

"A recurring point made by both sets of juvenile offenders was that no one was home when they came home from school. No one to complain to, or to brag to about the day they'd had; no one to supervise their activities," Crohnkhite says. "We heard this from kids of rich parents as well as poor parents."

Crohnkhite recently returned from a crime conference in Geneva, which has a population of 400,000.

"They had three homicides last year, and very little juvenile crime. They attribute this to the fact that they are on a European system where most businesses are closed between 1 and 4 in the afternoon. Parents are indeed at home when the children get out of school, which seems to make a difference."

Crohnkhite and others say kids "come home to TV sets, where they see things they can't have and shouldn't do. Combine this with the easy availability of handguns," and teen-agers' natural desire to stir up excitement, and we have a ready-made prescription for disaster.

Biochemical Factors

Since no definitive answers have yet been found by sociologists, criminologists or educators, Crohnkhite favors a closer look at possible biochemical imbalances.

"Medical researchers have found that monkeys who are violent lack a chemical in the blood called seratonin. They have also found, that children with low self-esteem have low levels of seratonin. Maybe we ought to work with the medical profession to help these kids. It would be better than what we do now."

"We have epic numbers of kids locked up . . . and yet they continue to kill."

Forrest Tenant, M.D. and Ph.D., a public health specialist who heads a chain of 29 drug treatment facilities in California, has formulated "a whole bunch of theories" about preventing teen-age crime.

"We need new ideas because the juvenile problem is immense. Science is going to have to dig in and come up with something that might help," he says.

"Self-esteem is absolutely chemically based. One's degree of motivation is also activated by biochemicals. I know of no one who has assayed these children's nutritional histories, or measured the vitamins, minerals, amino acids and various nutrients in their bodies. It is these substances that allow the body to make seratonin, which gives a person a feeling of motivation and self-worth."

"You test a successful athlete and he has very high degrees of seratonin because he eats properly. You test a gang member or a juvenile offender or a drug addict, and they have almost none. Problem kids eat tremendous amounts of carbohydrates—

> *"When it comes to juvenile crime, frankly nobody in the country and nobody in the world has the answer."*

pasta, breads, cereals—when they should be having 50% protein. Where's the beef, pork, veggies, eggs, cheese? It's not in their diets. This is not conducive to good mental health."

The System Is Also Responsible

Vincent Schiraldi, founder and executive director of the Center on Juvenile and Criminal Justice, a public policy think tank in San Francisco, disagrees with current trends.

"The diagnosis is that we've been too lenient [with delinquents] thus far. We should try them like adults. But California has not been lenient. We have the highest juvenile incarceration rate in the country—twice the national average. Kids here serve more time for every category of crime than adults—except for murder one and two. We have epic numbers of kids locked up here and yet they continue to kill.

"We should start holding the system accountable. If two out of three Toyotas broke down within a year of coming out of the factory, Toyota would be out of business. But if two out of three kids coming out of juvenile institutions reoffend, we build bigger juvenile institutions."

Schiraldi believes juvenile offenders can become solid citizens.

Children Deserve More Concern

Abu Qadir Al-Amin, now director of the supportive living program at the Center, was once on Death Row. He says: "At 14 I was considered incorrigible; at 15 I served nine months at a boot camp near Sacramento," after which he accidentally shot a man to death. "It was a petty theft. I had a gun, and a chain of events occurred that was not planned. I ended up on Death Row for two years and four months until the death penalty was declared unconstitutional."

Al-Amin says our society does not treat its children with the concern and constructive assistance they deserve. And it does not treat all children equally. Some are considered potential criminals before they ever break the law, he says, just because of their race or economic standing.

31

Donald Fuller, director of the Delinquency Control Institute at USC, sums it up.

"Rehabilitation is pretty much out of favor as a concept for juvenile offenders. Now the theory is that they'll learn if you lock them up for long enough. There are obvious problems with that. The criminal justice system has no resources to rehabilitate anyone. But all the existing theories have flaws. When it comes to juvenile crime, frankly nobody in the country and nobody in the world has the answer."

Girls Are Becoming More Violent

by Patricia Chisholm

About the author: *Patricia Chisholm is a staff writer for* Maclean's, *a Canadian news magazine.*

The waterfront park where Reena Virk was viciously beaten and left to drown looks like a Canadian dream: clumps of trees dot one shore, while attractive middle-class homes line the opposite bank. Residents of Saanich, just north of Victoria, know the place as a handy getaway for jogging, boating and family outings. But like many suburban parks across the country, it has two faces. After dark, it becomes a haunt for restless local teenagers looking for a place safe from prying adult eyes. Here, kids can engage in the typical rituals of an adolescent Friday night—exchanging gossip, smoking, maybe having a drink or making out—usually without incident. So it probably wasn't surprising that the 14-year-old Virk agreed to go off to the park with a couple of acquaintances on the night of Nov. 14, 1997, even though she had been in a nasty fight with some of their friends slightly earlier. On that occasion, another teenage girl stubbed out a lit cigarette on Virk's forehead, apparently over suspicions that the Grade 9 student had spread rumors about her. "She very much wanted to belong with the cool kids," recalls her friend Molly Pallmann. "That's because a lot of kids would bug her—I would see her crying in the hallways. Unfortunately, that led to her being killed. She was a sweet kid."

The horror of what happened next has sent shock waves across the country and attracted attention as far away as Sweden. Although some of the details remain unknown, it is clear that Virk was lured to the park at about 10 p.m. by two teens she met while hanging out at a convenience store a few blocks away. Once out of sight of passers-by, she was set on and so viciously kicked and beaten that she suffered multiple fractures, including fractured arms and a broken neck and back. According to a sister of one of the accused, she cried out, "Help me, I love you," during the assault. When her partly submerged body

Reprinted, with permission, from Patricia Chisholm, "Bad Girls," *Maclean's*, December 8, 1997.

was found more than a week later, a few hundred metres from where she was attacked, a few scraps of underwear was all that remained of her clothing.

Why Are Girls Committing More Violence?

Eight teenagers aged 14 to 16—seven of them girls—now face charges ranging from second-degree murder to aggravated assault, and Canadians are asking themselves some painful, seemingly unanswerable questions. Why was a young girl, with no history of violence, viciously murdered, allegedly by her peers? Why is violence among young girls sharply on the rise? And what, if anything, can be done to halt the trend? Sibylle Artz, Director of the School of Child and Youth Care at the University of Victoria and author of *Sex, Power & the Violent School Girl*, believes that too often, such cases are dismissed as the actions of a few bad eggs from dysfunctional families. But the behavior of many young girls, Artz suggests, is being twisted by profound cultural pressures their parents barely understand. Pressures to be sexy, to be popular—to be powerful. And when conventional methods of achieving those goals fail, more and more girls are turning to violence. "They are taking the attitude that the way to reach power is by being like males," Artz says. "If they can't get what they want, they become enforcers for the group. It's an ugly and painful thing."

That, many Canadians might respond, is an understatement. While the overall numbers remain small compared with boys, police are charging vastly more girls with violent crimes than they did 10 years ago. Since 1986, two years after the Young Offenders Act became law, assault charge rates for girls in British Columbia alone have more than tripled, rising to 624 in 1993 from 178 that year. And while not all experts agree that more crimes are actually being committed—some argue that public concern over youth crime is pushing officials into making more arrests—many say there is little doubt that common and aggravated assaults are on the increase. "Except for murder, I'm convinced that things have gotten worse," says Ray Corrado, a professor at Simon Fraser University's School of Criminology. "The context of the violence has also changed. It's more random, more vicious—and it's not just in the bad parts of town."

> *"When conventional methods of achieving [popularity and power] fail, more and more girls are turning to violence."*

Visibility and Unpredictability

Corrado cautions against jumping to the conclusion that violence among young girls is widespread. The vast majority do what young girls have always done: attend school, pursue hobbies, flirt—without getting into fights. And even among the minority who are violent, murder, Corrado notes, "is still incredibly rare." But he says there is a visibility—as well as an element of unpredictability—to teenage crime that can create a strong sense of intimidation among teens themselves. Often, such crimes occur or germinate in highly public places such as transit stops, 24-hour convenience stores, parks and malls. When tensions rise—among girls, a fight can be ignited by as little as a slight over appearance or competition for a boy—things can get out of hand very quickly. "It starts with kicking and punching and they all want to be part of it," Corrado says. "Then they panic."

"While the overall numbers remain small compared with boys, police are charging vastly more girls with violent crimes than they did 10 years ago."

Often, the fever seems to rise because of boys. To a chilling degree, many very young girls are desperate to be mated. Sue Johanson, a Toronto-based television sex therapist, has found that young girls are becoming much more aggressive in the pursuit of boys, inundating them with calls, letters, whatever it takes to get their attention—but with decidedly mixed results. "I have more guys say to me that the only reason they had sex was because a girl came on like blockbusters and it was the only way to get rid of her," Johanson says.

Violence—a Part of Adolescent Life

They go by their "mall" names of Fila, Crystal and Kat, and violence is something they accept as part of adolescent life. All three have scars on their wrists from suicide attempts; each talks about the importance of control in lives that, for the most part, are clearly out of control. The three hang out at The Storefront, a drop-in centre in the Marlborough Mall in northeast Calgary that offers counselling, job placement help and family services, as well as a place where kids can shoot pool, play a few arcade games and watch TV.

"There's a pretty big reason for violence among girls," says Fila, 15. "It's got to do with dominance and what you believe is yours. Usually it comes down to our boyfriends. First you threaten—'Don't touch him or I'll kill you.' And if that doesn't work you fight." Crystal, 16, and Kat, 15, say that clothes are also a flash point. There is even a hierarchy of most desired brands—Nike, Fila and Adidas. Kat says clothes matter because they reflect status and membership. "It's about belonging. You want to be part of a group, a gang. It's like your family," says Kat, who is in Grade 10. As for violence, Crystal says, "people don't listen if you say it nicely, so you have to put it bluntly and threaten them. And if that doesn't work, what comes next is to fight."

Fila, Crystal and Kat all profess the same tastes when it comes to music and movies. They love rap: their favorite singers are Puff Daddy, Mase and the recently murdered Tupac Shakur. "We like the black men and the words. They've got perfect bodies and they've got attitude," says Fila. "Yeah, and they're half-naked," adds Crystal. "They're risky. They've got this I don't care attitude, I'll just be who I am." The same kind of tastes are reflected in the movies they like, all based on gang life, such as *Gang Related*.

The Level of Threats Is Increasing

Although statistics in Calgary show no growth in the total number of violent crimes involving young girls, police say the level of threats and violence is increasing. On Nov. 21, 1997, a group of five 15- and 16-year-olds confronted four other girls between the ages of 12 and 14. Two of the younger girls were assaulted at a transit stop, one punched in the face and the other threatened that she would be thrown from the train platform if they did not give up their jackets—one a Nike, the other Le Château. As of Oct. 31, 1997, there had been 16 violent offences involving adolescent girls during the year. In 1996 during the same period, there were 22, and in 1995, only seven. "There clearly is more violence being shown by young girls than was the case years ago," says Staff Sgt. Dan Dorsey. "I left the streets in 1988 to work major crime, and when I came back this year, I could see there are far more female young offenders than was the case 10 years ago."

> *"Young girls are becoming much more aggressive in the pursuit of boys, inundating them with calls, letters, whatever it takes to get their attention—but with decidedly mixed results."*

Adolescent Girls and Self-Esteem

Dominance, control and the sanctity of the group: they are powerful motivators. And for adolescent girls, who often suffer a calamitous drop in self-esteem with the onset of puberty, a punch-up or two may seem like a small price to pay for being part of the gang. Seventeen-year-old Jaime Denike, who attends Gladstone Secondary School in east-end Vancouver, says that among teenage girls there is strength in numbers. "In a lot of instances, it will be one girl against one girl, but all their friends will end up getting involved," she says. Adds 15-year-old Zoe Verbauwhede: "Every single thing becomes a big deal." The Gladstone students agree that problems between teenage girls often arise from the intense need to conform. "In school, nobody can really be themselves," Verbauwhede says. "They'll be left out. So people try to act cool." Some teachers and students have been trained in conflict resolution techniques, contributing to a relatively safe environment at Gladstone, but the girls also say their is still an unwritten code not to snitch on peers—much like many of the Saanich students who did not report Virk's murder despite widespread rumors. "No one wants to be a rat," Denike explains.

For those who are inescapably different, life at school can mean unrelenting misery that eventually deteriorates into habitual violence. Marie, 16, speaks bitterly of the Oshawa, Ont., school where she was harassed from the age of 8 because of her thick glasses and short, round body. Such treatment can be particularly devastating for vulnerable kids, like Marie, who come from troubled families and have spent time in foster care. For the past four months [of 1997], she has spent many hours each day wrapped in a mangy sleeping bag, sitting on Yonge Street outside the Evergreen teen drop-in centre in Toronto's downtown core. Although she is five months pregnant, most nights she perches over hot air grates on city streets: she has been kicked out of all the local shelters because, as she says, her "roommates would start fights and I'd finish them."

Although Virk appears, at least on the surface, to have been a fairly normal schoolgirl, there are hints that she was caught in a similar, downward spiral of plummeting self-esteem. Some of her friends have acknowledged that she was self-conscious about her weight, and others have pointed out that she chafed under the rules of her parent's household—both are Jehovah's Witnesses of East Indian origin. About a year ago, she ran away from home and was placed in foster care. And earlier in 1997, her father Manjit Virk was charged with two sex offences against his daughter and one count of uttering threats. All three charges were stayed in August 1997 and the teen later recanted; her family said the charges were false, made by their daughter in an attempt to gain more freedom by being relocated to a foster home.

Girls Should Not Receive Special Treatment

Many prosecutors and social scientists caution against easier treatment for girls than boys. Halifax Crown attorney Catherine Cogswell has become impatient with such an approach. "What's facing the system is how to get out the message that violence is wrong and not to deal with girls with kid gloves," she says. "I have seen parents, police officers, social workers and judges be more lenient because the case involves a girl. I have walked away and thought, really, this is sexist."

> *"For adolescent girls, who often suffer a calamitous drop in self-esteem with the onset of puberty, a punch-up or two may seem like a small price to pay for being part of the gang."*

A sampling of Halifax-area cases vividly demonstrates the casual viciousness girls are capable of. In one incident, Cogswell recalls, a teenager stabbed her friend with a knife, puncturing her lung. By the time they got to court, neither could remember what the fight was about. And in 1996, when four boys gang-raped a classmate, a group of teens—including girls—stood by cheering. At the trial, one girl referred to the attack as "no big deal." According to her, "these things happen at school all the time."

Remorseless Girls Copy Violent Boys

Whatever the reasons, some teenage girls clearly are experiencing acute—at times uncontainable—levels of anger and are showing far more willingness to strike out. Researchers and clinicians are also discovering a chilling lack of empathy among young girls—a quality that, until recently, appeared to be more common among adolescent boys. Miriam Kaufman, a Toronto pediatrician and author of *Mothering Teens: Understanding the Adolescent Years*, says many girls she counsels seem devoid of even a basic moral sense. "It's as if right and wrong are not even part of their experience or vocabulary," she says. Such detachment appears to have been very much present among some of those charged in Virk's death: according to the mother of one of the accused, her daughter is a habitual troublemaker utterly lacking in remorse. "If you don't like this person, beat them up. Whatever you want you can have," she says, describing her daughter's mentality.

Trapped in Gender Stereotypes

According to June Larkin, a professor of women's studies at the University of Toronto who was also an elementary schoolteacher for 20 years, girls still feel trapped in gender stereotypes, despite 30 years of feminism. Many formal barriers to women may be down, she points out, but support for girls in nontraditional roles still remains weak. The result, she says, is that "if girls can't get equal, they'll get even." That attitude may pervert the notion of true equality, but it is hardly surprising, Larkin adds. "With few other

> *"Many prosecutors and social scientists caution against easier treatment for girls than boys."*

options, it's to be expected that some girls will adopt the violent behavior of dominant boys," Larkin says. She notes, however, that such tactics are almost always used against other girls. Boys, she says, are far more difficult to overpower and, in general, are impervious to insults. Girls, on the other hand, are deeply enraged by verbal attacks. Ironically, she notes, sexual put-downs, like "slut" or "whore"—the traditional language of sexism—are particularly popular with violent girls.

Parents Need to Wake Up

But according to many who work with distressed young girls, there is another, equally disturbing reason for their growing love affair with violence: parental neglect. Carey MacLellan, an Ottawa lawyer who frequently defends female young offenders, believes that parents must take much more responsibility for their children. Starting with the current obsession over clothes—wearing the right, usually high-priced jacket or shoes—parents should stop encouraging children to conform to peer ideals that are based on money. "There is a real nexus now between the clothing, gang behavior and crime," MacLellan says. "I think parents have to take responsibility for that—they are the ones paying for it." MacLellan also faults adults for failing to set limits, often rationalizing that they have no way to exert authority over their kids: "I have children calling their mother 'bitch,' and the parents just sit there. I have to walk away." MacLellan is also deeply concerned about the nonchalance he sees in many teens. "These kids, no matter what their behavior, have no fear of repercussions, none."

They may not, but many of the 800 people who packed a memorial service for Reena Virk certainly did. During his remarks at the service, Witness elder Richard Toews called Reena's death an "incomprehensible tragedy." The brutal slaying, he added, is a reminder that big-city crime can just as easily lurk in smaller cities like Victoria, no matter how blissful they appear. And that is a warning that might well be sounded in almost any community across the country.

Weapon-Carrying in Schools Is a Growing Problem

by Jennifer C. Friday

About the author: *Jennifer C. Friday is an assistant professor of psychology at Morris Brown College and a behavioral scientist at the National Center for Injury Prevention and Control, both in Atlanta, Georgia.*

Violence among young people is a growing problem in communities across America, taking a substantial toll in loss of life, physical and mental injury, and economic costs. The problem of violence in society is being brought into the school rooms around the country.

Young people are disproportionately represented both as victims and as perpetrators of interpersonal violence in the United States. Teenagers are more likely to be victims of violence than are persons in any other age group. The Bureau of Justice reports that 37 percent of the violent crime victimizations of youths ages twelve to fifteen years occur on school property.

Weapon-Carrying Is Becoming More Common

Weapon-carrying in schools reflects easy access to weapons in the community, their presence in many homes, and the apparently widespread attitude in American society that violence is an effective way to solve problems. Violence and weapon-carrying in schools also reflect the personal attitudes of students and their families. About one-half of the students in a New York City school survey reported that their families supported hitting back when hit and defending themselves if they have to, even if it means using a weapon. In another study of attitudes, nearly 40 percent of parents said they would tell their children "if someone attacked them, they should defend themselves, even if this means using a weapon."

Although weapons in schools is probably not a new phenomenon, few data are available to provide information about the magnitude of the problem and how it has changed over the years. It is perceived that more weapons are being brought to school, that they are increasingly lethal, and that more young people are being injured or killed because of them. On the basis of anecdotal evidence, opinion surveys, and news reports, gun-related incidents in schools appear to have risen over the last few years. Reports of weapons use appeared as early as 1978, in the first studies about victimization in schools. In 1986 about 20 percent of the personal victimizations in schools involved a weapon. Another trend is toward younger victims and perpetrators. . . .

The Prevalence of Fighting and Weapon-Carrying

Estimates of fighting and weapon-carrying in schools vary. The available studies have used a variety of methods, with varying student populations. Some are national studies, and some are limited to individual states or individual school districts. A number of studies have used questions from the Youth Risk Behavior Survey (YRBS) conducted by the Centers for Disease Control and Prevention (CDC). Those cited in this viewpoint represent the core of studies that have looked systematically at fighting and weapon-carrying in schools.

> *"Weapon-carrying by teenagers appears to be a frequent occurrence, according to studies."*

Fighting among students appears to be fairly common. Studies suggest that about one-half of all high school students have been involved in a physical fight, with a much smaller proportion reporting fighting on school property. In New York City, during the 1991–1992 school year, 21 percent of all physical fights involving public high school students occurred in school, 31 percent occurred while traveling to or from school, and 48 percent were unrelated to school.

CDC's 1993 Youth Risk Behavior Survey of 16,296 students in grades 9 through 12 nationwide indicated that 42 percent of the students were involved in a fight, somewhere, during the previous twelve months, and 16 percent of the students reported fighting at school. W. DeJong reported that 53 percent of students in a 1987 study said they had been in a fight with someone their own age in the past six months. The Joyce Foundation study conducted by LH Research reported that 20 percent of its respondents had been in a physical fight at school during the school year. During the 1991–1992 school year, 25 percent of New York City public school students in grades 9 through 12 reported having been involved in a physical fight.

Weapons Are in the Schools

Fighting behavior may be a contributing factor in weapon-carrying behavior. Students appear to view weapons as a means of protecting themselves if they get into a fight or of warding off possible attacks. According to a 1991 U.S.

Justice Department report, 2 percent of students during a six-month period had at least once taken a weapon to school to protect themselves from attack or harm. These weapons are often used to threaten, injure, or kill someone or oneself. According to R.J. Sampson and J.L. Lauritsen, individuals who use weapons to threaten other people are more likely to be the victims of property and violent offenses than those who do not use weapons.

Five studies conducted from 1990 to 1993 reported that an estimated 20 to 26 percent of students had carried weapons (anywhere), whereas five surveys conducted from 1989 to 1993 reported estimates of students carrying a weapon to school ranging from 2 to 13 percent. Another survey, which asked about the past year rather than the past thirty days, estimated that 22 percent of students had carried a weapon to school.

Weapon-carrying by teenagers appears to be a frequent occurrence, according to studies. The CDC's YRBS reported that in 1990 about 20 percent of all students in grades 9 through 12 reported having carried a weapon such as a gun, knife, or club anywhere on one or more days during the thirty days preceding the survey. Of these students, more than one-third (36 percent) reported carrying a weapon six or more times during the previous thirty days. Subsequent surveys showed increases in weapon-carrying among this population. In 1991 reports of weapon-carrying increased dramatically to 26 percent, although this rise may be due to a change in the structure of the question. There were slight declines in 1993, when 22 percent reported carrying a weapon. Also in 1993, nearly 12 percent of students reported having carried any weapon onto school property at least once in the thirty days prior to the survey.

The National Educational Goals Report found that in 1992, 9 percent of eighth-graders, 10 percent of tenth-graders, and 6 percent of twelfth-graders reported having brought a weapon to school at least once during the previous month. Of this group, 2, 4, and 3 percent, respectively, reported carrying a weapon on ten or more days in the previous month.

Gun-Toting Students

There is more variation reported in gun-carrying, specifically, than in weapon-carrying. In studies published between 1991 and 1993, from 5 to 35 percent of different student groups reported having carried a gun sometime at any location in the previous six months. The 5 percent is from a survey of students in grades 11 and 12 in South Carolina, and the 35 percent is from a survey of high school age males living near a juvenile correctional facility.

J.F. Sheley and J.D. Wright, in their survey of male inmates of juvenile correctional facilities and males from a public high school near the facilities, looked primarily at gun acquisition and possession. Both groups of males reported a significantly higher prevalence of weapon-carrying both in and away from school. While the study is not generalizable to the male population, it provides some information about youth who live in high-risk settings.

The 1990 CDC YRBS showed that 4 percent, or one in twenty-four, students carried a firearm for fighting or self-defense during the thirty days preceding the survey. In 1991 this figure increased to 6 percent; in 1993 it rose to 8 percent, or roughly one in thirteen students.

Across the studies, carrying a gun *to school* seemed to show the smallest variation. In the seven studies that asked about carrying guns to school, between 4 and 9 percent of students reported having carried a gun to school during the past thirty days. These figures are similar to ones found in other studies. The 1987 National Adolescent School Health Survey reported that 6 percent of eighth- and tenth-grade male students had carried a handgun to school during the year, and 2 percent had carried a handgun to school every day. An Illinois survey of thirty-one schools in 1990 disclosed that one in twenty students had carried a gun to

> *"Despite the perception that nonurban schools are free of violence, communities of all sizes, ethnic makeup, and socioeconomic status have experienced violence in schools."*

school sometime during that year. In the LH Research study done for the Joyce Foundation, 15 percent of students reported carrying a handgun in the last thirty days, and 4 percent said they had taken a handgun to school that year.

In a study done in ten inner-city high schools in four states, Sheley and associates found that 22 percent of the students said they had carried a gun outside of school, and 6 percent had carried a gun to school "now and then."

The Demographics of Weapon-Carrying

In general, weapons (including guns) are more likely to be carried by younger than older students, by males more than by females, by blacks more than by Hispanics, by Hispanics more than by whites, and by those in urban more than in suburban or rural geographic locations.

Age: Most studies about weapon-carrying in schools have looked at students in grades 9 through 12, and all show the same basic trend: younger students are more likely than older students to be in fights, to carry weapons, and to be victimized. Current data suggest that both physical fighting and weapon-carrying decrease as grade level and age increase. Ninth-graders are much more likely than twelfth-graders to be in a fight or to carry weapons in and around school. The 1991 YRBS reported that 9.1 percent of ninth-graders, 8.6 percent of tenth-graders, 7.4 percent of eleventh-graders, and 6.6 percent of twelfth-graders carried a gun during the thirty days preceding the survey.

Gender: In all surveys, male students are much more likely than female students to carry weapons. The 1993 YRBS suggests that males are three times more likely than females to carry weapons, and the MetLife survey reports males are five times more likely than females to have carried a weapon. The proportion is even higher for males when gun-carrying behavior is considered.

CDC reports that males are nearly eight times more likely than females to carry guns anywhere.

Race and Ethnicity: Black students are more likely than Hispanic or white students to be involved in a violent incident and are also more likely to carry a weapon. Black and Hispanic students are more likely than white students to be victims of violent acts involving weapons at school. Black and Hispanic students are also more likely than white students to carry a gun.

Geographic Location: Despite the perception that nonurban schools are free of violence, communities of all sizes, ethnic makeup, and socioeconomic status have experienced violence in schools. L.D. Bastian and M. Taylor found equal percentages of central city (2 percent) and suburban (2 percent) students report violent victimization at school, compared with 1 percent of rural students. (Violent victimizations are largely composed of simple assaults and involve attacks without weapons.) Other studies show similar proportions of students involved in fights and carrying weapons among students in urban centers and suburban areas. LH Research reported that 19 percent of central city school students have been in a fight in the past year, compared with 20 percent of suburban school students. In the same study, 62 percent of central city young people reported that they could get a gun, compared with 58 percent of suburban and 56 percent of small-town and rural students. Seventeen percent of students in the central city schools carried a handgun in the past thirty days, compared with 15 percent of suburban students.

Types of Weapons Carried to School

Weapons confiscated from students across the country include firearms, such as guns, starter guns, and toy pistols; knives; brass knuckles; box cutters; mace; pipes; smoke bombs; slapsticks; ax handles; tire irons; a sock with a pool ball inside; scissors; hatchets; hammers; razor blades; and bullets.

Students are more likely to carry knives than any other weapon. In 1990 about one-half (55 percent) of all high school students who reported carrying weapons to school indicated that they had carried a knife or razor. In the New York City Public School Survey, 16 percent of the students reported they had carried a knife or razor anywhere, and 7 percent reported they had carried a handgun. Nationwide, 11 percent of students reported carrying a knife or razor, and 4 percent reported carrying a firearm in the previous thirty days. Among eighth- and tenth-graders, almost 7 percent of boys and 2 percent of girls reported carrying knives to school nearly every day.

Weapons in schools are brought in by teachers as well as by students. A small portion of public school teachers (2 percent) has indicated that they have carried a weapon to school. This percentage is consistent for teachers in all regions of the country and all (urban, suburban, or rural) locations. Among teachers who took a weapon to school, mace was the reported weapon of choice; 44 percent of the school teachers in the MetLife sample reported bringing it to school to protect themselves. Twenty-six percent of the teachers brought knives to school, and about 5 percent, or one in one thousand, teachers brought handguns.

Reasons for Weapon-Carrying

When students were asked why they carried weapons, the primary response was to protect themselves against possible aggressors. Other reasons cited were showing off to impress friends; to make themselves feel important; and to emulate their friends. Teachers, students, and law enforcement officials believe that students carry weapons for four main reasons: (1) for protection while going to school; (2) for impressing their friends; (3) for self-esteem; or (4) for protection in school. Lou Harris found similar reasons. When asked, "What is the single most important reason some students carry a weapon?" 41 percent of the students answered "for protection against possible attacks by other people," 34 percent said to "show off and impress their friends," 10 percent "because it makes them feel important," 8 percent "because they are angry and want to hurt someone," and 4 percent "because their friends carry weapons."

> *"A survey of New York City public high school students found that 85 percent of students who carried a weapon said they did so to protect themselves against attack by others."*

A survey of New York City public high school students found that 85 percent of students who carried a weapon said they did so to protect themselves against attack by others. Students who carried a weapon in school were also more likely than other students to believe that threatening to use a weapon and carrying a weapon were effective ways to avoid a physical fight. They were more likely to say they would feel safer during a physical fight if they had a knife or a handgun.

In the National Crime Survey, less than 20 percent of students reported fear of being victimized. Victims of violent crimes were three times more likely to be afraid than those who were not. Younger students were more likely to fear an attack than were older students.

Methods for Reducing Weapon-Carrying

Preventing violence and weapon-carrying in schools is complicated by numerous variables that play into the root causes of such behavior. Nonetheless, many efforts are underway to try and address some of the causes. Efforts to reduce weapon-carrying focus on three broad prevention and intervention categories: (1) education; (2) legal and regulatory change; and (3) environmental modifications.

Education: Education activities generally serve to provide information and teach skills. Most of the educational efforts are focused on the general area of violence prevention. These efforts are geared toward reducing the incidence of violence in schools, which would in turn reduce the need for students to bring weapons to school. Many schools are starting an assortment of violence-prevention programs, including conflict-resolution curricula; mentoring programs; and general education about violence and its impact on the lives of students, their families, and their communities. Neither their effect on weapon-carrying nor their effect on violence reduction has been established.

Legal and Regulatory Change: Legal and regulatory activities focus on the laws or rules that may lower the risk of violent behavior and of students' carrying weapons. These include regulations that focus on the use of and access to weapons by students, such as enforcement of current weapons laws, the Drug Free Act, and the Gun Free School Zones Act.

Schools and their jurisdictions are making a better effort to enforce existing weapon laws. The Brady Bill, for example, is designed to help limit who has access to guns. The Gun Free School Zone Act of 1990 prohibits the possession of a firearm in a school zone (within one thousand feet from the grounds of any school).

Legal and regulatory activities also include instituting dress codes—something many schools have done. Dress codes have been instituted in some schools not only as a way of preventing weapons coming onto school property, but also as a means of reducing violent behavior. Some schools have banned baggy clothing, overcoats, sweatpants with elastic around the ankles, metal jewelry, leather, and special brand-name garments. In addition, some schools are introducing uniforms as means of reducing the threat of and actual violent behavior that has occurred because of clothing and the wearing of gang colors in school. The Baltimore City School District instituted a dress code, backed up by penalties, and was able to lower the incidence of firearm- and weapon-related incidents in its jurisdiction. They reported 55 firearm-related incidents in 1987, 35 in 1988, and 28 in 1989.

Environmental Modifications: Environmental changes include metal detector programs, security patrols, and school surveillance methods. In the MetLife study, 31 percent of teachers reported their schools had made random checks of book bags, backpacks, and lockers as a means of reducing weapon-carrying in their schools. Twenty-eight percent of the teachers in the study also said that their schools had hired security guards or police to patrol in and around the school. Five percent said that their schools used hand-held metal detectors, and 2 percent indicated that their schools made students walk through metal detectors to enter the buildings.

About one-fourth of large urban school districts in the United States use metal detectors to help reduce weapon-carrying in schools. Metal-detector systems in schools vary. Walk-through or portal metal detectors that require each person who enters the building to pass through are expensive and can be time-consuming. Most schools use either hand-held metal detectors or walk-through lanes that randomly select entering students. Metal detectors may provide a false sense of security; at the same time, they may have the opposite effect. The mere presence of metal detectors in a school may imply to some that the environment is unsafe and therefore that some protection may be necessary.

Some schools use security personnel, teachers, other students, and volunteer parents to patrol hallways and playgrounds. Others have used school surveillance methods, including closed-circuit televisions, random searches, and see-through bags as ways to ensure that students do not bring contraband items on campus.

Closed-circuit television is used more often in very large schools, especially in urban centers, than in smaller school settings. The television monitors are strategically placed in and around school buildings and on school property, especially buses, and they are usually monitored from the principal's office or in the school security office if there is one.

Instead of regular backpacks and book bags, some schools require students to bring bags that are made of clear materials such as plastic or mesh that will allow easy viewing of their contents. Schools are also allowing random searches of books bags and lockers as a means of controlling weapons in schools; others have removed lockers completely.

The Effectiveness of Methods

Very few of the prevention methods have been evaluated. Because those that have been evaluated at some level have produced mixed results, it is difficult to say which methods have been effective. According to student reports, there is some indication that violent crimes have occurred about as frequently in schools using security measures as in schools without these measures. Sheley and associates report a similar finding.

Metal detector programs are fairly new and have undergone some limited evaluation. Early results indicate that students who attended high schools with metal detector programs were as likely as students who attended schools without such programs to have carried a weapon anywhere, but were less likely to have carried a weapon inside a school building or while going to or from school. Although metal detectors may reduce the number of weapons that come onto school grounds, they do not appear to reduce

> *"Although metal detectors may reduce the number of weapons that come onto school grounds, they do not appear to reduce . . . violent behavior."*

either weapon-carrying off of school property or violent behavior such as threats or physical fighting at or away from school. New York City schools have reported some successes with their metal detector program. Weapon-related incidents have decreased, school attendance has increased, and students anecdotally reported an increased sense of security as a result of the metal detector program.

Despite the fact that many large urban school districts currently employ elaborate physical security measures (including the use of metal detectors, often at a cost of millions of dollars), there have been no rigorous, controlled evaluations of their effectiveness in reducing violence-related injuries and deaths. Moreover, many of these security measures have been challenged through the courts. Some, such as the Gun Free School Zones Act, have been upheld while others are still being debated.

The Problem Needs Examination

Few data exist to document long-term trends or to accurately assess the incidence and prevalence of violence and weapon-carrying behavior in schools across the country. It is difficult to identify trends because there is no standardized reporting system for school violence. Data on weapon-carrying in schools are fairly limited. Systematic data collation is recent, and trends for periods longer than five years are virtually nonexistent. The YRBS has been done three times in the past four years and provides some trend data, but most of the other surveys are one-time studies. Data limitations include the sizes and representativeness of the samples and survey response rates.

More work needs to be done to assess the reliability and validity of data collected by self-report methodology. One way to verify the self-report data is to collect other objective data from secondary sources. Some examples of this are to match hospital/clinic records with students' reports of being treated for an injury, or to use qualitative methods such as focus groups to assess some of the reported information. Still, many of the programs to reduce violence and weapon-carrying behavior in schools simply have not been in place long enough to permit thorough evaluation of their effectiveness.

Violence and weapon-carrying are not simply school problems. The root causes of these behaviors involve issues whose solutions require cooperation among the school, community, and public and private agencies that serve the community. Schools need to build alliances with their communities. Safe schools require safe communities. School children who fear for their lives are more likely to want to carry weapons, and the biggest threat to effective education is an armed student body.

Youth Violence Is Not Increasing

by Children's Defense Fund

About the author: *The Children's Defense Fund is a national organization that works to educate the nation about the needs of children, especially poor and minority children.*

In many ways, fear *for* our children's safety was twisted into fear *of* our children in 1996. Truths about violence and youths were obscured by politicians' and media hyperbole portraying today's young children as a coming wave of "superpredator" youths. In fact:

- After a big increase, violence committed *by* youths has decreased recently for the first time in a decade. While no amount of brutality by or against young people can be tolerated, honest examinations of demographics, crime trends, and the potential of prevention efforts do *not* indicate that today's young children should be objects of fear tomorrow.
- Children and youths are 10 times more likely to be victims *of* violence than to be arrested *for* violence.
- Crimes committed with ever-more-available guns account almost entirely for the terrible surge of violent crime by youths that the nation experienced from 1987 through 1994.
- The most punitive of the currently popular responses to youth crime—such as "three-strikes-and-you're-out" laws that would count an act of juvenile delinquency as a strike, and laws that would put children in adult courts and adult prisons—are less cost-effective than common-sense prevention, individualized justice, and graduated sanctions.

The best news for violence prevention in 1996 was found in communities that showed they can do much to reclaim safety for children. Although Congress pulled back from funding prevention efforts in 1996, in many areas communities took steps to protect children by creating safe havens after school, on weekends, and in the summer; participating in community policing; and developing programs that work with courts to hold juvenile offenders accountable and help rehabilitate them. And although Congress was a reluctant participant in 1996, incremental gun control laws continued to gain momentum at the federal and state levels, and stepped-up enforcement of existing gun laws by police and communities has begun to make a difference and to slow the illegal firearm trade that is robbing too many of our children of their childhoods and even their lives.

Children as Victims of Violence and Gunfire

More than 1.6 million 12- to 17-year-olds reported that they had been the victims of violent crime (other than murder) in 1994 (the most recent year for which data are available by age). That total, as bad as it is, does not include another very pervasive form of violence against children—abuse at the hands of their own parents or caretakers. Most children who suffer violence, whether in their homes or communities, are victims of adults. Four of five juveniles murdered in 1994 were killed by adults, and a majority of *all* violent victimization of 12- to 17-year-olds is committed by adults.

"For a decade, guns drove an appalling rise in child deaths."

For a decade, guns drove an appalling rise in child deaths. The number of children who died each year because of gunfire nearly doubled between 1983 and 1993. In 1993, the year for which the most recent complete data are available, 5,751 children under 20 died from gunfire—one child every hour and a half, or the equivalent of a classroomful of children every two days. Although more than half the children who died from gunfire that year were White, Black male 15- to 19-year-olds suffered the greatest proportionate toll. Young Black males are now five times as likely as their White male counterparts to be victims of gunfire.

Nearly two-thirds of the child gun deaths were homicides. The number of children murdered by guns tripled between 1984 and 1994, while the number of children who were victims of non-gun homicides remained flat. After homicide, the largest cause of youth gun deaths is suicide. Guns are used in two out of three youth suicides, and are far more likely than other methods of suicide attempts to cause death. Black male youth suicide rates have skyrocketed, driven by a 300 percent increase in gun suicides between 1980 and 1992. Accidental shootings present another danger to children: Gun accidents killed 526 children in 1993, more than one child each day.

Juvenile Offenders

For nearly a decade, beginning in the mid-1980s, juvenile violent crime—and public concern about it—mounted steadily and rapidly. Between 1985 and 1994, juvenile arrests for violent crime (murder, forcible rape, robbery, and aggravated assault) rose 75 percent. But juvenile arrests for violent crimes were *down* 2.9 percent in 1995—the first drop in a decade. Most encouragingly, arrests of youths for homicide fell dramatically in both 1994 and 1995, down 22.8 percent since 1993. And the earliest reports for 1996 indicate another big drop in homicides in general in big cities and, likely, in homicides by juveniles.

A combination of factors is believed to have contributed to these reductions in youth violence, including increased partnerships between schools, community groups, parents, and law enforcement agencies; stepped-up efforts to keep adults from providing guns to children illegally; improvements in medical technology and experience that may keep alive more children with serious gun injuries; and other societal changes, such as a subsiding of the crack trade and a major drop in all crime and homicide in most big cities (New York City had fewer homicides in 1996 than in any year since 1968).

At the same time that efforts to reduce youth violence are beginning to bear fruit, some commentators—focusing on particularly heinous but isolated crimes by a few youths, and on population projections for the future—proclaimed a "coming wave of superpredators" or "a teenage time bomb." But no teenage population boom is coming: In 2010, the percentage of juveniles, relative to the total population, will be 7 percent—the same as it is now and has been every year since 1989, and lower than the level before 1989.

The recent increase in violent crimes by youths has been concentrated among a very few children, primarily in severely stressed communities. Less than one-half of 1 percent—one in 200—of all 10- to 17-year-olds were arrested for violent offenses in 1994. Of all youths arrested, 19 of 20 are arrested for nonviolent crimes. And about one-third of all juvenile homicide arrests occur in just four cities: Los Angeles, Chicago, Detroit, and New York. Nationwide, 80 percent of counties had no juvenile homicides in 1994, and another 10 percent had one.

> *"In fact, the real wave that has swept away so many of our children . . . has been the tidal wave of guns into communities."*

In fact, the real wave that has swept away so many of our children, as both victims and perpetrators, has been the tidal wave of guns into communities. *Gun* crime is virtually the only type of youth crime that has risen over the past decade. While juvenile arrests for homicides with guns have quadrupled, juvenile arrests for homicides *without* guns haven't risen at all since 1984. And other weapons-related offenses have risen as steeply as homicides. By contrast, property crimes, by far the most common offenses committed by juveniles (outnumbering violent crimes 5-to-1), have remained flat over the decade. What we have been witnessing, then, has been not a drastic overall change in youth crime, but essentially a very sharp and very serious increase in crime with guns. Because juveniles have increasingly easy access to guns, what formerly would have been a fist fight or

51

knife fight, or a serious act of delinquency, now too often involves a gun and is far more likely to result in death or a homicide arrest.

Violence Prevention Efforts Can Reduce Violent Crime

With youth population rates flat and youth violent crime rates apparently beginning to fall, the opportunity is ripe to increase investments in proven prevention strategies for teenagers and young children, so they can become nonviolent youths who achieve success in their families, schools, friendships, and activities.

Research and evaluations of community programs are proving that parental and community action can do a great deal to keep children safe—that children who are kept busy with positive activities and watched over by caring adults have better odds of staying out of trouble and out of harm's way, and becoming successful adults, than children without those opportunities. Such actions not only reduce violence, but can reduce drug and alcohol abuse, school dropout, and early sexual activity, as well. . . .

Boston Pulls Together to Save Children

Not one child was murdered with a gun in 1996 in Boston; one young child, tragically, was beaten to death by an adult relative. Although one death is still too many, that's a big improvement, compared with the 16 child homicides Boston faced in the peak year of 1993. What is Boston doing right? And how can other cities do the same?

Deborah Prothrow-Stith, M.D., assistant dean at Harvard's School of Public Health, reports that Boston's efforts to prevent violence began in 1982, when the Boston Violence Prevention Project developed a training module in violence prevention. Over the years, hundreds of city residents received this training, and learned broader violence prevention concepts to adapt to their communities. Many of those trained then launched prevention initiatives that, in turn, affected thousands of Boston-area youths—initiatives that included youth organizations like Teens Against Gang Violence; summer opportunities at the Boys & Girls Clubs and at basketball camps; and congregation-based programs like the Ten-Point Coalition, where congregants mentor delinquent youths and assist their families.

> *"The steep decline in youth homicides indicates that violence prevention has taken hold in Boston."*

By the 1990s, the mayor's office began to provide significant support for violence prevention, funding streetworkers, community centers, and a Safe Neighborhoods micro-grants fund. The city also aggressively pursued federal funds for violence prevention, including money from the U.S. Departments of Justice, Education, and Health and Human Services. Some of this training and funding was targeted to communities hardest hit by violence, such as Roxbury and

Dorchester. But the violence prevention movement rippled throughout the Boston area, as a broad range of professions and communities made violence prevention a priority and participated in coalitions cutting across these lines.

Leadership in law enforcement also was critical. According to Jim Jordan, director of Strategic Planning and Resource Development for the Boston Police Department, community policing restored accountability to a mistrusted police force and led to improved relationships between police officers, probation officers, and social service workers and the community. Working with other agencies, police have been able to identify at-risk youths and respond to a neighborhood's particular needs, whether it be to break up a drug trade, monitor youths on probation, or provide more youth activities. In addition, the Bureau of Alcohol, Tobacco, and Firearms (ATF), on the heels of the 1993 Brady law, provided federal support in interrupting the supply of illegal guns to Boston. Local grassroots leadership on gun control provided critical political support for these efforts.

Ultimately, all of these individual efforts have come together and grown to have a big impact on Boston's children and the safety of their communities: 16 children were murdered in 1993, six in 1994, four in 1995, and one in 1996. But as youth worker Ulric Johnson of the Adolescent Wellness Program emphasizes, the roots of violence—poverty, discrimination, hopelessness, and family breakdown—must be attacked to truly reduce all forms of violence against children, now and in the future.

Still, the steep decline in youth homicides indicates that violence prevention has taken hold in Boston, involving coalitions, broad public education, investments in prevention, new laws, and new strategies for enforcing old laws. But it all started with just a few people, committing to saving children from more violence. And, in the end, that's the central lesson to be learned from the Boston experience. As Prothrow-Stith says, "Just get started."

The Problem of Youth Violence Is Exaggerated

by Eric R. Lotke

About the author: *Eric R. Lotke is a research associate at the National Center on Institutions and Alternatives.*

The headlines create the impression of a nation in crisis. *Juvenile homicide hits all-time high,* they declare. *Scourge of youth violence sweeping the nation.* Politicians lament the death of our youth and vow to keep neighborhoods safe. Teachers warn students to shun attractive clothing, fearing they will be shot by children who plan to make it their own. Rarely have alarm bells rung so loudly or so long; even good news like the recent decline in juvenile homicide was followed by warnings that the worst is yet to come.

Two problems of juvenile violence face our nation. The first problem is that certain neighborhoods have suffered from tremendous increases in youth violence. In these neighborhoods, youth homicide has doubled or even tripled in the past decade. The increase in homicide is itself distressing, and it suggests other troubles lurking beneath.

The second problem is our national response to the first problem. This problem arises from sympathy for the victim and fear of victimization; it ends with a loss of perspective on the small scale and a limited range of youth violence. Although American homicide rates are high and youth homicide is rising, only a tiny fraction of Americans run a real risk of homicide, and only a tiny fraction of those homicides are committed by children. Most cities that show rapid increases in youth homicide have changes on the scale of three homicides increasing to six homicides—a genuine "doubling" but not one that warrants nationwide fear. In the sarcastic words of *L.A. Youth,* a newspaper of inner city teens: *Exclusive . . . The Shocking Truth! Did You Know? Many Young People Have Never Shot Anybody! . . .*

Informal surveys around dinner tables often reveal a belief that the juvenile killers are numbered in the hundreds of thousands. Many people are surprised by our finding that *approximately 940 children were convicted of personally taking the life of another human being in the entire nation in one full year. . . .*

Crime Rates

Overall crime rates in America have been stable or slightly declining for most of the past twenty years. Victimization surveys reveal roughly the same rate of robbery and aggravated assault in 1992 as they did in 1973, and burglary rates declined precipitously through the 1980s. Homicide arrest rates were the same in 1993 as they were in 1973. Overall victimization rates seldom change more than a few percent each year, and the change is more often downward than upward.

> *"[There is] a loss of perspective on the small scale and a limited range of youth violence."*

The declining victimization rates may come as a surprise to Americans accustomed to hearing that crime is on the rise. Part of the misconception stems from relying on police records of arrests to show crime trends. Police record keeping has improved over the years, as staffing has increased and file keeping has been computerized. Much of the supposed increase in crime is explained by changes in methodology rather than actual changes in victimization rates. For instance, between 1973 and 1992, police statistics showed a 120% increase in the rate of aggravated assault. Direct surveys of the American population, however, indicate that rates of aggravated assault *declined* 11% during that period.

When it comes to juvenile crime, arrest trends have been relatively similar to adult arrest trends in recent years. In 1982, juveniles comprised 18% of all arrests; in 1995 they comprised 18.3% of all arrests. From 1972 to 1995, the percentage of overall index crimes—serious crimes such as murder, robbery and rape—cleared by the arrest of a juvenile decreased from 27.3% to 22.1%. In the area of property crime, juvenile clearances decreased significantly from 33.8% to 25.0%. For violent index crimes only there has been a slight increase from 13.2% to 14.1%. Thus, trends in juvenile crime mirror the overall trend of general stability and marginal declines.

Furthermore, the vast majority of juvenile crime involves non-violent offenses, primarily relating to property or drugs. Only 6 out of 100 juvenile arrests are for violent crimes (the same as adults). Among the small number of violent offenses, the majority are assaults—a very flexible crime category that often involves mere threats or fights. Arrests for murder and rape constitute less than one-half of one percent of juvenile arrests.

Yet the *overall* crime trends mask specific trends within particular demographic groups. When the focus is narrowed to juvenile homicide, the picture shifts to genuine and shocking increases. Youth homicide arrest rates have doubled just since the late 1980s, with the increases sweeping across racial and ethnic lines. In the four short years between 1987 and 1991, the arrest rate for homicide among white youth increased by 79%, and the rate among African American youth increased by 121%. These increases are most troubling in the communities that already suffer from high rates of homicide and other violent crime. In 1992, the victimization rate for homicide among African American teenagers was nearly eight times the victimization rate among white teenagers, and five times the victimization rate for the general population.

Most of the increase in juvenile homicide involved firearms. Between the 1970s and the mid 1980s, the rate of youth homicide was essentially stable, and the weapons used in the offense were closely split between guns and other weapons. In 1987 that started to change. The number of juvenile homicides involving a firearm started to spiral upwards while the number of non-firearm homicides held steady. Virtually all of the additional youth homicides since 1987 involved guns, so that in 1994 nearly 80% of the youth homicides were committed with a firearm. Four times as many children were killed with a gun in 1994 as in 1984.

Nonetheless, these rapid increases in youth homicide are highly site-specific and do not present the overall threat to public safety that many people perceive. Eighty-two percent of the counties in America experienced *zero* youth homicides in 1994; 92% experienced zero or one. Just four cities—Chicago, Los Angeles, New York and Detroit—account for nearly *one-third* of the juvenile homicide arrests nationwide, even though they account for only *one-twentieth* of the country's juvenile population. Even in these high homicide cities, the rates of increase are large but the actual numbers are relatively small. Most states experience just a handful of homicides by juveniles in the course of a year; many states experience none at all, and large states like New York experience just over one hundred. Finally, the increases may finally be coming to an end: data for 1995 suggest that arrests of juveniles for homicide and other violent crimes have started to decline.

> *"The vast majority of juvenile crime involves non-violent offenses, primarily relating to property or drugs."*

How Many Children Kill?

Nobody knows exactly how many children kill in the course of a year in America. Estimates run from as low as 1000 to as high as 3000. To put the matter in perspective, an average year in America sees a total of between 20,000 and 24,000 deaths by homicides. Thus, children appear to commit as little as 5% or as many as 15% of the annual homicides in America. . . .

According to the FBI Uniform Crime Reports (UCR), which tabulate arrests nationwide, 2560 juveniles were arrested for a homicide offense in 1995. Arrests are frequently used as a measure of crime by politicians and the press. For example, a 1996 cover story in *U.S. News & World Report* warns: "Teenage Time Bombs: Violent Juvenile Crime Is Soaring—and It Is Going to Get Worse." The statistics behind the warning? "The number of youths under 18 *arrested* for murder tripled between 1984 and 1994."

Unfortunately, such headlines assume too tight an equivalence between arrests and offenses. The number of arrests and other data provided by police are so sensitive to police practice that they often measure police conduct better than the underlying offense.

One problem is that police often arrest several people en route to identifying a single perpetrator. Such duplicative arrests can cause a single homicide to appear as several homicides in statistics based on arrests. Another problem is that juveniles often act in groups. It only takes one person to pull a trigger, but more people may be associated with the act: some in the car alongside the triggerman; others who refuse to cooperate with a police investigation. The police may arrest all these actors in their effort to identify the triggerman and determine the various degrees of involvement and culpability. This practice can make a single incident appear to be several incidents when, at the end of the year, the police department simply reports a gross number of homicide arrests. Similarly, an additional arrest is counted each time a person is taken into custody, notified or cited to appear in court—even if multiple citations occur for the same underlying incident.

> *"These rapid increases in youth homicides are highly site-specific and do not represent the overall threat to public safety that many people perceive."*

Such problems can be aggravated in the context of serious crimes and high levels of public concern, which often lead the police to intensify their enforcement practices and increase the frequency of their arrests. If crime is measured by arrest, the heightened enforcement will appear to be heightened crime. The apparent increase in crime can lead to increased arrests, which may lead in turn to an appearance of higher crime in a self-perpetuating upward spiral.

Arrest rates can, of course, provide a crude measure of crime rates because they often reflect a response to genuine criminal behavior. Arrest rates cannot, however, provide too much detail. In the context of extremely fine questions like the number of a single, exceedingly rare type of crime by people of a single age group, the error introduced by arrest statistics may outweigh their accuracy. An increase of a few hundred arrests (in a nation of 270 million people and 15,000 police departments) can create the appearance of a nationwide crime wave. . . .

A Careful Look at Violence

The number of actual killers is bound to be smaller than the number of children involved in homicides because several people are often involved in a single offense. Although there is seldom a legal or statistical difference between the person who pulled the trigger and the sidekick, many people find an ethical distinction. The question always remains: would the sidekick have pulled the trigger? Indeed, might the fact that the sidekick did *not* pull the trigger, and may not even have had a gun, indicate that the sidekick acting alone would not have killed the victim? These questions are unanswerable, but it seems needlessly clumsy to attribute to the accessory the same ethical qualities as the principal. The ultimate question is how many children are personally and individually responsible for taking the life of another human being.

The best source of data for determining individual responsibility is the FBI Supplementary Homicide Reports (SHR). Its detailed breakdown reveals that just half of the juvenile offenders acted alone; a quarter acted as one of a pair; and the last quarter acted as part of a group of three or more. If those ratios are applied to the number of children convicted of a homicide offense, it leads to the conclusion that approximately 940 youngsters personally and individually took the life of another human being nationwide in 1992.

Furthermore, 10% of all youthful homicide offenders killed their parents, often in the context of abusive relationships. While these are not justifiable homicides, they are also quite different from the random or gang-related killings so many Americans fear. Another half of the children killed acquaintances. Sometimes the acquaintances were abusive parent-equivalents, like the mother's boyfriend; sometimes they were rival drug dealers—the statistics do not say. But as terrible as it is to kill a family member or acquaintance, these offenses too differ from those often portrayed in the evening news. Acquaintance killings are not random, motiveless or unfathomable. All too often they begin as petty disputes over trivial issues between hot-headed teens; with firearms present, the dispute sometimes escalates into a murder. Applying the SHR ratios to convictions suggests that 535 children were known to be principally responsible for killing somebody they knew nationwide in 1992.

So who are the cold blooded predators of the evening news? How many children spray gunfire into crowds or lie in wait to ambush unsuspecting pedestrians? The answer is twofold: more than a country would wish, but not as many as might appear from the mass media. Subtracting the 12% of the offenses about which nothing is known, 31% of the juvenile homicides were committed against a stranger. That means in the entire nation in 1992, a total of 410 children were convicted of such an offense; of them, 290 children personally committed the crime. . . .

The problems seen on the evening news or referenced by politicians on tour may appear unmanageable—but analysis reveals that the number of children involved is not so large and the solutions are not so far off that hope must be abandoned. With a little creative energy, this nation can help its children to navigate the difficult path through adolescence in this turbulent and troubled time.

Teens Are Unjustly Blamed for an Increase in Violence

by Mike Males

About the author: *Mike Males, a social ecology graduate student at the University of California, Irvine, is the author of* The Scapegoat Generation: America's War on Adolescents.

In previous decades, American politicians and social scientists predicted waves of violence stemming from "impulsive" blacks, volatile Eastern European immigrants, "hot-blooded" Latin Americans, and other groups "scientifically" judged to harbor innately aggressive traits. In each case, the news media joined in vilifying whatever temporarily unpopular minority politicians and pseudo-scientists had flocked to blame.

And in each case, the branding of disfavored population groups as inherently violent has been disproven. (See Stephen Jay Gould's *The Mismeasure of Man* for examples.) In each case, violence has been found to be a straightforward function of poverty and income disparity.

Here we go again.

Experts have identified a 1990s demographic scapegoat for America's pandemic violent crime: our own kids. A media scare campaign about the coming "storm" of "teenage violence" waged by liberal and conservative politicians and experts alike is in full roar.

Creating Scandals

Blaming "a ticking demographic time bomb," *U.S. News & World Report* (12/4/95) warns of "scary kids around the corner." The "troublesome demographic trends" are a growing adolescent population.

"A Teenage Time Bomb," *Time* announced (1/15/96), quoting Northeastern University criminologist James Alan Fox's view of teenagers as "temporary sociopaths—impulsive and immature." Added *Time:* "If [teens] also have easy access to guns and drugs, they can be extremely dangerous."

Reprinted, with permission, from Mike Males, "Wild in Deceit," *Extra!* March/April 1996.

Other top-quoted criminologists, like UCLA's James Q. Wilson and former American Society of Criminology president Alfred Blumstein, are in full agreement with Fox: Young equals violent. And top political officials concur. The *Los Angeles Times* (12/18/95) noted FBI Director Louis Freeh and other authorities' alarm over "the fact that the crime-prone 16-to-24-year-old group will grow dramatically over the next decade—which Freeh cited as an 'alarming indicator of future trends.'"

The trendiest demographic scapegoater is the centrist Brookings Institution's John DiIulio, Jr., anointed "The Crime Doctor" and "one of Washington's in-vogue thinkers" by the *L.A. Times* (5/2/95). "More male teenagers, more crime. Period," is his message. A new breed of youthful "super-predators" menaces the nation, so vicious even hardened adult convicts are scared of them, DiIulio said.

Creating Bias

Journalists ought to be aware they are pouring gasoline on a fire they have already fanned. A 1994 Gallup Poll (*Gallup Poll Monthly,* 9/94) found that American adults already hold "a greatly inflated view of the amount of crime committed by people under the age of 18," with the most salient reason "news coverage of violent crime committed by juveniles." The average American adult believes that youths commit 43 percent of all violent crime in the U.S., three times the true figure of 13 percent—and, as a result, a large majority is eager to harshly punish juveniles.

> *"Experts have identified a 1990s demographic scapegoat for America's pandemic violent crime: our own kids."*

Responsible journalists would be looking to reverse this dangerous misimpression they have helped create. Just the opposite is occurring.

In the scare campaign against adolescents, the news media not only uncritically repeat official claims, they actively embellish them with sinister cover stories and apocalyptic tales of suburban mayhem. The message is screamed from headlines, magazine covers and network specials: Adolescents are "wild in the streets" (*Newsweek*, 8/2/92); teens everywhere are "killer kids" (*Reader's Digest,* 6/93).

Though casting a few paeans to details like poverty, discrimination and abuse, the media scare campaign declares that violence is innate to teenagers and the coming mayhem is inevitable. Therefore, the only real solution, articulated by former Robert Kennedy aide Adam Walinsky (*Atlantic*, 7/95), is spending tens of billions to hire five million more police officers and suspending basic civil rights to combat the "epidemic of teen violence."

Unnatural Aggression

The problem with the 1990s teen-violence scare campaign is not that its prediction of a more violent future is wrong—it may well be correct. The problem is its wrongheaded explanation for why violence is rising.

There is no such thing as "youth violence," any more than there is "black violence" or "Italian violence." The recent rise in violent crime arrests among youths is so clearly founded in social conditions, not age-group demographics, that experts and officials have had to strain mightily to ignore or downplay them.

> *"The average American adult believes that youths commit 43 percent of all violent crime in the U.S., three times the true figure of 13 percent."*

The social scientists receiving the most media attention "argue that teenage aggression is natural." (*Newsweek,* 8/2/92) If it is, we would expect teens all over the world to be violent. That is far from the case.

Murder, the most reliably reported crime around the world, is typically committed by killers very close in age to their victims (unless the victims are children or the elderly). In the 19 largest industrial nations outside the U.S., the 40 million young males aged 15 to 24 committed just 800 murders in the most recent reporting year (World Health Organization, *World Health Statistics Annual,* 1994). In these other Western nations, which have a total of 7,100 murders a year, the typical killer is age 30 or older, far beyond the teen years.

In stark contrast, the U.S.'s 18 million 15-to-24-year-old males accounted for 6,800 murders in 1992. American murder peaks at age 19. U.S. 15-to-24-year-olds are 16 times more likely to be murdered than their counterparts in other Western nations. (U.S. adults have a seven times' greater murder risk.)

So U.S. experts, politicians and their media parroters couldn't be more wrong: There is nothing innately violent about teenagers. There is something extremely violent—hysterically so—about the United States. Not even similar "frontier cultures" such as Canada and Australia have murder tolls remotely approaching ours.

Clearly, there are reasons other than "Teen age" that explain why nine out of 10 young men who murder in the world's 20 largest Western countries are Americans. Here American social scientists and the media dispense some of the most absurd escapisms as "explanations."

Favorite Villains

The favorite conservative and pop-psychology villain (from right-wing media critics like Michael Medved and William Bennett to officials of the Clinton administration) is media violence, and the cure-all is more restrictions on TV, movies, books and music available to youths. But the media in most other Western nations are as violent as America's or more so. Efforts by U.S. experts to explain why Japan has extraordinarily violent media but extraordinarily low societal violence (9 million Japanese teens accounted for just 35 murders in 1992) are the essence of lame. (See James Q. Wilson's illogic in the *L.A. Times,* 6/25/95.)

The favorite liberal scapegoat is America's gun proliferation. "Whereas illegal firearms were not easily available to 12-year-olds just a few years back, guns can now be obtained in any neighborhood by almost any youngster who has a yen for one," the *L.A. Times* reported (9/9/95), summing up expert opinion. The panacea is another age-based restriction: tougher laws to keep guns away from youths.

True, Europeans and Japanese do not routinely pack heat. And Californians, in a state with 4,000 murders in 1994, purchase 300,000 to 400,000 handguns every year.

But if violent media and guns "in every neighborhood" were the reasons for teen violence, we would expect affluent white families to have the most murderous kids. White households are nearly twice as likely to harbor guns, and one-third more likely to subscribe to blood-dripping cable TV channels, than black and other non-white households (*Statistical Abstract of the U.S. 1995*). Yet in California, where whites are the plurality race, non-whites account for 87 percent of all teen homicides and 80 percent of all teen arrests for violent crimes. How do those who blame media violence, gun availability, and/or "inherent teenage aggression" explain that?

Poverty Violence

The major factor, buried in teen-violence stories and rarely generating any remedies, is poverty. The biggest differences between the U.S. and the 19 other relatively peaceful industrial nations cited above are youth poverty and extreme disparities in income between rich and poor. The 1995 Luxembourg Income Study found that the U.S. raises three to eight times more children in poverty than other Western

> *"There is no such thing as 'youth violence,' any more than there is 'black violence' or 'Italian violence.'"*

nations. The U.S. has the largest and fastest-growing gap in income between its richest 5 percent and poorest 5 percent of any industrial society (*U.S. News*, 8/28/95).

One figure summarizes the real U.S. violence issue. In 1993, 40 million Americans lived below the official poverty line (which itself understates the true rate of poverty). Half of these are children, and six in ten are non-white. While most impoverished people are not violent, there is no question among criminologists that the stresses of poverty are associated with much higher violent crime levels among all races and ages.

(That poverty is linked to crime should not come as a great surprise. After all, during the Great Depression murder spiraled upward—peaking in 1933 with a rate of 9.7 murders per 100,000, higher than 1993's 9.5 per 100,000 rate. See U.S. Census Bureau, *Historical Statistics of the United States*.)

If you divide the number of violent crimes by the number of people living in destitution, the phenomenon of "teenage violence" disappears: Adjusted for poverty, 13-to-19-year-olds have almost the same crime rate as people in their 40s, and have a crime rate well below that of those in their 20s and 30s (Bureau of Justice Statistics, *Sourcebook of Criminal Justice Statistics 1994;* U.S. Census Bureau, *Poverty in the United States*, 1993).

The same adjustment for poverty sheds light on an issue that moderates and liberals seem afraid to discuss—the disproportionate amount of crime committed by non-white teens. "It's increasingly clear that everyone's kids are at risk," the Rand Corporation's Peter Greenwood told the *L.A. Times* (9/6/95)—which reprinted the meaningless comment under the blaring headline, "A New Wave of Mayhem."

> *"Blaming concocted 'innate' teenage traits for violence opens up a wide array of political and agency profiteering to 'treat' the problem."*

Neither Greenwood nor the *Times* explained why, if "everyone's kids are at risk," a black youth is 12 times more likely to be murdered than a white youth, or why 31 California counties with a combined population of 2.5 million reported zero teen murders in 1993 (California Center for Health Statistics, 1995).

In fact, teen murder rates for whites are low and falling; non-white teen murder rates are high and rising. In 1975, 97 white youths and 240 non-white (including Hispanic) youths were arrested for homicide in California. In 1994, homicide arrests among white youths had fallen to 60, but among non-white youths had doubled to 482 (*Crime & Delinquency in California*, 1975–1993, and 1994 printout).

But notwithstanding Charles Murray's racist *Bell Curve* theories, non-white "dysgenics" is not the explanation for the disparity. If one adjusts the racial crime rate for the number of individuals living in extreme poverty, non-whites have a crime rate similar to that of whites at every age level.

The raging anecdotal campaign to portray affluent youths as out of control (see *New York Times Magazine* 10/8/95; *L.A. Times*, 9/6/95), and the far-out-of-proportion hype accorded the pathetic suburban Lakewood Spur Posse, are attempts to hide the fact that the issues are the same as they have always been: poverty and racism.

Masking the Issues

Why is "teen violence" deployed by politicians and experts through a compliant media to mask the real issue of "poverty violence"? Because in Washington, as *U.S. News & World Report* (11/6/95) notes, "reducing child poverty, much less eradicating it, is no longer a paramount priority for either political party."

Instead, the focus is on the sort of proposals put forward by the conservative Council on Crime in America (*Reuters*, 1/16/96): more police, more prisons, longer sentences imposed at younger ages. That states like California, Texas and Oklahoma have imposed exactly such get-tough measures for two decades and suffered record increases in violent crime appears to have little impact on the debate.

We don't want to spend the money to reduce youth poverty. But blaming concocted "innate" teenage traits for violence opens up a wide array of political and agency profiteering to "treat" the problem. Admitting that the issue might be that 45 percent of black youth, and 40 percent of Hispanic youth, grow up in poverty is not on the official agenda—so it is not on the news media's agenda, either.

The Extent of Youth Violence Has Been Distorted

by Barry Krisberg

About the author: *Barry Krisberg, president of the National Council on Crime and Delinquency, is the author of* Crime and Privilege *and* Juvenile Justice: Improving the Quality of Care.

Fear of crime is palpable. Americans now rate crime as the most important public policy issue. Responding to the citizenry, politicians are rushing head-long toward massive investments in more police and prisons. . . .

Fear Affects Public Policy

Public policy is being fashioned on an anvil of fear. The public debate has been energized by extensive media coverage of terrible crimes (the killing of tourists in Florida, the kidnapping and murder of Polly Klaas in California, the killing of the father of basketball star Michael Jordan). Discussions of crime policy, whether in Washington, D.C., or in state capitals across the nation, have not been informed by data or thoughtful analysis. Legislators and the media seem to be gripped by a kind of moral panic reminiscent of the McCarthy period—then we were convinced there was a communist spy behind every door, now we fear the "predatory criminal" who has just been released from prison.

What is truly frightening about the current crime debate is its hysterical nature. Moreover, many of the proposals being adopted are enormously expensive and will radically diminish public funding for schools and health care, higher education and economic development. For instance, a sentencing law aimed at recidivists enacted in California (the broadest version of "Three Strikes" proposed so far) will double the state's prison population, requiring the taxpayers to fund a prison expansion equal to *the entire amount of state funding for all public universities and colleges in California*. Few elected officials opposed

Excerpted from Barry Krisberg, "Distorted by Fear: The Make-Believe War on Crime," *Social Justice*, Fall 1994. Reprinted with permission.

this law even though the fiscal implications were well known to them.

At the federal level, the Congress has passed a $30 billion crime bill to be funded by "savings through reductions in the federal work force." It is noteworthy that President Bill Clinton's budget called for these same savings to be used to reduce the federal deficit. Further, this same Congress refused to pass a much smaller job stimulus package due to concerns about inflation.

Much worse than the fiscal implications of the new crime war are the forecasted impacts on our communities. Proposed sentencing legislation would add over 1.5 million inmates to the nation's prison system. Over half of these additional inmates will be young African American males—the equivalent of 20 football stadiums full of young men going into prison. One can only speculate on the horrendous consequences of these policies for the poorest families in our communities. Other proposals designed to put children as young as 13 in prison may mean a return to practices of state-sanctioned child abuse not seen since the 19th century.

What Crime Wave?

An ABC television documentary asked the provocative question, "Are We Scaring Ourselves to Death?" This show contrasted the media's near obsession with crime at a time when crime rates are actually declining. Stories of violence, sex crimes, and drugs are the usual lead stories on local television news shows. Crime stories dominate front pages of newspapers. Almost every night, "virtual reality" television shows such as "America's Most Wanted," "Cops" and "Rescue 911" take us into the front seat of a police car to witness crime scenes. We are presented with the dramatic retelling of horrible crimes and, as electronic voyeurs, we get to sample the tragic suffering of family members whose loved ones have been brutally murdered.

Despite the terror engendered by this media assault and the often over-heated anti-crime rhetoric of politicians, there is scant evidence that the nation is in the grip of a "crime epidemic." The National Crime Survey, conducted by the U.S. Justice Department, reveals that crime rates have actually fallen over the past 20 years. Levels of violent crime in 1992 were similar to those recorded a decade ago. In 1992, the rate of property crimes was at the lowest level since this survey was begun in 1973. Rates for violent crimes such as rape, robbery, and assault were lower than those reported 10 years ago.

> *"There is scant evidence that the nation is in the grip of a 'crime epidemic.'"*

While the United States possesses a very high murder rate compared to most industrialized countries, the homicide rate has not fluctuated much in the last 20 years. In 1973, the murder rate was 9.4 per 100,000; in 1993, the rate was 9.3 per 100,000.

The media seem particularly obsessed with violence by young people. We have all heard the message—young people nowadays are more vicious, more cold-blooded than ever before. It is alleged that very young adolescents are becoming the major crime threat in America. The facts contradict these myths. Juveniles represent a small and declining part of serious crime in America. During the last 10 years in which violent arrests were virtually unchanged, the juvenile share of these arrests increased by 0.3%—hardly a crime wave.

The Statistics Are Inaccurate

The statistics presented on youth violence are inflated because juveniles tend to be arrested in groups—thus, 10 juveniles might be arrested in connection with one drive-by shooting. Even if nine of the 10 are subsequently released, the police will record this event as 10 juveniles arrested for homicide. Similarly, the data on the alleged huge increases in violent arrests for very young children are exaggerated because any increase in the frequency of a rare event will appear as a large percentage increase.

Over the last decade, juveniles comprised a smaller share of all arrests. Whereas 18% of arrests in 1982 involved juveniles, by 1992 this proportion had declined to 16%. Juveniles are primarily arrested for property crimes—violent crimes account for only 5.6% of all juvenile arrests. Adults are 4.5 times more likely to be arrested for violent crimes than teenagers.

> *"Juveniles represent a small and declining part of serious crime."*

What *has* increased is the number of children being murdered or committing suicide. Researchers indicate that the availability of handguns and assault weapons is behind this tragic development. The number of youths involved in violent conflicts is not increasing; however, the increased firepower in youthful hands is escalating the lethality of these confrontations. It is also important to note that children are more likely to be the victims of violence than the perpetrators. It is estimated that as many as 5,000 children die each year as a result of abuse and neglect by parents and guardians. Children face greater dangers from adults than from teenagers.

Excessive Leniency?

The story of an American teenager arrested for multiple cases of vandalism in Singapore has generated worldwide attention. The 18 year old was tortured and coerced into pleading guilty. He then received "caning" by a martial arts expert—a punishment that causes permanent disfigurement and often leads to unconsciousness. Caning has been universally condemned as torture by most international human rights organizations.

This case and the presumed low crime rate in Singapore have fueled a discussion of the excessive leniency of the U.S. justice system, particularly our juvenile court system. Here again, the facts run contrary to the myths. The imprisonment rate in the United States is higher than any European nation. Only China locks up a greater proportion of its citizens than the U.S. Further, sentences meted out in American courts are much harsher than those in other industrialized nations.

The alleged leniency of the juvenile court is likewise more myth than reality. For instance, a comparison of two Department of Justice studies reveals that the odds of being convicted of a violent crime are higher in juvenile courts than in criminal courts. In California, young people sent to the Youth Authority will serve more time for violent offenses than will adults sentenced to prison for the same crimes. Moreover, studies on youngsters who are transferred to adult courts have consistently shown that many of these youngsters receive lighter sentences than if they would have remained under the jurisdiction of the juvenile court.

Chapter 2

What Causes Youth Violence?

The Causes of Youth Violence: An Overview

by Richard A. Mendel

About the author: *Richard A. Mendel is a freelance writer and researcher who specializes in poverty-related issues.*

Over the past several decades, and especially since the federal Juvenile Justice and Delinquency Prevention Act passed in 1974, extensive research has identified the common characteristics of chronic offenders, the conditions—personal, familial, societal, or educational—that seem to contribute to delinquent behavior, and the factors that seem to prevent repeat offenders from "growing out of it" and returning to the straight-and-narrow, like the majority of other youths who get into trouble.

Perhaps most striking is the finding that the pathways toward crime are well-marked. Across subcultures, over time, the behavior patterns leading to chronic criminal behavior are distinct—and they almost always involve serious behavior problems in early childhood.

"In early childhood, some boys and girls begin to show patterns of aggressive behavior in their family, in their schools, in their interaction with peers, or in their activities in the community. They pick fights with their brothers and sisters, scream at their parents, verbally attack their teachers, bully their peers, and intimidate younger children in the neighborhood," writes Ronald Slaby, a crime prevention expert at the Education Development Center and Harvard University. This behavior is "the best predictor of chronic delinquent offending and violence in adolescence."

A Common Progression of Problems

Most children who display antisocial tendencies do not go on to become juvenile delinquents or career criminals—most do not. But those who do become chronic offenders typically follow a common progression of increasingly serious behaviors: problems begin with defiance, lying or bullying, followed by fighting

Excerpted from Richard A. Mendel, "Why Prevention? A Brief Look at Youth, Crime, and Public Policy," in *Prevention or Pork? A Hard-Headed Look at Youth-Oriented Anti-Crime Programs*, a publication of the American Youth Policy Forum, Washington, D.C., 1995.

among individuals or gangs, and then serious violent behavior starting with aggravated assault and leading (in some cases) to rape, robbery, and perhaps homicide. Early alcohol abuse (often marijuana abuse as well) precedes the slide into violence for the vast majority of serious offenders. Subsequent violent behavior is often associated with use of other illicit drugs such as cocaine and heroin.

"Adult antisocial behavior virtually *requires* childhood antisocial behavior," explains Lee Robins. Yet, for the most part, children who display warning signs of violence receive little focused attention. They may be punished by parents or teachers, or suspended from school, but seldom are they engaged in a well-designed program to address the underlying causes of their problem behavior.

Critical Risk Factors

What is it that leads these youth to violence? Here again, the work of criminologists, psychologists, sociologists, and public health scholars sheds light. Through hundreds of studies their research has identified critical risk factors in five domains:

Family: "Children who demonstrate antisocial behavior come from very nonsupportive families at two extremes: either the family is repressive and abusive, or it seriously neglects the child from the early years on," reports Joy G. Dryfoos, a leading scholar on adolescence. Surprisingly, parental neglect is almost as strong a predictor of subsequent violence as physical abuse, and parental rejection is the most powerful predictor of all. In one study, 50 percent of children rejected by their parents went on to commit serious crimes, versus only 20 percent of abused and neglected children.

> *"Across subcultures, over time, the behavior patterns leading to chronic criminal behavior are distinct—and they almost always involve serious behavior problems in early childhood."*

As veteran criminologist Travis Hirschi has put it, "the closer the child's relationship with his parents, the more he is attached to and identified with them, the lower his chances of delinquency." This finding holds in one- and two-parent families alike. As studies have concluded, "Parental absence due to divorce or separation has been found to have either a small or inconsistent association with adolescent delinquency," while marital conflict in two-parent families "is strongly associated with juvenile delinquency and conduct disorder."

Neighborhoods and Peer Groups

Neighborhood: Growing up in an underclass neighborhood is closely correlated with increased risk of delinquency. Of course, most poor people are not criminals. Prevalence of drugs, crime, guns, and poverty have been identified as causes of delinquency, as has the lack of positive role models, thriving community-based organizations, quality schools, adequately funded social services, cohesive community leadership, and safe and constructive recreational opportunities. "The inclination to violence springs from the circumstances of life among the ghetto poor—the lack of jobs that pay a living wage, the stigma of race, the fallout from rampant drug use and drug trafficking, and the resulting alienation and lack of hope for the future," writes Elijah Anderson, a University of Pennsylvania urban anthropologist who has spent many years observing and documenting the often dangerous and deviant behavioral dynamics of the inner city.

> *"Growing up in an underclass neighborhood is closely correlated with increased risk of delinquency."*

Peer Groups: Frequent association with delinquent and drug-using peers or participation in a youth gang are also critical indicators of delinquency. Unlike adult crime, the majority of youth crime is committed in groups. In fact, writes Delbert Elliott, "The strongest and most immediate cause of the actual onset of serious violent behavior is involvement with a delinquent peer group. It is here that violence is modeled, encouraged, and rewarded; and justifications for disengaging one's moral obligation to others are taught and reinforced." Membership in a youth gang is an especially powerful risk factor: though gangs can provide youth a sense of belonging, plus some safety from real dangers, extended involvement in a gang leads to "exceptionally high rates of delinquency," write David Huizinga, Rolf Loeber, and Terence P. Thornberry.

School Ties

School: "While patterns of behavior learned in early childhood carry over into the school context, the school has its own potential for generating conflict and frustration and violent responses to these situations," Elliott writes. "During junior and senior high school, a clear adolescent status hierarchy emerges, and much of the violence at school is related to competition for status and status-related confrontations. Ability tracking also contributes to a collective adaptation to school failure and peer rejection by grouping academically poor students and those who are aggressive troublemakers together in the same classes. Delinquent peer groups tend to emerge out of these classes and individual feelings of anger, rejection and alienation are mutually reinforced in these groups."

Though there is some evidence that delinquent behavior subsides somewhat in the months immediately after dropping out (due to reduced feelings of failure and frustration), the overwhelming overrepresentation of school dropouts among the nation's prison population confirms the powerful ongoing link between school failure and criminal behavior.

Individual factors: In addition to these external factors, several individual characteristics can also predispose youth to violence. Hyperactivity and attention deficit disorder are closely correlated with delinquency, as is low intelligence. Many children who exhibit behavior problems demonstrate maladaptive beliefs, thought processes, and behavior patterns that predispose them to violence. Children may attribute hostility to peers where none is intended. They may lack basic problem-solving skills or the ability to identify non-violent solutions when social problems arise. They may hold beliefs justifying violence in a wide variety of situations, and they may resort to violence quickly in conflict situations. "Under conditions of high emotional arousal," reports Harvard's Ronald Slaby, "aggressive individuals are likely to default almost automatically to learned stereotypic patterns of behavior that are often both violent and inappropriate for the situation." These social skill deficits have been the focus of several delinquency programs in recent times—some with highly successful results.

Resiliency Against Risk

These risk factors explain much about who becomes a criminal and who doesn't. They provide important clues for the formulation of effective prevention strategies. If prevention can improve parenting skills and family cohesion in high-risk households, if it can reduce (or ameliorate) the negative influences youth experience in their neighborhoods and schools, if it can intervene to inhibit the formation or expansion of deviant peer groups, prevention can make a major contribution to our nation's struggle against crime.

Yet these risk factors tell only part of the prevention story. "A striking finding of studies of risk factors associated with offending is that many adolescents who are exposed to risk factors do *not* become delinquent," reports the Congressional Office of Technology Assessment. "Studies have found that a positive temperament, including positive mood and a tendency to evoke positive responses in others, a high IQ, positive school and work experiences, high self-esteem, some degree of structure in the environment, and one good relationship with a parent or other adult reduce the risk factors associated with offending."

> *"Many children who exhibit behavior problems demonstrate maladaptive beliefs, thought processes, and behavior patterns that predispose them to violence."*

"Research has demonstrated that healthy bonding is a significant factor in children's resistance to crime and drugs," explain David Hawkins and Richard Catalano of the University of Washington. "Strong positive bonds have three important components: (1) *attachment*—positive relations with others; (2) *commitment*—an investment in the future; and (3) *belief* about what is right and wrong, with an orientation to positive, moral behavior and action."

Preventing Youth Violence

"A variety of social experiences may contribute to violence. . . . Yet none of these social experiences or sources of social interaction, singly or in combination, will inevitably lead to violent behavior for all individuals," writes Ronald

Slaby. "Much like a physiological immune system, learned patterns of psychological mediation are capable of succumbing to, neutralizing, or counteracting the impact of experiences that act as violence toxins."

This potential for resiliency, this capacity of youth to overcome troubling influences and develop into healthy, productive, law-abiding adults, provides a second critical underpinning for prevention. Not just a means to treat behavior disorders or solve social problems, prevention can also be a vehicle for building up this social "immune system" in high-risk youth—creating a moral compass, so to speak, a commitment to prosocial values combined with the skills, knowledge, and thought processes necessary to avoid the temptations and pressures that lead to violence.

"Understanding [the] risk factors [for violence] is a first step toward identifying effective means of prevention," write Hawkins and Catalano, whose "social development strategy" underlies the comprehensive approach to serious, violent, and chronic juvenile offenders advocated by the Office of Juvenile Justice and Delinquency Prevention. "Equally important is the evidence that certain *protective factors* can help shield youngsters from problems. If we can reduce risks while increasing protection throughout the course of young people's development, we can prevent these problems and promote healthy, pro-social growth."

A Lack of Moral Values Causes Youth Violence

by Don Feder

About the author: *Don Feder is a syndicated conservative columnist for the* Boston Herald. *He has also written articles for the* National Review, Human Events, *and* Reason.

Thinking about the three Norwegian children who killed a classmate, a question I was asked at the close of a college speech came to mind.

In the chilly cradle of social democracy, little Silje Marie Redergard, a 5-year-old girl, was kicked, stoned and left to freeze to death by three boys, ages 5 and 6. Norway's prime minister blamed Silje's death on "free market" violence, specifically those combative capitalists, the Teenage Mutant Ninja Turtles.

Terrible as it is, the Scandinavian tragedy is child's play next to the everyday horrors enacted in America's cities.

Typical Theories

The Centers for Disease Control and Prevention reports that while the overall homicide rate remained fairly steady between 1985 and 1991, the murder rate for 15- to 19-year-olds jumped 154 percent.

The cultural elite has its usual unedifying explanations. Interviewed on *CBS This Morning*, CDC director Dr. David Satcher noted, "Easy access to guns for teen-agers is certain[ly] a major factor."

Were guns less prevalent in our society in 1985? Did teens of the mid-'80s not know where to obtain firearms or how to use them? Satcher's analysis confuses cause and effect. A teen-ager who picks up a gun does so volitionally. The question Satcher begs is why more teens are grabbing guns today.

Troubling Climate

Equally predictable is an article in the Oct. 21–23, 1994, *USA Weekend*, by Alex Kotlowitz, author of *There Are No Children Here,* commenting on kid killers.

Reprinted from Don Feder's November 16, 1994, column, "Teen Murder and the Poverty of Values," as it appeared in the *Conservative Chronicle*. Reprinted by permission of Don Feder and Creators Syndicate.

His solutions to juvenile murder? Keep schools open evenings. Attract working people back to inner-city neighborhoods and "get involved yourself: We're all neighbors." Thank you, Mister Rogers.

Why are these kids so violent? Kotlowitz would say it's because they're desensitized by the violence they see around them. Because they're poor. Because they're not getting enough counseling.

> *"Our poverty—one which makes us particularly susceptible to the crime contagion—is a poverty of values."*

But where did the climate of violence that's traumatized kid killers originate? Poverty? Compared to the poor of the Depression era, the poor today live like royalty. So why did the crime rate decline during the 1930s?

Depressed neighborhoods? Turn-of-the-century immigrant slums and the shanty-towns that dotted the Southern landscape of 30 years ago were positively pacific compared to the mean streets of contemporary urban America.

Moral Poverty

Our poverty—one which makes us particularly susceptible to the crime contagion—is a poverty of values. In this regard, the question from a collegian at the end of a speech was apropos.

I said a moral reversion to the '40s and '50s would be an absolute blessing for this nation. In the question and answer period came the predictable challenge. Did I really believe people were more moral a generation ago, and if so, why?

That Americans generally were better behaved can't be denied. In the days of Dwight Eisenhower, we didn't need "The Club" to retain possession of our autos. Women could walk city streets at night in relative safety.

Indulgence's Faults

Human nature didn't change in the course of four decades. People were just as covetous, lecherous and violence-prone in 1954 as they are in 1994. Teens were every bit as rebellious and hormone-driven then as now.

The difference? Society changed all of its red lights to green lights. Once we taught sexual restraint through our schools and popular culture. Now we teach indulgence.

Once we taught personal responsibility. Now we teach that if you do something despicable, it's everyone's fault but your own. Were you an abused child? Do you lack an adequate education, a meaningful job, self-esteem?

The results of these lessons are glaringly apparent in the young, who are impressionable and haven't lived long enough to learn by experience. Adults mouth clichés. Children live them.

We tell them they're not responsible for their conduct, that the world owes them everything from material possessions to happiness, to trust their feelings, then wonder that they act on these beliefs with murderous consistency.

In this regard, the Jimmy Stewart movie *Mr. Smith Goes To Washington* contains a powerful message.

Jefferson Smith, an idealistic young senator, has been framed by Claude Rains's character because Smith threatens to expose the latter's crooked schemes. Smith is filibustering to prevent his expulsion. He's been on his feet for days, pleading his innocence to an indifferent Senate. Finally he collapses from exhaustion.

Rains leaps up and—after attempting suicide—confesses his guilt in an anguished voice: My cronies and I are thieves but "not that boy!"

We Need Shame

Given the moral climate of the times, viewers found this credible. Corrupt as Rains's character was, he still had a sense of shame, instilled by his parents, church, teachers—someone.

That is what too many of our children lack. Give it to them now. Give it to them quickly, or they will seem positively angelic beside the monsters they breed.

Illegitimacy Contributes to Youth Violence

by Allan C. Brownfeld

About the author: *Allan C. Brownfeld is a syndicated columnist and a contributing editor for the* St. Croix Review.

Those, such as Attorney General Janet Reno, who repeatedly speak of the "root causes" of crime rather than the need to remove offenders from society, rarely confront the nation's skyrocketing illegitimacy rate—which is clearly a basic *cause* of crime, family dissolution, and social disarray.

From 1960 to 1988 the rate of children born to unmarried women soared from 5 percent to 26 percent. For blacks it is approximately 70 percent. The divorce rate has more than doubled in a generation. At any given moment, about a quarter of American children are living in a single-parent family. In 1975, among married couples with children, 41 percent of the mothers worked; in 1991 the figure was 64 percent.

Children with absent fathers and working mothers get little attention. They also commit more crime and are more likely to be victimized by crime. The arrest rate for teenagers ages 14–17 in 1960 was 47 per thousand. In 1991, it was 132. The "victimization" rate of males ages 16–19 was an incredible 121 percent, up from 89 percent as recently as 1988.

Crime Stems from Single-Parent Families

David L. Levy, president of the Children's Rights Council and author of the book *The Best Parent Is Both Parents*, reports that new research indicates that neither poverty nor race but the fragile structure of the American family is the primary cause of crime. Douglas A. Smith and G. Roger Jarjoura published findings in the *Journal of Research in Crime and Delinquency* analyzing victimization data on over 11,000 individuals from three urban areas. They discovered that the proportion of single-parent households in a community predicts its rate of violent crime and burglary while poverty level does not. Furthermore,

Reprinted, with permission, from Allan Brownfeld, "The Growing Illegitimacy Rate: A 'Root Cause' of Crime Many Prefer to Ignore," *St. Croix Review*, May 1994.

the percentage of non-whites in an area has "no significant influence on rates of violent crime."

The Children's Rights Council of Georgia correlated demographic data and found that states with the highest number of single-parent households—such as New York, Georgia, Alabama, Louisiana, and Washington, D.C.—also had the lowest child well-being rating and increasingly high rates of crime. States with the smallest number of single-parent households were New Hampshire, Vermont, North Dakota, and Iowa. Here, crime rates were low and child well-being rates were high.

David Levy points out that even a poor state like West Virginia has high ratings for child well-being due to a high percentage of intact families. "The assumption heretofore that poverty is the problem has been refuted," he said. "Poverty is the symptom, and the two-parent family is the solution." America needs to move toward encouraging family formation and preservation, and in the event of separation/divorce or unwed parents, the child's right to two parents and extended family that marriage would have facilitated must be protected.

Illegitimacy Rates Keep Rising

Much controversy resulted from an article in the *Wall Street Journal* by American Enterprise Institute senior fellow Charles Murray entitled "The Coming White Underclass." Murray recalled that when Senator Daniel Patrick Moynihan (D-N.Y.) wrote his 1965 warning about the disintegration of the black family (for which he was accused of "racism"), 26 percent of black births were to unwed mothers. Today, the figure among whites is 22 percent—only 4 percentage points lower. At the same time, the percentage of black births out of wedlock has soared to 68 percent which has resulted in a criminal underclass in urban areas. Murray now predicts that illegitimacy rates will increase as rapidly among low-income whites in the 1990s as they did among low-income blacks in the 1960s. "You will have an underclass that is about four or five times the size of the one we have now," he says.

"Children with absent fathers and working mothers get little attention. They also commit more crime and are more likely to be victimized by crime."

In Murray's view, "Illegitimacy is the single most important social problem of our time—more important than crime, drugs, poverty, illiteracy, welfare or homelessness because it drives everything else."

The Welfare System Is Failing

One element contributing to the growing illegitimacy rate is the welfare system—which rewards single women for having children. Former Secretary of Education William Bennett notes that, "The current system is a complete failure. We have spent enormous sums over the past three decades on welfare programs and what do we have to show for it? An underclass which is much larger, more violent, more poorly educated and which consists of many more single families."

President Bill Clinton's expressions of concern about these trends illustrates, Bennett points out, a widespread "acknowledgment among experts in the field that a strong link exists between social pathologies, exploding rates of illegitimacy, and welfare payment to single mothers. . . . Welfare may not cause illegitimacy, but it does make it economically viable. There is hardly any question anymore that illegitimacy rates would fall, probably dramatically, if payments . . . were stopped. Welfare is illegitimacy's economic life-support system."

> *"Illegitimacy is the single most important social problem of our time—more important than crime, drugs, poverty, illiteracy, welfare or homelessness because it drives everything else."*

Beyond this, declares Bennett, there is now "agreement on an important moral principle: Having children out of wedlock is *wrong*—not simply economically unwise for the individuals involved, or a financial burden on society, but morally wrong."

Concern Among Liberals

For many years, Democrats, especially liberal Democrats, refused to discuss growing illegitimacy rates and family breakdown. The programs they have so eagerly supported—such as value-free sex-education programs and the distribution of condoms in the schools—have conveyed an "anything goes" attitude toward sex and marriage. When former Vice President Dan Quayle discussed this subject, citing the bad example of television character Murphy Brown's decision to have a baby out of wedlock, he was ridiculed. Now, even the most radical members of the Clinton Administration are having second thoughts, at least in their public rhetoric. Thus, Secretary of Health and Human Services Donna Shalala said in an interview that, "I don't like to put this in moral terms, but I do believe that having children out of wedlock is just wrong."

Things have become so bad that even liberals, who promoted a philosophy which led to this societal collapse, are lamenting current trends. A member of President Clinton's welfare-reform task force says that, "You couldn't even *talk* about this stuff in a Democratic setting until very recently. There's been progress. People aren't talking about illegitimacy as an alternative lifestyle anymore."

Thus far, however, only the rhetoric has changed. The Department of Health and Human Services has created an animated condom for use in advertising and the Justice Department has lowered the standard of what constitutes child pornography. . . .

It is clear that the fabric of our society is in serious danger of unraveling. Those who brought it to this point are unlikely to be the ones to change course. Still, the fact that the nation is prepared to focus upon these negative trends is at least a first step in their resolution.

The Lack of a Structured Family Life Causes Youth Violence

by Emilio Viano

About the author: *Emilio Viano teaches at the School of Public Affairs of the American University in Washington, D.C., and is the author of* Critical Issues in Victimology.

In today's rapidly changing world, people frequently move in and out of local communities. What was once a homogeneous rural village becomes a "boom-town," attracting people with different lifestyles and placing difficult demands on existing values, norms, institutions and services. Generational and demographic changes affect many rural areas. Young people depart for the cities, leaving their elders behind. In cities, young adults may move out of the neighborhood to another one, and their aging parents cannot follow them. They face the challenge of having to accept, respect, and interact with newcomers who are frequently from a different race, ethnicity, or religion.

In both the rural and urban situations, conflict and anomie may fester as established folkways and mores confront the challenge of a multiplicity of lifestyles, values, and norms. There is no question that in today's world, more than ever before, the stability of many communities and their support functions are challenged by vast population migrations, political upheavals, shifts in economic power and productivity, and dramatic improvements in the ease of travel.

The Importance of Community

Weak connections to the larger environment, or its failure to provide needed resources to a community, may entrap the members and begin a negative process fueled by the community's disempowerment. The more a community is denied resources and services, and the more its residents are blocked from acquiring

Excerpted from Emilio Viano, "Empowering the Family," *Peace Review*, vol. 6, no. 2 (June 1994). Reprinted by permission of Carfax Publishing Ltd., PO Box 25, Abingdon, Oxfordshire OX14 3UE, United Kingdom.

needed skills, self-esteem, and communal ties, the more powerless the community becomes and the greater the potential for disorder, conflict, and crime. Identity, competence, self-direction, and relatedness are essential elements for the health of any community.

The family, as the most intimate and influential environment in which human development takes place, is an essential building block of the community and, ultimately, of society. But the definition, structure, and functions of the family are in a state of flux and change.

To understand crime and violence we need a perspective that examines the intricate way in which certain factors interact to negatively affect certain individuals, families, and their social interconnections. Our inquiry must be multidisciplinary, using insights and approaches provided by epidemiology and human ecology. We can consider crime and violence as a kind of disease. Epidemiology approaches disease by examining the web of causation—or multiple interacting factors—rather than by seeking a unique, root cause.

Human ecology shows us that families and the external social structure can generate both pro- and antisocial behaviors by individuals and groups. What we know about child development suggests that the family is an institution in society whose health is far more important for preventing crime and violence than the state of its justice system. But we cannot talk credibly about the family's importance without sufficiently considering how structural elements in society—such as political, economic, educational, and religious institutions—affect the family task most clearly connected to crime and violence: child rearing and development.

> *"The family, as the most intimate and influential environment in which human development takes place, is an essential building block of the community and, ultimately, of society."*

Let's begin with child development. Through competent child raising, potentially violent and generally dangerous human forces can be controlled. Besides its biological makeup, the newborn is given a capacity to form relationships and an aggressive quest for survival. What makes us human is our interconnection, be it linguistic, cultural, political, or religious. The environment for most humans includes, most closely, family, friends, neighborhood, and school and then, less evidently, laws, social attitudes, and institutions.

The capacity of heads of households to satisfy basic needs for themselves and their dependents helps shape the family's psychological and social feeling of ability, competence, and contentment. Thus, the family, as the society's basic building block and its primary agent of socialization, can play a significant role in either crime production or prevention.

Variations of Familial Crime

Crime within the family, as a category, applies to those criminal situations in which both the perpetrator and the victim are members of the same family. The expression "within the family" encompasses acts between parents, between siblings, between parent and child, and between generations. The full range of crimes can take place within the family. They might include crimes of assault, such as spouse abuse, child abuse, sibling violence, co-wife fighting (in polygamous societies), and elderly abuse; or other crimes, such as child kidnapping, larceny, robbery, theft, extortion, embezzlement, child selling, infanticide, child pornography, prostitution, vandalism, arson, and even murder.

Violent crime within the family is strongly influenced by broader cultural patterns of violence among people who reside in the same community. For example, one can expect to find more wife abuse in communities where men altercate with one another when drunk, where women fight with other women, where men fight with other men, and where young women are put through hurtful initiation rites. Considerable progress has been made in several countries in labeling as crimes certain family behaviors that were previously overlooked, such as spouse and child abuse and forced sex in marriage. Although there have been calls to criminalize these behaviors, no similar calls have been made for criminalizing the property crimes that also take place within the family.

"Youth who have strong bonds with parents and teachers and who expect rewards from legitimate activities in the future have low rates of delinquency."

Crimes against the family encompass those events where either an individual or a group not connected to the family perpetrates a crime against the family as a group. These crimes affect more than one member of the family, take place in the family domain, or entail family possessions. The assortment of crimes against the family is considerable: burglary, larceny, car theft, swindling, kidnapping, hostage taking, mass murder, and racial, religious, ethnic, or political persecution.

Crimes by the family refer to criminal acts carried out by a family as a group against nonmembers The idea of a family as a criminal enterprise might sound strange. But the family mirrors major trends in society. Thus, if a society is belligerent and violent, the family is likely to be violent as well. The family also furnishes role models for deviant behavior and may even expressly teach its members how to be deviant. For example, when parents use physical force to deal with children or each other, they are teaching family members to use violence themselves, either inside or outside the family.

How central criminal activity is to family life varies considerably. In some cases, otherwise law-abiding family members may commit a crime once while under the influence of alcohol consumed at a wedding, funeral, or other family reunion. In other cases, two or more family members may be regularly involved in criminal activities, such as when two siblings, who hold jobs, also sell drugs or smuggle goods, distribute pornographic materials, operate confidence schemes, or burglarize residences. Sometimes the entire family may engage in crime as their way of making a living. Also, some crimes have historically been connected with families, like feuds and vendettas.

Deviance and Punishment

Sanctions are necessary to prevent criminal behavior. But for sanctions to be effective, it is not necessary or desirable for them to entail corporal punishment or legal intervention. Actually, the most effective sanction is receiving disapproval from those we most care about. The strongest sanctions come from the interactional costs of losing one's reputation or social attachments.

Formal sanctions, in themselves, have little capacity to change behavior. First, what authorities may consider as punishing or rewarding may be interpreted very differently by the intended targets of the sanctions. Sanctions derive their power from individuals' need to win the approval or avoid the disapproval of their group. Official social control works only to the degree that it negatively affects our network of interpersonal relationships. When it does the opposite, such as when getting arrested, sentenced, and incarcerated is considered a rite of adult passage or a badge of honor, it is totally ineffective.

Deviants and potential deviants look to significant others in their personal environment far more than to official rules when they weigh the outcome of their acts. Informal punishments are more effective than formal ones, because the latter work only to the extent they damage one's reputation and social ties. People whose social status is such that sanctions will diminish their position in their relevant group will be quite responsive to control strategies.

Disgrace in Families

On the other hand, penalties—threatened or applied—that do not discredit have little power. Sanctions may be annoying or physically painful but they will have little lasting effect if they do not disgrace. Threatened or actual penalties from friends and family are the best forecasters of the impact of sanctions. These sanctions have an immediate effect. Instead, when the standards of subgroups run counter to official values, they cancel out the effectiveness of formal sanctions. When punishment from intimates is expected, deviant behavior is infrequent. People are more worried about their reputation in the eyes of family, friends, and coworkers than about formal legal authority.

According to Allan Y. Horwitz, "Social integration predicts the effectiveness of preventive social control." Those who are strongly integrated into a powerful informal group will be most influenced by its system of rewards and penalties. Youth who have strong bonds with parents and teachers and who expect rewards from legitimate activities in the future have low rates of delinquency. This may be particularly true of women. Generally, women are more sensitive than men to interpersonal relationships, personal reputations, value connectedness, and intimacy. Young people who have few connections with family and school, but serious ties with nonconformist mates, show the highest rates of deviant behavior.

The Power of Group Control

Thus, groups (and therefore, families) that are small, close, and tightly drawn together have the strength to affect reputation and bonding. Thus, they can exercise the most powerful social control and command allegiance to shared norms. These groups are more likely than any other to have members who want to do what is right in the eyes of their leaders (parents) and mates. Penalties in these groups elicit more attachment costs and reputational harm than in less interconnected groups.

In *Crime, Shame and Reintegration* (1989), John Braithwaite argues that societies that foster strong interconnections and communal obligations among their members are the best equipped to promote preventive social control. The Japanese are often recognized as more likely to be intertwined in closely knit groups that inhibit deviant behavior through informal social controls. Their presumptive control is reflected in unspoken communication in Japan. People who correctly belong do not have to be told. They understand instinctively what the group wants.

The importance of belonging is learned early in life and is a paramount Japanese value at all levels. The emphasis on teamwork and on offering each other support has positive implications for the low overall crime rate in Japan. Japanese family relations are very important to the role of the group; family members have a strong sense of responsibility for one another.

"The weakening of adult supervision, the rise of the automobile, and the growth of an independent youth culture have reduced the informal controls over adolescent activities."

The Japanese criminal justice system relies on the power of informal social control and on the threat of being shamed and ostracized. Rather than deterrence, it emphasizes "reintegrative shaming." Individuals are shamed into abiding by the obligations of their social environment, and their groups have an equal obligation to assume responsibility for their deviant members.

As societies evolve from traditional to modern, they have increasing difficulty in exercising effective social control. When individuals are not highly dependent on groups, they get fewer returns from conforming and suffer less bonding and reputational costs from punishments. The reduced dependence on the group that characterizes modern life allows individuals to ignore the opinions others have of them.

Groups themselves are weakened and therefore less able to impose informal penalties that support legal sanctions. Interpersonal relations become more individualistic and less oriented toward collective obligations. Under these circumstances, groups are less able to exercise preventive control.

The weakening of adult supervision, the rise of the automobile, and the growth of an independent youth culture have reduced the informal controls over adolescent activities. Compared to their parents and grandparents, teenagers now spend considerably more time in unsupervised activities with other adolescents. As a result, youth deviance is rapidly escalating in the contemporary world. Adults are also more likely to engage in deviant activities in the absence of any group dependency. To reverse this trend, and to reconstitute one of the most effective mechanisms for crime prevention, we must focus on rejuvenating the family.

Gangs Perpetuate Youth Violence

by Nina George Hacker

About the author: *Nina George Hacker is the assistant editor of* Family Voice, *a monthly publication that promotes traditional and Judeo-Christian values.*

In December 1996, Los Angeles police arrested a 14-year-old gang member on charges of dousing two 11-year-olds with alcohol and setting them on fire.

Time was, juvenile offenses consisted of truancy, shoplifting, "drag" racing, petty vandalism, or underaged drinking and smoking. Occasionally, a fist-fighting "rumble" made the news if one gang member pulled a switchblade knife on another. But killings were rare, and drugs were virtually unknown. Jump ahead to today's generation of adolescents, whom Princeton scholar John J. DiIulio, Jr. characterizes as "fatherless, godless and jobless."

As a result, says criminologist James Alan Fox, we are seeing a veritable "epidemic" of criminal violence by juveniles, especially the "superpredators"— who *"kill and maim on impulse,* without any intelligible motive." They are kids whose faces are empty and hard, their eyes reflecting anger and hurt. "Bonded to no one, with no hope for the future, no fear of justice and absolutely no respect for human life," writes Arianna Huffington, chairman of the Center for Effective Compassion. They are teens like the gang who, in 1989, savagely beat, then repeatedly stabbed and raped a jogger in New York's Central Park— leaving her for dead. Later, one of the attackers told prosecutors, *"It was fun."* In 1994 alone, the FBI says, more than 114,000 persons under 18 were charged with *rape, robbery,* and *aggravated assault.* What has happened to America's kids?

Armed and Dangerous

Twelve percent of teens in a 1996 Harris poll reported carrying a weapon— and as many as three out of four had seen or been in fights involving weapons. Even colleges—traditionally havens of quiet congeniality—are battling sharp

Excerpted from Nina George Hacker, "Gangs: When Families Fail," *Family Voice*, February 1997. Reprinted with permission.

increases in student crimes such as murder, rape, and illegal drug trafficking. One university official blamed the rise on drug use and violent behavior by middle and high school students who bring their bad habits onto campus.

According to a recent Justice Department study, children *under the age of 15* accounted for one-third of all juvenile crime arrests in 1995. Not only are the perpetrators getting younger and younger, so are their targets: In 1996 one in four victims of violent crime was between the *ages of 12 and 17*. Consider the following true stories from recent news accounts:

> *"California authorities characterize today's youth gangs as 'heavily armed . . . involved in drug trafficking, witness intimidation, extortion, and bloody territorial wars.'"*

- Five boys, aged 13 to 14, *brutally tortured* another 13-year-old boy for hours in the west coast *home* of one of the attackers.
- In Virginia, a 13-year-old boy was charged with three counts of *extortion* and one count of *robbery* after threatening schoolmates.
- A 16-year-old Washington, D.C.-area girl was sentenced to life in prison for the gang-ordered *killing* of a 14-year-old classmate—she was *stabbed more than 40 times*.

Between 1983 and 1993, murders committed by *14- to 17-year-olds* rose a whopping *165 percent*. During that same time period, juvenile arrests *doubled*, with an estimated 2.7 million teenagers arrested in 1995. Today, youths under the age of 25 commit *nearly half* of all violent crime, reported David G. Walchak, president of the International Association of Chiefs of Police. Moreover, close to one quarter of U.S. students surveyed by the Justice Department say they knew someone who died violently.

Not surprisingly, many of these deaths are gang-related. Describing "a violent and insidious new form of organized crime," California authorities characterize today's youth gangs as "heavily armed . . . involved in drug trafficking, witness intimidation, extortion, and bloody territorial wars." When Metropolitan Life surveyed police, students, and teachers, 93 percent attributed violence in schools to gang membership. And, according to Chief Walchak, street gangs have been a significant factor in the increase in homicides by juveniles.

Gang Activity Explored

How extensive *is* gang activity? The Justice Department claims there are over 120,000 gang members in 1,436 gangs nationwide. But in 1995, the *Washington Times* reported more than 350,000 gang members on the west coast. And the National School Safety Center estimated 125,000 gang members just in Los Angeles. Some "supergangs"—or "nations"—include thousands of members.

No longer exclusively an inner-city phenomenon, gang networks have infiltrated even small towns and the nation's most comfortable, secure suburbs. For instance, the latest federal crime statistics identified more than 20 gangs in Montgomery County, Maryland, one of the most affluent areas in the U.S. And two of the largest, most notorious gangs, the rival "Crips" and "Bloods," now terrorize 58 cities in 35 states across the country—with an estimated 70,000 members in Los Angeles alone. Often, writes researcher Robert Maginnis, "gangs are formed in prison and then emigrate to the streets."

Most gangs are racially or ethnically segregated, and the majority are African American or Hispanic. White gangsters tend to be neo-Nazi skinheads or "punk" rockers into "heavy metal" culture and anarchic rebellion. Gang structure revolves around territories ("tagging" and defending one's turf to the death) and/or money-making activities (robbery, extortion, drug dealing). Specific gang clothing, colors, signs, tattoos, and graffiti are used to distinguish one gang from another.

The gang's energy is fueled by their music. While black "gangsta" rap glorifies killing, the brutal abuse of women, and disrespect for authority, white punk and heavy metal artists promote random violence, sadism, and satanic worship. Gang-influenced movies and comic books transmit gang language, symbols, and traditions.

Nihilistic thinking pervades the gang mentality. Social scholar Cornel West comments: "The frightening result is a numbing detachment from others and a self-destructive disposition toward the world. Life without meaning, hope, and love breeds a cold-hearted, mean-spirited outlook that destroys both the individual and others."

Who Joins Gangs?

Typically, "gangsters" are males as young as eight and rarely older than 22—most are either killed or imprisoned before age 25. "Partying and fighting, the core activities of a gang, are what draw many young males," Maginnis observes. Girls tag along as auxiliary members, although some are now forming their own all-female gangs—with names like "Nasty Girls Crew." According to *Newsweek*, almost all crime is now committed by males between the ages of 15 and 35. However, the most recent Justice Department figures indicate rapidly rising crime rates for teenaged girls as well. In 1995, females accounted for one-fourth of all juvenile crime.

> *"Nihilistic thinking pervades the gang mentality."*

In October 1996, two Maryland girls, 12 and 14—the youngest to ever be charged—were arrested for armed carjacking.

Jack Levin, a criminologist at Northeastern University, found that girl gangs are now imitating boys' physical violence: "For the slightest reasons, a dispute over a boyfriend, a challenging glance, girls will get into violent confrontations where they used to have [only] verbal [disputes]."

Gang members, girls or boys, "will *kill* over trivial matters—a jacket, some sneakers, a dirty look," says James Fox. "For them, murder is just not the taboo it once was." Yancey Griggs, director of Juvenile Hall in Detroit, laments: "Twenty years ago a youngster would shy away from a killer. . . . Today kids flock around [him]. He's a big shot, a hero, and he shows no remorse, no sense of wrong." Twenty-five percent of seventh through tenth graders polled in 1996 agreed: "Most young kids admire gang members."

Home Away from Home

Many see gang membership as a way of acquiring power and protection from the crime and violence they fear in their communities. But the primary draw of gangster "families" is their offer of the identity, acceptance, security, and attention so many kids are not getting at home. Black street gangs will call each other "cuz" for "cousin." And gang members' loyalty to one another, even unto death, presents a strong appeal to abused or neglected children.

"Gang members' loyalty to one another, even unto death, presents a strong appeal to abused or neglected children."

A 1995 Heritage Foundation survey showed that a substantial majority of teenaged criminals are from broken and single-parent households. In gangs, the older male leader often functions as a surrogate father—from whom his devoted "homeboys" will accept parent-like discipline and even punishment. "Gangs provide a sense of belonging and fraternity," says John King, a Maryland police captain. The paradox, he added, "is that the gang's approach for achieving these things is illegal and destructive to the gang member, the family unit and the community."

Former president Lyndon Johnson said: "The family is the cornerstone of society. . . . When the family collapses, it is the children who are usually damaged. When it happens on a massive scale, the community itself is crippled." Today we are seeing the result of our crippled society in the massive rise of gangs that—tragically—give children a home away from the home their parents have failed to build.

Television Violence May Cause Youth Violence

by Mary A. Hepburn

About the author: *Mary A. Hepburn is a professor of social science education and head of the Citizen Education Division at the Carl Vinson Institute of Government at the University of Georgia in Athens.*

With an average national TV viewing time of $7^1/_4$ hours daily, the prevalence of violence in broadcasts is a serious concern. Television programming in the United States is considered the most violent in advanced industrialized nations. Violence is common in TV entertainment—the dramas that portray stories about crime, psychotic murderers, police cases, emergency services, international terrorism, and war. The dramas are played out in highly realistic scenes of violent attacks accompanied by music and other sounds that churn up emotions.

Violence Sells

As the realism and gore in the screen images of TV entertainment have intensified, local news cameras have also increasingly focused directly on the bloody violence done to individuals in drive-by shootings, gang attacks, and domestic beatings. Why must these visual details be presented in the news? Why does a typical television evening include so many beatings, shootings, stabbings, and rapes in dramas designed for "entertainment"?

Producers of programming ascertain that scenes of violent action with accompanying fear-striking music can be counted on to hold viewers' attention, keep them awake and watching, and make them less likely to switch channels. The purpose is to gain and maintain a large number of viewers—the factor that appeals to advertisers. The generations of younger adults who have grown up with daily viewing of violence in entertainment are considered to be "hooked." A program has more commercial value if it can hold more viewers, and programmers attempt to ensure high viewer attention with doses of violent action in the program. How does all of this violence affect young people?

Excerpted from Mary A. Hepburn, "TV Violence: Myth and Reality," *Social Education*, September 1995. Reprinted with permission of the author.

The Influence of Television

Several decades ago, a few psychologists hypothesized that viewing violence in the unreal television world would have a cathartic effect and thus reduce the chances of violent behavior in the real world. But other psychologists began to doubt this notion when their research with children revealed that much action on the TV screen is perceived as real by children. L.R. Huesmann and L.D. Eron, who studied the effects of media violence on 758 youngsters in grades 1 through 3, found that children's behavior was influenced by television, especially if the youngsters were heavy viewers of violent programming. Television violence, according to the researchers, provided a script for the children to act out aggressive behavior in relationships with others. The most aggressive youngsters strongly identified with aggressive characters in the TV story, had aggressive fantasies, and expressed the attitude that violent programs portrayed life as it is. These children were also likely to perform poorly in school and often were unpopular with their peers.

Exposure to Violence Can Lead to Violence

Huesmann and Eron state that television is not the *only* variable involved, but their many years of research have left them with no doubt that heavy exposure to media violence is a highly influential factor in children and later in their adult lives.

Research in the field of public communications also supports the conclusion that exposure to television violence contributes to increased rates of aggression and violent behavior. B.S. Centerwall analyzed crime data in areas of the world with and without television and, in addition, made comparisons in areas before and after the introduction of TV. His studies determined that homicide rates doubled in ten to fifteen years after TV was introduced for the first time into specified areas of the United States and Canada.

> *"Generations of younger adults . . . have grown up with daily viewing of violence in entertainment."*

Observing that violent television programming exerts its aggressive effects primarily on children, Centerwall noted that the ten- to fifteen-year lag time can be expected before homicide rates increase. Acknowledging that other factors besides TV do have some influence on the quantity of violent crimes, Centerwall's careful statistical analysis indicated, nevertheless, that when the negative effects of TV were removed, quantitative evidence showed "there would be 10,000 fewer homicides, 70,000 fewer rapes, and 700,000 fewer injurious assaults."

Researching Themselves

Centerwall has also brought to light important research literature that has been little known among social scientists and educators concerned about television violence. In the late sixties, as a result of public hearings and a national report implying that exposure to TV increases physical aggression, the large television networks decided to commission their own research projects. NBC appointed a team of four researchers, three of whom were NBC employees, to observe more than two thousand schoolchildren up to three years to determine if watching television programs increased their physical aggressiveness. NBC reported no effect. Centerwall points out, however, that every independent researcher who has analyzed the same data finds an increase in levels of physical aggression.

> *"Research ... supports the conclusion that exposure to television violence contributes to increased rates of aggression and violent behavior."*

In the study commissioned by the ABC network, a team at Temple University surveyed young male felons who had been imprisoned for violent crimes. Results of these interviews showed that 22 to 34 percent of the young felons, especially those who were the most violent, said they had consciously imitated crime techniques learned from television programs. It was learned that, as children, felons in the study had watched an average of six hours of TV per day, about twice as much as children in the general population at that time. Research results were published privately by ABC and not released to the general public or to scientists.

Violent Shows Affect Boys

CBS commissioned a study to be conducted in London and ultimately published in England. In the study, 1,565 teenaged boys were studied for behavioral effects of viewing violent television programs, many of which were imported from the United States. The study revealed that those who watched above average hours of TV violence before adolescence committed a 49 percent higher rate of serious acts of violence than did boys who had viewed below average quantities of violence. The final report was "very strongly supportive of the hypothesis that high exposure to television violence increases the degree to which boys engage in serious violence."

Five types of TV programming were most powerful in triggering violent behavior in the boys in the London study: (1) TV plays or films in which violence is demonstrated in close personal relationships; (2) programs where violence was not necessary to the plot but just added for its own sake; (3) fictional violence of a very realistic kind; (4) violent "Westerns"; and (5) programs that present violence as being for a good cause. In summarizing the implications of the study, the research director made it clear that the results also applied to boys in U.S. cities with the same kind of violence in TV programming.

The Evidence Is Finally Revealed

For about fifteen years, these studies have received little attention. Each was either filed away or distributed to a very limited audience—not to the general public, the research community, or the press. Today, that seems eerily similar to the fate of tobacco company research on the ill effects of smoking, the results of which were also disseminated only to a small select group. The Commission on Violence and Youth of the American Psychological Association recently communicated the above-mentioned and other supporting research to its members. It concluded that evidence clearly reveals that viewing and hearing high levels of violence on television, day after day, were correlated with increased acceptance of aggression and more aggressive behavior. The commission noted that the highest level of consumption of television violence is by those most vulnerable to the effects, those who receive no moderating or mediating of what is seen on the screen.

> *"Evidence clearly reveals that viewing and hearing high levels of violence on television . . . correlated with increased acceptance of aggression and more aggressive behavior."*

This information is of great significance to social studies educators. Yet it is only since 1993 that the network-funded studies of the seventies and eighties have been gaining some attention in journals that reach educational professionals. In January 1994, an article in the *Chronicle of Higher Education* pointed up the huge "education gap" that exists between the effects of television violence that have been conclusively documented by psychological and medical researchers and what the general public knows. According to the article, "Until recently, researchers' voices have been drowned out in the din of denial and disinformation coming from executives of the television and movie industries, whose self-serving defense of violent programming has prevailed."

Shirking Responsibility

TV industry spokespersons argue that violent programs are a mere reflection of the society, and that any effort to modify programming would interfere with First Amendment guarantees of freedom of the press. Others claim to be giving the public "what they want" and take no responsibility for the effects on viewers. Another response from the networks is that parents or families must take the responsibility for preventing viewing of violent programs. In none of these defenses are the networks willing to recognize research information that shows that an appetite for violence has been stimulated by the glorification of violence and a daily diet of violent programs broadcast into every home in America.

Many Factors Can Cause Youth Violence

by Randi Henderson

About the author: *Randi Henderson, a freelance writer in Maryland, is a former reporter for the* Baltimore Sun. *She frequently writes on medical, social, and psychological issues.*

Editor's note: The names of the children interviewed for this article have been changed to protect their privacy.

Shakeela is six years old, and what she remembers most about walking into the room where her dead aunt's body lay was the blood.

"When I went in the house and I saw my Aunt Julie, I saw the blood dryin' up," she says, looking down at her small hands clasped on the table in front of her and describing what she knows about her aunt's murder by her uncle last year. "He was tryin' to scare her, but he killed her."

Sadness and fear are in Shakeela's voice, but not surprise. The violence that punctuated her aunt and uncle's relations was not news to her. "My mom and I used to go to her house when my uncle was shoppin'," she says. "We'd pack up to take her to my house. But he come home and he said, 'Freeze! Where are you goin'?' He didn't like her goin' out."

The pixie-faced first-grader is sitting in a blue vinyl chair at a long table in a narrow white room in the Spelman Building in southeast Philadelphia. On this rainswept night, she is sharing memories about her aunt's death with two other children who have also experienced the violent death of family members. The group, facilitated by two students from the University of Pennsylvania, is a component of the city's Grief Assistance Program. Usually there are at least twice this many children, but the fierce rains have kept the others home.

The Spelman Building also houses the offices of the medical examiner for the state of Pennsylvania. Just a short distance from the room where Shakeela and the other children talk, her aunt's body was autopsied.

Excerpted from Randi Henderson, "Caught in the Crossfire," *Common Boundary*, January/February 1995. Reprinted by permission of the author.

There is a glaring incongruity here: The promise and innocence of young life contrast sharply with the disillusion and ugly finality of violent death. But such contrasts are the everyday content of the lives of Shakeela and the other children in this group. This fact becomes apparent as they talk about trying to keep themselves safe in the place that most children think of as a secure sanctuary: their bedrooms.

Fear Resides

Joseph, age eight, speaks of the pain he has felt since his father's murder nearly three years ago. His father, while on the way to work, was caught in crossfire that erupted after an argument between two men in a crime-ridden, drug-steeped section of north Philadelphia. "Sometimes I think the man [who killed my father] is gonna break out of jail and beat up all the guards and come to my house and try to get me and my mom and my sister," solemn-faced Joseph says in a flat, almost expressionless tone. "I'm scared to go upstairs if I have my window up, 'cause sometimes I think he gonna go right through my screen."

"He can't go through your screen." Shakeela reassures him.

"Oh, yes he can," Joseph replies.

"Then keep your window closed."

"It be hot."

Latonya, seven, whose pretty face is topped by a floppy denim hat with the front brim pinned up by bright flowers, debunks the notion of safety offered by a closed window. "He could bust the window," she offers. She then considers whether plastic over the window would afford protection, but Joseph finds little comfort there.

"He could shoot through the window" he says, "and a bullet might get me."

"Then you be dead," concludes Latonya, who sucks a finger as she talks.

Joseph argues that he wouldn't be dead if shot in the arm or leg, but concedes that a bullet in his head or mouth would certainly be fatal. He adds, "You get shot in the throat, you might live."

And somehow, with the spontaneity of children, the conversation shifts to favorite foods (pizza and French fries), then to school, basketball, and other details of their daily lives.

> *"Pizza, school, basketball and violent death [are staples] in the lives of . . . [many] children growing up in this country today."*

Pizza, school, basketball—and violent death. Staples in the lives of Joseph, Latonya, and Shakeela—and tens of thousands of other children growing up in this country today.

Children's Reality

The centuries-old image of children as symbols of innocence is colliding with contemporary American life. The children whose relatives have been murdered may represent extremes, but their experiences are only degrees removed from those of most of their inner-city contemporaries, and their suburban and rural peers aren't immune, either. Children's lives today are saturated with violence: in their homes, in their neighborhoods and schools, on television, in movies and video games, and in the lyrics and the beat of the music they listen to.

Marian Wright Edelman, founder and president of the Children's Defense Fund (CDF), uses stark images to define the problem in CDF's 1994 report, *The State of America's Children.* From the scenes she sketches, she might well have been listening to the conversation of Shakeela, Joseph, and Latonya:

> Violence romps through our children's playgrounds, invades their bedroom slumber parties, terrorizes their Head Start centers and schools, frolics down the streets they walk to and from school, dances through their school buses, waits at the stop light and bus stop, lurks at McDonald's, runs them down on the corner, shoots through their bedroom windows, attacks their front porches and neighborhoods, abuses them or a parent at home every few seconds, and tantalizes them across the television screen every six minutes. It snatches away their parents at work, and steals their aunts, uncles, cousins, brothers, sisters, and friends. It saps their energy and will to learn, and makes them forget about tomorrow. It nags and picks at their minds and spirits day in and day out, snuffing out the promise and joy of childhood and of the future which becomes just surviving today.

Living Horror

The violence that Edelman sees is an active, dynamic force, and a powerful one, breeding a mix of terror and despair that stalks children's souls. Wanda Henry-Jenkins, a nurse, a minister in the African Methodist Episcopal Church, and the daughter of a murder victim, sees this effect on a daily basis. Henry-Jenkins is founder and executive director of the Grief Assistance Program of the Philadelphia medical examiner's office.

"Think about what children are like," she suggests. "They make monsters out of shadows on the wall. Well, those shadows are real when someone close has been murdered. It's no longer just in their minds. These children have actually lived a horror that other people only dream about. They immediately lose the sense of the world as a safe place to live in. And guess what—they're right. You do your best to make safe places in your life, but the world and the people in it are not safe, because you have discovered an evil part of humanity."

The possibility of safety retreats even further when a peer is killed. "I look in that casket, I don't see my peer—I see me," Henry-Jenkins says. "They stay home all the time, they don't want to go out and play anymore, they lose their childhood. The innocence is all gone. No more naiveté—all of it's wiped out."

Deficiency of Hope

Like Wanda Henry-Jenkins, Larry Watkins sees the results of children's continual exposure to violence. Watkins is a social worker who oversees Washington, D.C.'s Youth Trauma Services Team, which provides street-side intervention and follow-up counseling for children touched by violence. He borrows from the psychiatric lexicon for his assessment of the problem. "What I see in these children," Watkins says, "is a spiritual deficit disorder. . . . [They have] no belief in a Higher Power and no concept of wrong or right."

"These young people look at TV images of the good life in America, then they look at the blight in their own lives," explains Thomas Blagburn, director of community policing for the District of Columbia and a member of the Youth Trauma Services Team. "They're angry and they're confused." The constant exposure to violence hardens them, he says. "The violence escalates. You slap women. You fight. You kill. And then you go down to McDonald's and have a fish sandwich and think nothing about it."

> *"[Children] make monsters out of shadows on the wall. Well, those shadows are real when someone close has been murdered."*

Adds his colleague Al-Farabi Ishaq, another social worker on the team: "A newly identified population of young black males are being socialized not by their families but by the 'hood. 'If I don't have a meal to go home to, I don't have to go home,' they reason. 'I can just hang on the street with my homeys.' And these homeys, the homeboys, develop a spiritual bond among themselves," he explains. "These children have a self-image so depleted of positive reinforcement that it's not hard to understand the need to hang out.

"I have seen the lives of so many young people destroyed," he continues. "I have seen the survivors as unable to go on as the victims lying dead. These victims may not be dead, but they're maimed in a way we haven't yet begun to understand. We don't know what kind of human beings these survivors will be."

From the other side of the country, Charles Clemons, a pediatrician and emergency-medicine specialist in Richmond, California (just north of Oakland), also speaks of the impact of violence in terms of deficits. "Similar to people who suffer from protein deficiency or vitamin deficiencies, adolescents in inner cities in this country are suffering from a deficiency of work and hope and love." Clemons, who is vice president of Physicians for a Violence-Free Society, argues that our social/economic milieu "teaches kids that crime pays and that they'd better maximize their gratification today because they may not have a tomorrow."

Darrell, a sixth-grader at the Barclay School in Baltimore, echoes these sentiments, but in simpler language, when he describes how violence affects him: "It make me feel like nobody. You ain't safe no more. You got to walk the streets watchin' your back, makin' sure nothin' ain't gonna happen to you. But you can't always watch your back.

"You should be able to go outside and know that you gonna be all right. And know that you gonna survive. But you go out, you don't even know if you gonna live for another hour."

Tracing Violence

This situation did not appear overnight. From the tax rebellions of the 1700s to the Plains wars and gun-toting outlaws of the last century to the gangsters and gangs of this one, violence has been a consistent theme of American life. And while violence is not uniquely American, its prevalence in this country gives it a salience unmatched elsewhere in the world. . . .

What the statistics bear out is that today's children are not only victims of and witnesses to violence but perpetrators as well. Who better illustrates this than Robert "Yummy" Sandifer, the 11-year-old from Chicago's South Side who killed and was killed within the space of three days in 1994? Yummy, nicknamed for his love of junk food, was the son of a crack addict who had been arrested 41 times for prostitution. The boy's history of abuse and neglect was well known to Chicago's social-services system. He hung with the Black Disciples and had a reputation as one of the gang's meanest fighters, despite his age and size. When 14-year-old Shavon Dean was shot and killed, the story came out that Yummy had been directed to go after members of a rival gang but had mistakenly shot the neighborhood girl. Street talk connected the murder to the Black Disciples, and the police started closing in on the gang. Yummy became expendable. His body was found under a viaduct in a puddle of bloody mud.

Societal Influence

How does a child become entangled in such a brutal and savage web?

"What happens to kids reflects the society in general," says Arnold Goldstein, a clinical psychologist, the director of the Center for Research on Aggression at Syracuse University, and the author of several books about gangs. "We are an exceedingly aggressive country, and the kids get a steady diet of this from peers, from parents, from siblings, and from mass media. There are plenty of ways aggression is being taught, and plenty of teachers. It's where we're at as a country, and we shouldn't be surprised when it shows up in our most impressionable citizens—the kids."

Few other experts would discount the societal influence Goldstein speaks of, but all agree that there's more to the story. "It's a piece of a big, huge puzzle," says Laura Ross Greiner, project coordinator at the Center for Studies and Prevention of Violence at the University of Colorado. "You can have one child grow up in a very violent home and not be a violent adult. Another child brought up in a violent home will grow up to perpetuate the pattern of violence. A lot of things influence behavior that the child grows into, including home environment, community environment, conventional norms, and individual temperament and personality."

"In some sense violence does cause violence, but it's much more complex," concurs John E. Richters, chief of the conduct-disorder program at the National Institute of Mental Health. Richters brings a unique personal perspective to his research, which has recently focused on the effects on children of living in violent neighborhoods. Richters describes himself in his younger years as an "anti-social, violent kid," a high-school dropout with a felony record that included drug and theft charges. When he reached his late 20s, he reassessed his life; continued his education through high-school equivalency, college, and graduate school; and began advancing his career steadily to its current level. "I'd done my empirical work already," he notes. He feels that while direct cause-and-effect links remain elusive, the role of witnessing and experiencing violence in the creation of violent behavior may be important. "It can be a factor that increases the likelihood that a kid will engage in violence," he says. "If what you've been exposed to for a good part of your life is people resolving the problems they face by resorting to violence, and that's all you've seen, then you will naturally adopt those strategies for dealing with problems. It's regrettable but perfectly understandable."

Frightening Effects

As varied as the causes of violence among children are its damaging effects on their psyches. Says Arnold Goldstein: "Some kids learn to be aggressive from the environment of aggression. In a truly pragmatic sense, they see that aggression very often works. Some kids have an increased sense of vulnerability, an increased sense of distrust and mistrust. Not, by the way, necessarily ill advised. And the third effect, which in some ways is the scariest, is the desensitization. A callousness. A sense that this is like breathing and eating, just part of the way it is."

James Garbarino, former director of the Erikson Institute for Advanced Study in Child Development in Chicago and current director of the Family Life Development Center at Cornell University, agrees. He researched the psychological effects of violence on children and compared the impact of what children are experiencing in America's cities to the experiences of those in war zones such as Palestine and Northern Ireland. Garbarino observed that both groups exhibit clearcut symptoms of Post-Traumatic Stress Disorder. These children experience intrusive and recurrent recollections and dreams of the violence; they become

> *"Our social/economic milieu 'teaches kids that crime pays and that they'd better maximize their gratification today because they may not have a tomorrow.'"*

numbed and unresponsive to the world. They may have exaggerated startle responses and trouble sleeping and concentrating. They wet their beds and regress to sucking their thumbs. They often fail in school.

But, Garbarino adds, "what I'm most concerned about are consequences that go beyond the narrowly psychological to the philosophical. There's an effect on future orientation. Kids have a declining confidence in the future. They've given up on the ability of adults to protect them. A kid in Michigan once said to me, 'If I join a gang, I'm 50 percent safe. If I don't join a gang, I'm zero percent safe.'

"In extreme form we see what people call 'terminal thinking'—most graphically illustrated when you ask a kid, 'What do you plan to be when you're 30?' and he says, 'Dead.'" . . .

Looking for Troubled Children

In Washington, D.C., the Youth Trauma Services Team cruises the streets of the roughest sections of the southeast and southwest quadrants, looking for trouble or responding to calls where children may be involved. "We wade into the grief with a hand on the shoulder and a pat on the head," says Thomas Blagburn of the team, which includes police, social workers, clergy, and psychologists.

Their reception by the children has been overwhelmingly positive, Watkins has found. "They greet us like we're the ice-cream man," he says. "Even the perps, the kids packing guns and carrying drugs, are receptive. They know we're there to help them, not bust them."

> *"We are an exceedingly aggressive country, and the kids get a steady diet of this from peers, from parents, from siblings, and from mass media."*

Threats from Home

But even as help may come on the streets, many children know that another setting—one where police and social workers are much less likely to show up—is equally threatening. For all too many American children, the violence that threatens them is found at home.

In the Barclay School—an elementary/middle school in a Baltimore neighborhood bordered on the north and west by upscale, gentrified homes and Johns Hopkins University, and on the south and east by boarded-up houses, businesses, and a thriving street-corner drug trade—Shaunita, a forlorn and teary-eyed little girl pleads with her principal to protect her from the violence she fears awaits her at home.

Principal Gertrude Williams is trying to reassure the girl that she's not being suspended. It's almost the end of the day, and her grandmother, who is her guardian, has been called to take her home; that's all.

"She gonna beat me. I know she gonna beat me, and I didn't do anything," Shaunita wails, fearful and quivering. "I was wrong for walkin' out of class, but I don't need to be beat."

"Sometimes I try to intercede, but sometimes that does more harm than good," Williams says of the violence that she knows goes on behind the closed doors of the homes of many of the students in her school. Describing Shaunita as a "plucky little girl" who has lost her spirit as her mother has been consumed by a drug habit, the principal sometimes seems to share the girl's despair at the daunting forces to be overcome. Although a number of programs are in place to intervene with at-risk children and to educate parents who will listen, Williams feels that the biggest job must be done on an ongoing basis by the classroom teacher. "We're working on getting teachers to see beyond the books and see the hurt kid inside, and to be more mindful of the fact that they're dealing with a child who has been physically and mentally abused," she explains.

Domestic Violence

Domestic violence is the most difficult form of violence to quantify. The Kelly Miller Junior High students, more than willing to relate gory details of violent acts they have witnessed on the streets, become much more reticent when asked about violence in their own homes. Most acknowledge that it is something they at least know of. But child- and spousal-abuse statistics probably represent only the tip of the iceberg of domestic abuse, and a third form goes largely unreported. "The violence of siblings toward siblings is something that's not paid much attention to," points out Albert J. Reiss Jr.,

> *"In a child's psyche, the experience of domestic violence interacts with other exposures to violence in a number of different ways."*

a Yale University sociologist and chairman of the 1992 National Academy of Sciences Panel on the Understanding and Control of Violent Behavior. "I keep hoping someone is going to play that up one of these days."

In a child's psyche, the experience of domestic violence interacts with other exposures to violence in a number of different ways. First is the model of behavior he or she is presented with. "Aggression and violence are learned behaviors," says Leonard Eron, a professor of psychology at the University of Michigan, a research scientist at the university's Institute for Social Research, and chairman of the American Psychological Association's Commission on Violence and Youth. "Youngsters who are exposed to this kind of behavior begin to feel that it's an appropriate way to solve problems, to get things that they don't have, to vent their frustrations."

Children Need Security

Equally important is the fact that children being raised in violent homes may not have an adult family member to whom they can turn for security and reassurance. Such an adult is critical for helping children process and move beyond the horrors they witness around them. Psychoanalyst Anna Freud's studies of British children who survived bombings during World War II found that those who maintained close contact with their parents during the bombings were less disturbed than children who had been separated from their parents and sent to the countryside for safety, even though the latter group was in less physical danger. A study of children who lived through the massacres of the Pol Pot regime in Cambodia found that those who did not live with a family member were the most likely to develop Post-Traumatic Stress Disorder and other mental-health problems.

The irony of these findings is clear: All too often the children who encounter violence in their communities are exactly the ones who cannot count on dependable adult relationships to help them through. "Even more than

> *"The reality is, if you don't stand up for yourself, you get victimized. For a lot of kids, it's the only way to survive."*

eradicating drugs and alcohol, what many of these kids need is a sense of family," says D.C principal Ron Hasty. Fortunately, according to Jacqueline Wallen, an associate professor of family studies at the University of Maryland who has investigated the mental-health consequences of violence on children, a number of studies have documented the protectiveness of low-income parents toward their children. "If something happened near the day-care center, they'd all rush to the center and bring their children home to keep them safe. Or they would organize systems for the kids to get to school safely." She adds, "You don't have to be a genius or have tons of free time to be able to be helpful to your kids. But you do have to have some ability to listen to them and to help them feel safe. Sometimes it's just physically being near them that's really important."

Despair and Acceptance

While social workers, educators, psychologists, and physicians conduct studies and devise and implement programs in a search for an antidote for violence, or a way to prevent it, the children themselves seem to accept its inevitability.

"I like to go to the basketball courts, but I can't go anymore because they be shootin' around there," says Joseph, the Philadelphia boy whose father was murdered, in a matter-of-fact voice. The shooting he's talking about isn't baskets.

"They tell me when there's a shooting, they just drop down," says Napoleon Hendrix, a 15-year veteran of the San Francisco Police Department's homicide squad, of the children with whom he has contact. "I say, 'This is a terrible way to live.' They say, 'Man, this is the '90s.'"

When asked if there are any safe neighborhoods, Darrell, the seventh-grader from the Barclay School in Baltimore, doesn't hesitate: "Not where I go." Then he adds wistfully, "I think there are safe neighborhoods out in the country, but I don't have no way to get there."

There is little hope in these children's words, or promise for the future. Even some professionals seem overwhelmed. With all the work being done, the programs being developed, and the attention devoted to the problem, James Garbarino still describes current social conditions as being in a kind of "free fall."

And when Jacqueline Wallen tried to set up a program in schools to help children deal with the violence they saw and experienced, she found that "it seemed almost like setting up a first-aid station at Dachau. It's like trying to palliate pain in an untenable human situation."

Part of her despair comes with the observation that as destructive as violence is, for some children the consequences of nonviolence could be equally destructive. "The reality is, if you don't stand up for yourself, you get victimized. For a lot of kids, it's the only way to survive. And I think parents are stumped. I get calls from teachers who want to know what to recommend to parents who say, 'My child has to fight back; otherwise they'd cream him.'"

There are a few optimistic notes being struck, however. Some of the many programs underway are beginning to show evidence that they are influencing children positively, indeed palliating the pain that Wallen speaks of. The Centers for Disease Control and Protection (CDC) and several independent agencies are implementing evaluation efforts to determine what works and what doesn't.

One principle is already clear. A problem with many causes and manifestations needs to be attacked comprehensively on many fronts for a solution to succeed.

Chapter 3

How Can Youth Violence Be Reduced?

CURRENT CONTROVERSIES

Reducing Youth Violence: An Overview

by Craig Donegan

About the author: *Craig Donegan is a staff writer for* CQ Researcher, *a weekly news and research publication of Congressional Quarterly.*

Yes, 16-year-old Tiana Hutchins acknowledges, she and her girlfriend were breaking the 11 p.m. weekday curfew for teenagers in Washington, D.C. But they were just walking and talking in the neighborhood, she says.

"We were only two blocks from my house when a police car pulled up," she recalls. "He said, 'Where ya'll going? Ya'll ain't supposed to be out this time of night. I can lock you up!'" The next time, the officer warned, he'd take them in.

The incident so upset Tiana, a high school junior, that she agreed to be the lead plaintiff in an American Civil Liberties Union (ACLU) suit challenging the city's curfew.

Tiana offers her own solution to violent youth crime. "Forget the curfews," she says. "Tighten up on the bad kids. Show them they can't be arrested one morning and out on the street the next day. Get on the parents to make their kids come to school. Have after-school recreational programs and community-service projects. Put more security in the schools."

Prevention or Punishment

Tiana's wide-ranging prescription embraces elements of the two basic approaches being advocated to reduce juvenile crime in America: prevention and punishment.

Prevention advocates insist that the only way to stop juvenile crime is to attack it before it starts, through early intervention in the lives of at-risk children. They call for prenatal care and parenting classes for young mothers as well as full use of social services such as Medicaid, Head Start and Aid to Families with Dependent Children (AFDC).

After at-risk children reach school age, prevention advocates say, education

Excerpted from Craig Donegan, "Preventing Juvenile Crime," *CQ Researcher*, March 15, 1996. Reprinted with permission.

must play a key role in shaping youngsters' lives by offering in-school programs that teach conflict resolution, social skills and how to resist gangs and drugs. Violence-prevention curricula "must be a long-term and consistent" part of education, the Rev. Jesse Jackson and other civil rights leaders, educators and policy-makers said at a national conference on youth violence.

"We don't have to raise children to be violent or criminal because this is a preventable problem," says Deborah Prothrow-Stith, assistant dean of government and community programs at the Harvard University School of Public Health. "If we admit this as a society, then we will become very creative about preventive strategies."

> *"The two basic approaches being advocated to reduce juvenile crime in America [are] prevention and punishment."*

Moreover, says Marcia Chaiken, a respected social-policy researcher in Alexandria, Va., "prevention is more cost-effective than punishment. We have strong evidence from research that for the vast majority of at-risk children, approaches such as teaching parents good parenting skills combined with early education and youth development can prevent later delinquency."

Harsher Punishments

Law-and-order advocates say that preventing youth crime hinges on harsher punishment, such as trying juveniles as adults and locking them up longer. Today, the political mood leans toward punishment. Sen. John Ashcroft, R-Mo., who called for tougher sanctions in his Violent and Hardcore Juvenile Offender Reform Act of 1995, reflects that mood. "A small and increasingly violent segment of the teenage population roams free, committing violent and serious offenses without being held accountable for their actions," Ashcroft told colleagues in August 1995 in proposing the legislation.

The push for harsher punishments has been influenced by the dramatic rise in violent crimes committed by youths—including murder, forcible rape, robbery and aggravated assault. According to the Justice Department, the arrest rate for children ages 10 to 17 who committed violent crimes doubled from 1983 to 1992—and could double again by 2010.

Get-tough advocates say youth crime could get even worse because of the expected increase in the under-18 population from 69 million Americans in 1995 to 74 million in 2010. "Americans are sitting on a demographic time bomb," writes John J. DiIulio Jr., director of the Brookings Institution's Center for Public Management. "The large population of 7-to10-year-old boys growing up fatherless, Godless and jobless—and surrounded by deviant, delinquent and criminal adults—will give rise to a new and more vicious group of predatory street criminals than the nation has ever known."

To stop the impending flood of "superpredators," DiIulio would protect schools with metal detectors, guards and other security measures; keep violent repeat offenders in jail or detention for longer periods; and target government crime-prevention resources to cities that really need them.

Combination Measures

Cities and states have reacted to youth crime with a mix of get-tough and prevention measures, among them curfews, laws holding parents accountable for their children's delinquent behavior and requiring school uniforms.

A 1995 survey by the National Conference of Mayors shows that the number of youth curfews has increased by 45 percent since 1990. Of the 387 cities that responded to the survey, at least 270 have curfews. Curfew supporters cite its success in New Orleans, where a dusk-to-dawn curfew for youths under 17 reportedly drove down crime 27 percent during restricted hours.

Yet some critics of curfews say that street-smart delinquents can lie their way around curfew requirements. Because most curfews have exceptions, including school-sponsored activities and evening jobs, "There are all sorts of things you can say to legally prohibit a police officer from taking you into custody," says Barry Krisberg, executive director of the National Council on Crime and Delinquency. "The only kids who get caught are the poor schnooks who don't know what they're doing." Other curfew critics, including the ACLU, question their constitutionality.

For their part, schools are using metal detectors to keep out guns and knives, video cameras to record violent confrontations and spot trespassers and uniformed police to keep the peace. A growing number of schools are requiring students to wear uniforms to eliminate clothing that signifies gang membership—or can be mistaken for gang "colors." The idea is to eradicate distinctions between kids in gangs and those who are not, and to lessen the visible disparities between children of affluence and those from poorer families. . . .

Punish Now, Prevent Later

In addition to supporting curfews and uniforms, a number of state legislatures have increased criminal penalties for violent crimes by youths. In fact, from 1992 to 1994, 27 states passed laws to make it easier to prosecute children as adults, according to a 1995 National Governors' Association (NGA) report.

> *"Cities and states have reacted to youth crime with a mix of get-tough and prevention measures."*

Many states also have approved community-based prevention programs, such as employment training, mentoring and after-school recreational and academic programs. But lawmakers' support for such programs has usually hinged on passage of tougher penalties for violent juvenile offenders, according to the NGA report. "Almost only when coupled with more punitive initiatives do the preventive measures get approved," says co-author David E. Brown, an NGA senior policy analyst. . . .

If prevention efforts give way to more emphasis on punishment, warns Peter W. Greenwood, executive director of the Criminal Justice Program at the Rand Corporation, then DiIulio's time-bomb nightmare could come true. Treating juvenile criminals as adults, he says, is how "we'll get our superpredators: They'll come out of our adult institutions."

As educators, lawmakers and law enforcement experts grapple with the problem of juvenile crime and violence, these are some of the questions being asked:

Do curfews prevent juvenile crime?

A majority of Americans consider curfews as legitimate tools for keeping young people out of harm's way and reducing crime. And cities that use curfews are high on them, too. According to a 1995 U.S. Conference of Mayors survey, 56 percent of the cities with curfews rated their curfews as somewhat or very effective while only 14 percent considered them not effective.

The Washington Metropolitan Police Department reports that felony arrests in the city during curfew hours declined 34 percent from July 16–Sept. 30, 1995, compared with the same period for 1994.

"Everybody claims they work," Krisberg says, "but I'd love to see some research studies." Most juvenile crimes, he notes, occur between 3 p.m. and 6 p.m. Nevertheless, he says, a well-enforced curfew might limit certain youth crimes, such as auto theft.

After reviewing the literature on curfews, Greenwood says he still does not know if they prevent crime. "I've never seen any systematic evidence to show they work," he says.

"I find it very hard to believe that a curfew could have any significant effect on teenagers who are selling drugs, stealing cars or carrying a gun," says Arthur Spitzer, legal director of the ACLU in Washington, D.C. "The very thought that they would be deterred by a $500 fine against their parents is laughable when these kids

> *"Almost only when coupled with more punitive initiatives do the preventive measures get approved."*

are facing up to 10 years in the pokey. A kid won't look at the Rolex he's just stolen and say, 'Oh, I've got to get home. It's 11 o'clock.'"

Do Curfews Work?

When it comes to protecting innocent people, Spitzer says, a curfew "is not the way we do that in this country. We don't say to all women you must be home at 10 p.m. so you won't be raped. People make these decisions for themselves, and parents can do so for their own kids, but the City Council can't control 50,000 kids."

Some critics say curfews are not always enforced evenhandedly, which leads to public cynicism and undermines any effectiveness they may have. "Curfew laws tend to be applied in racially disparate ways," Krisberg says, with youths in middle-class or affluent white neighborhoods virtually immune from curfew enforcement.

Many cities report that curfews work best when parent participation is strong—whether voluntary or forced (through fines and mandatory counseling). But that's still not enough. says Edwin Delattre, dean of Boston University's School of Education and an adjunct scholar at the conservative American Enterprise Institute. Successful curfews require broad, active community support, he says.

> *"Many cities report that curfews work best when parent participation is strong—whether voluntary or forced (through fines and mandatory counseling)."*

"Without adequate [staff] resources for police to enforce them, curfews are largely useless," Delattre says. They will be enforced sporadically, he says, and cities will divert resources once meant for curfews into police activities that satisfy political needs or get more media coverage. "That makes a mockery of the curfew and breeds public cynicism toward law and the police," Delattre says.

Moreover, he adds, curfews that work have communities that recognize youth crime as everybody's problem—not just a problem for those who live in high-risk neighborhoods.

Parents Are Responsible

Does punishing parents for their children's delinquent behavior prevent juvenile crime?

There is growing support for the theory that getting parents more involved in their children's lives is crucial to stemming youth crime. Indeed, some hard-liners say that punishing parents for their children's crimes is the place to start.

Paul J. McNulty, president of the First Freedom Coalition, a Washington anti-crime group, wants relatives to be required to sign agreements in which they promise to keep juvenile offenders on the straight and narrow. "Family members and friends would sign a contract with the court agreeing to forfeit particular assets if a juvenile offender fails to comply with the court's requirements," McNulty writes. "All who sign the bond would then have financial incentive to supervise the juvenile offender closely to ensure compliance."

In several cities with curfews, including Washington, parents whose children violate the curfew can be charged with a misdemeanor, fined up to $500, required to attend parenting classes and assigned to community-service work.

In San Antonio, Texas, first-time curfew violators receive warning tickets. Second offenses require parents to meet with social workers and a third violation results in formal charges that can mean a $500 fine for the parents.

Police in Huntington Beach, Calif., charge parents $36 per hour to "babysit" for curfew violators held in custody. In Paterson, N.J., the parents of children who skip school must attend school with their kids. In Oregon, parents of children under 15 who commit crimes can be fined up to $1,000, made to pay $2,500 in restitution and required to attend parenting classes.

A Question of Responsibility

The Oregon law appears to be working, supporters say. Mayor Ken Hector of Silverton reports that after an initial flurry of arrests, the number of parents summoned to court quickly dropped to zero. Silverton educators have reported more parents getting involved in school activities. And enrollments in parenting classes have increased.

"Our goal should not be to incarcerate kids but to use the authority of the law to get parents to fulfill their responsibilities, even if that means a judge ordering a parent to participate in counseling," says Howard Davidson, director of the American Bar Association's Center on Children and the Law. "When kids get arrested for shoplifting, or are truant from school, the focus should be on bringing in the parents, not punishing the kids."

But Douglas Bandow, a senior fellow at the libertarian Cato Institute, says that "We should never lose sight of the fact that crime is an individual responsibility" and that juvenile offenders must ultimately account for their actions. Moreover, he says, punishing parents is likely to affect juvenile crime only where it is least needed—in cities, towns or neighborhoods that already have cohesive community and family structures.

"There is growing support for the theory that getting parents more involved in their children's lives is crucial to stemming youth violence."

Rand's Greenwood says that police and city officials offer anecdotal evidence that holding parents accountable works, but "I can't find any studies that tell me yea or nay."

It may be a good idea in principle, adds Krisberg, but in practice it could make careless parents resentful and even more likely to abandon their children. "If somebody calls up and says, 'I've got your kid here, and when you show up you're going to get a $350 ticket,' plenty of people are going to say, 'Keep him,'" he says.

Involve the Parents

Poverty also complicates the picture, Krisberg says. "If the parents are poor—if dad's not working and mom's got a minimum-wage job—then what does parental responsibility amount to?"

In such cases, says Davidson, communities should provide evening counseling sessions to help troubled parents regain control of their delinquent children. Child care also should be available, he says. "The question is one of priorities," Davidson says. "Do we really care about getting parents involved when kids seem to be out of control? And I don't just mean the mothers. I mean the fathers, too."

Most parents want to do the right things for their children, says University of Minnesota law professor Barry Feld. "To the extent that they don't," he says, "it's because they are too trapped by circumstances."

Krisberg and his colleagues found that programs that teach parents how to discipline and care for the health of their children can reduce anti-social behavior in kids. When combined with school-based programs that teach at-risk children how to follow rules, control anger and communicate effectively, parent training can also prevent juvenile delinquency and violence.

"Rather than simply use a punitive approach, the courts can use their power to make parents attend proceedings with their children and to tell them, "This is your responsibility, and we're going to see if we can't help you meet it,'" says Harvard's Prothrow-Stith.

Schools Play a Part

Are school programs on violence reduction, conflict resolution and peer mediation effective?

Supporters call programs to reduce violent and criminal behavior among schoolchildren the "fourth R" of American education.

Anti-violence and mediation courses have proliferated since the late 1980s, when Prothrow-Stith introduced her "Violence Prevention Curriculum for Adolescents." Instruction in violence prevention often revolves around videotapes depicting staged violent situations and methods for avoiding fights and resolving disputes non-violently.

Conflict-resolution programs also have grown in popularity, with more than 5,000 programs operating in elementary and secondary schools throughout the United States, says Judy Filner, program director for the National Association for Mediation in Education. While violence prevention focuses on teaching children to control their own behavior, conflict resolution emphasizes interpersonal skills that students must have to manage potentially explosive situations from beginning to end.

In peer mediation, the most popular mediation program, students are used to defuse conflicts between other students. "The students are not policemen," Filner says. "It's just a small number of kids who learn mediation skills and then intervene to help resolve conflicts between other students, when everyone agrees."

Classroom programs in conflict resolution, which can last from six weeks to an entire semester, are also growing in popularity. Iowa, Illinois and Ohio have statewide programs in conflict resolution, and Texas has adopted legislation that endorses conflict-resolution courses for all the state's public schools, Filner says.

Resolving Conflicts Effectively

Until recently, however, there was no hard evidence that such programs work. Now, says Prothrow-Stith, two new studies suggest that conflict resolution and violence-prevention curricula do make a difference. One of the studies reports that suspension rates dropped by up to 70 percent in two schools that introduced her violence-prevention curriculum, she says.

For violence- and conflict-resolution courses to work, she adds, they must acknowledge that Americans live in a social and cultural context that encourages fighting. They have to recognize that the country recently had "a kick-butt, make-my-day president" and that it is inundated by Power Rangers on television and in movies telling kids that violence is the way to solve conflict. A successful program also recognizes the reality that in some families, parents tell their children, "You go back outside and you beat him up, or I'm going to beat you."

> *"For violence- and conflict-resolution courses to work, . . . they must acknowledge that Americans live in a social and cultural context that encourages fighting."*

"It's important to accept that anger is normal, but to know there are many ways to respond to it and that fighting is the response where you often lose more than you gain," she says.

To drive home the point, Prothrow-Stith includes the teenage version of cost-benefit analysis in her program, asking kids to think about what they gain and what they lose if they resort to violence. "Conflict-resolution works," she says, "but it is a very small piece of a larger prevention pie—it's probably not going to help the kid who's holding up a McDonald's."

No Scientific Proof

In their review of mediation-program evaluations, however, Krisberg and his colleagues report they found no scientific evidence that such programs work. In fact, anti-social and delinquent behavior reportedly increased in some peer-counseling approaches, in which students were led in group settings to give mutual support for socially acceptable behavior.

"I'm not surprised at the results," says Krisberg. "Most of these programs were not designed with kids in mind but were basically designed by and for adults."

While stressing that the findings on peer mediation are piecemeal, Krisberg relegates the talk-it-through approach to "the warm and fuzzy" category. Young people are very good at talking about the dangers of drugs and violence, he says, but the kids he has talked with tell him their peers are not good at mediating conflicts. "They feel that peer mediation tells them the adults can't help them," he says. "They want the teachers to step in."

Practical Aspects

Yet Prothrow-Stith says students are better than adults at knowing where, and when, trouble is brewing. Because of that, they can be very useful to one another, and to their teachers, in stopping fights before they get started. "Too often, the teachers find out about these conflicts after the shouting starts or a crowd is gathering," she says. "It is more difficult to prevent something worse at that stage."

Schools with large numbers of immigrants, particularly from non-Western cultures, present mediation programs with the biggest challenge. "Their cultural styles don't necessarily lend themselves to middle-class, white chit-chat, which is what some of these programs are about," says Krisberg.

Then there is the problem of actually getting students to the sessions. "You set up a 10-session curriculum, and the kids may attend three or four," Greenwood says. To make matters worse, "You might not get the truly at-risk kids in the programs to start with."

But Prothrow-Stith doesn't think instruction should be limited only to at-risk students. "It's for everybody," she says, "because if we were all better at handling conflict and anger, then America would be a less violent place."

Rehabilitation Programs Can Reduce Youth Violence

by Mary Dallao

About the author: **Mary Dallao** *is an editorial assistant for* Corrections Today, *a publication of the American Correctional Association.*

Before 19-year-old "Ben" was arrested for a felony, he says no one could tell him what to do. "I'd heard it all before," he says, "but I really didn't listen. I was hard-headed. Sure, they brought people to tell me stuff, but I just blew them off because I thought I knew it all. It was always just another person telling me how to live my life."

Ben's attitude changed in 1994 when he was sentenced to two years with Colorado's Youth Offender System (YOS) instead of serving his four-year sentence with the department of corrections. YOS aims to rehabilitate juvenile offenders who are charged with violent weapons-related offenses and convicted as adults.

Through a four-phase program, YOS provides young offenders with a comprehensive package of boot camp–style orientation, academic instruction and cognitive development. Some call it a "second last chance."

Now in phase three of the program, Ben is on his way to becoming a free member of society. His last day in phase three will be August 10, 1996. Looking back on his experience with YOS, Ben thinks the program works because it fosters a positive peer culture. Young people in the program dictate the rules to each other, and this sense of accountability to a peer group seems to sink in better than reprimands from authority figures.

In the Beginning

Richard Swanson, deputy director of YOS, says the idea for the Youth Offender System resulted from a 14-point plan issued in 1993 by Colorado Gov. Roy Romer after a particularly violent summer. Downtown Denver had fallen victim to high-profile teenage crime, and Swanson says kids were killing each other over something as trivial as a Bronco football jacket. Romer's 14-point

Reprinted from Mary Dallao, "Colorado's Youth Offender System Offers Juveniles a 'Second Last Chance,'" *Corrections Today*, August 1996, by permission of the American Correctional Association.

plan demanded that state agencies develop nontraditional ways of dealing with juvenile violence because typical methods had failed.

Colorado needed a solution that didn't involve juvenile courts. Swanson says juvenile courts can be self-defeating—especially in urban areas, which are hotbeds of gang cultures. The violence, seriousness and sophistication of juvenile crimes continue to increase in these cultures. Older youths and adults often use young people to commit crimes based on the understanding that juvenile courts will not punish them.

"YOS has touted itself as the third tier of the criminal justice system—the middleman between adult and juvenile corrections for young offenders ages 14 to 18."

"Our society has developed a use of juvenile courts and a needs-based, rather than deeds-based, response to juvenile crime that, in a way, recruits young people into a gang, which, in turn, recruits them into criminal acts," Swanson says. While he is quick to emphasize that juvenile courts do well with traditional youth issues, Swanson believes that sophisticated violent crime requires special attention. It demands the accountability of adult courts, yet requires more intervention than the custodial adult model allows.

The Third Tier

YOS has touted itself as the third tier of the criminal justice system—the middleman between adult and juvenile corrections for young offenders ages 14 to 18. The third tier acts as a deterrent for young offenders. Juveniles convicted of violent crimes and tried as adults are sent to YOS at the court's discretion, and they can be revoked back to the adult system if they don't cooperate.

Of 190 youths who have participated in YOS since its inception in 1993, Swanson says only ten have been sent back to the adult system. Most of these requested the move because they "wanted to be treated like men"; the rest seem thankful to have avoided this fate.

"Kids come in here, and they're pretty well scared to death," he says. "They see the adults in the other sections of the facility, and they feel very lucky to be here. If these same kids were sent to adult prison, the probability of them being victimized would be very high."

Hell Days and GEDs

Ben says his first day with YOS was hell. Literally.

The Induction, Diagnostic and Orientation (IDO) phase of YOS—the boot camp phase—lasts for 30 to 45 days. On his first night, Ben was locked in his room with a piece of paper covering the window so he couldn't see out. At 2 o'clock, the door was opened, and the young offenders were herded down to the cell block to do calisthenics.

"I threw up," Ben says. "They just push you and push you, and make you do all kinds of exercises and drills. It's hard when you're not in shape."

The first day of YOS is called "Hell Day," and it's the day when juveniles learn that the staff means business.

After calisthenics, Ben got his head shaved.

"When I was locked back in my cell after Hell Day, I was so tired," he says. "I just kept asking myself, 'How did I ever mess up this bad?'"

Induction into YOS has several goals: identifying disruptive individuals, instilling rituals and protocol, introducing teamwork and cultivating high standards of conduct. After the boot camp phase establishes these rules and sets barriers, discipline becomes less rigid as the program progresses.

Phase one focuses on education, as well as the development of a positive peer culture in a modified therapeutic community; phase two offers job development and pre-vocational experiences; and phase three provides six to 12 months of intensive community supervision.

Ben got his GED during the second phase of the program. He says he stopped going to high school in ninth grade. Through the YOS education program, Ben earned his degree in four and one-half months. He is especially proud of this achievement because he says school has never really "clicked" with him.

> *"We teach [young offenders] vocational skills and offer them ways to avoid relapse. We try to give them self-esteem and hope for the future."*

Today, Ben talks about his future. He hopes to finish college, buy his own house, marry his girlfriend and own his own business as a jeweler. He thinks his attitude has changed.

"My mind-set before YOS was different," he says. "I always felt bored and helpless—like there was nothing I could do to get up in the world. I think I'm much better off now. I'm independent, and I'm not as much of a follower."

The Future of Juvenile Corrections?

Swanson says only time will tell if YOS is the future of juvenile corrections. Because the program has been in existence only since 1993, empirical evidence is not available to document its success. So far, Swanson reports that about five individuals have completed the entire program.

"All we can tell you is that, if you look at evaluations of programs for similar offenders, you'll find that we've captured these documented program strengths and put them all together in one comprehensive package," he says.

Still, some critics of YOS beg to differ. Juvenile court judges sometimes oppose YOS because they believe many offenders are too young to be involved in such a regimented program. The juvenile system often disagrees with the decision to place juveniles in YOS without first committing them to the Division of Youth Services.

And the program is expensive. It costs about $50 per day to maintain an adult in the Colorado Department of Corrections. The cost for YOS is almost double this amount.

"The truth of the matter is, we won't know if it's worth it for another five or six years," Swanson says. "But, in terms of planning, we have everything social science knows about that can turn a kid's life around. We teach them vocational skills and offer them ways to avoid relapse. We try to give them self-esteem and hope for the future. I think we capture all these elements in a way no other program does."

Reforming the Juvenile Justice System Can Reduce Youth Violence

by Nick Gillespie

About the author: *Nick Gillespie is an assistant editor for* Reason, *a political and social affairs magazine.*

In Chicago, a 14-year-old girl is shot to death by an 11-year-old gang member who is in turn found dead a few days later, two bullets in the back of his head; his suspected killers are 14 and 16. In Fuquay-Varina, North Carolina, a 13-year-old boy is accused of beating a 22-year-old female neighbor with a mop handle and then raping her. In Somerset, Pennsylvania, a 14-year-old is charged with hammering nails into the heels of a younger boy.

Youth Violence Is Rising

These hellish snapshots flesh out the disturbing statistics on juvenile crime rates: Between 1983 and 1992, reports the FBI, juvenile arrest rates for violent crime jumped 128 percent for murder and non-negligent manslaughter (versus 9 percent for adults); 95 percent for aggravated assault (versus 69 percent); and 25 percent for rape (versus 14 percent). Adding to the fear is the sense things are only going to get worse.

As a Washington, D.C., Superior Court judge told *Time*, "Youngsters used to shoot each other in the body. Then in the head. Now they shoot each other in the face." Little wonder then that, as the *Los Angeles Times* puts it, "the rising demand for a crackdown on juvenile criminals" is "one of the most powerful trends in campaign 1994."

Harsher Punishment May Not Work

But it is far from clear whether the most politically salable reform, lowering the age at which offenders can be tried as adults (as 20 states did in 1993 alone), will have much, if any, effect on violent juvenile crime. Designed to let courts impose longer sentences on children (typically, convicted juveniles cannot be incarcerated beyond their 25th birthday, regardless of the crime), it is inherently a rearguard action.

"The more draconian the sentence," writes UCLA criminologist James Q. Wilson, "the less (on the average) the chance of its being imposed; plea bargains see to that. . . . The most draconian sentences will . . . tend to fall on adult offenders nearing the end of their criminal careers and not on the young ones who are in their criminally most productive years."

A More Effective Juvenile Justice System

What is needed instead is a juvenile justice system that teaches young criminals responsibility for their behavior at every turn, rather than exculpating juveniles categorically until a final heinous act is committed. The current system, an artifact of Progressive-era politics, sees juvenile status as a defense against criminal responsibility. Accordingly, youthful offenders are usually given a number of "free rides" or "diversions" before any serious

> *"What is needed . . . is a juvenile justice system that teaches young criminals responsibility for their behavior at every turn."*

punishment is meted out. When sentencing does take place, the courts are often barred from using previous arrests and convictions in deciding on punishment. And since virtually every state seals or expunges juvenile records, offenders need not worry about prior convictions haunting them in the adult world.

This is exactly wrong. As Peter W. Greenwood of the RAND Corporation notes, "Studies of responses to punishment suggest that initial low levels of punishment and gradual escalation desensitize subjects and make them less likely to respond."

Raise the Cost of Crime

There is nothing particularly mysterious or elusive about reducing the incidence of juvenile crime. It will respond to the same thing that works with "adult" crime: raising the costs of criminal behavior, thereby making it less attractive as an alternative to lawful behavior.

Between 1950 and 1992, according to Justice Department statistics, the number of serious crimes per 100 people rose from 1.2 to 5.9, while the expected days in prison (the average sentence for serious offenses adjusted for the probability that offenders are actually sent to prison) dropped from 24 to 8. The only time during that period that serious crime rates (including juvenile ones) slowed was during the 1980s, when expected days in prison rose. Such consistent inverse correlations suggest that criminal behavior is ultimately a choice, not an inevitability.

120

Long-Term Patterns

It is particularly important for youthful offenders to learn that criminality is a choice, since long-term patterns of violent criminal behavior generally begin during the juvenile years and grow in intensity—it is rare when a murder, rape, or assault is a criminal's first crime. About one-third of all boys in the United States will be arrested before turning 18. While most will not be arrested again, for those who are, each successive arrest places them at higher and higher chances of being detained in the future, culminating in 90 percent probability for those with five or six arrests. University of Pennsylvania criminologist Marvin Wolfgang has identified the latter as the "chronic offenders," the 6 percent of boys who account for more than 50 percent of all arrests.

> *"Raising the cost of criminal behavior [will make juvenile crime] less attractive as an alternative to lawful behavior."*

Each arrest, then, is an opportunity to deter the educable and incarcerate the incorrigible. By taking past criminal behavior and other meaningful contextual information into account at the sentencing stage and by maintaining a permanent, open record, the juvenile justice system can teach the youthful offender that "present-orientedness"—a trait common in criminals of all ages—is a weak guide at best, a self-defeating one at worst.

Reform the System

A variety of well-defined and sequenced sanctions, including individual mentoring, formal probation, at-home supervision, community service, non-secured group homes, and short-term incarceration in military-style boot camps or locked facilities, would allow the system to screen out salvageable offenders while providing long-term lock-up for those who remain a violent threat to society. These reforms come neither easily nor cheaply, but they are effective.

"We are terrified," writes UCLA's Wilson, "by the prospect of innocent people being gunned down at random, by youngsters who afterward show us the blank, unremorseful faces of seemingly feral, presocial beings." Violent youthful offenders are indeed "presocial beings." The current juvenile justice system does little to change that.

Training in Conflict Resolution Can Reduce Youth Violence

by Kim Nauer

About the author: *Kim Nauer is a staff writer for* City Limits, *a monthly publication concerning neighborhood revitalization.*

Walking home from school along the bustling corridor of Pennsylvania Avenue in East New York, there doesn't seem to be much of a chance of being assaulted. The light is still bright at 3 p.m. and the streets are filled with adults attending to their late afternoon business.

Even so, kids pull their voices out like box cutters, taking aim at a new enemy or an old friend who has crossed their thin line of tolerance. Whether these small altercations end quietly or with someone in the hospital depends as much on the target as the instigator. On this cold November afternoon, as three girls approach, the attack begins with a giggling taunt from the leader.

"She got sti-tches!"

Never slowing their gait, the girl and her friends pepper Maxine, a 15-year-old steel reed of a girl, with insults and the promise of a future beating. Maxine keeps walking, her mouth locked in a thin smile, her gaze fixed on the corner ahead. "Remember me?" is the last phrase she hears from the encounter as the barrage fades from earshot. "Remember me. You had better remember me. . . ."

"They was just talking," Maxine mumbles. "I have a fight with that girl." It started over nothing, she says. They used to be friends. But a few weeks ago the two began quarreling. It led to a shoving match and before Maxine knew it she was in the hospital, getting four stitches put into her lip.

Obviously, from the apparent pride her nemesis took in this work, now nearly healed, the fight is not over. But Maxine seems resigned to a life of sidestepping such incidents. "Every part of Brooklyn, Queens, the Island—anywhere you go, it's not different. Everywhere you go, it's a violent place."

Excerpted from Kim Nauer, "Motive and Opportunity," *City Limits*, December 1995. Reprinted with permission.

Chapter 3

Unavoidable Violence

Violence is part of the wash of daily life for kids in East New York, a 5.6-square-mile patch of Brooklyn with the distinction in recent years of having one of the city's highest homicide rates. A survey of 850 sixth, seventh and eighth graders at East New York's Intermediate School 302, conducted in January 1995 for the U.S. Centers for Disease Control and Prevention (CDC), sought to determine how prevalent anger and violence are in young people's everyday lives. The results were stunning.

Thirty-three percent of the children claimed to have "badly beat" someone in the previous four months. Twenty-six percent said they had carried a weapon at least once during that period. Fifteen percent claimed

> *"Since the early 1980s, educators and social workers have been experimenting with dozens of different ways to steer children away from violent behavior."*

to have threatened someone with a weapon. Fifteen percent claimed to have robbed someone and 13 percent said they had been arrested.

If these numbers sound like the bravado of pre-teens talking tough, the results gathered from an additional 36 pages of psychological testing—designed to ferret out possible motivations for violent behavior—show something deeper at work. Half of the students surveyed exhibited symptoms of severe post-traumatic stress syndrome, a relentless cycle of recalling then repressing the memory of a traumatic incident. Another 27 percent showed mild to moderate symptoms. Less than a quarter of those surveyed seemed to be thinking in peace.

The survey, conducted by Mark Spellmann and Gerald Landsberg at the New York University School of Social Work, marks the beginning of a push by the CDC to pin down what works and what doesn't in the untested world of "violence prevention." The researchers are teamed with Manhattan-based Victim Services to measure how likely it is that victims of violence will turn to violence themselves and what effect a program of antiviolence education, counseling and organizing can have on these children.

Steering Kids Away from Violence

Since the early 1980s, educators and social workers have been experimenting with dozens of different ways to steer children away from violent behavior. Such efforts—ranging from conflict resolution curriculums to intensive parent counseling—have received warm media attention but little in the way of scientific scrutiny.

That has changed with the rising teenage homicide numbers. Today, says CDC spokeswoman Mary Ann Fenley, murder is the second leading cause of death for 15- to 24-year-olds behind the long-time leader, car accidents, and gaining fast. While it's important to continue finding better criminal justice so-

123

lutions, she says, the problem will not be solved until policy makers find some way to prevent future generations from turning to violence. "We need to be able to give the nation some hope that these projects are going to make a difference."

Motivation for Aggression

For social scientists and biologists, the goal of violence research is to define the roots of motivation. Why does a shove in the hallway cause one child to shove back and another to simply apologize?

Some argue, controversially, that heredity shapes brain chemistry and therefore plays an important role in how angry or aggressive a person is. More in the mainstream are physiologists who study both behavior and brain chemistry. They maintain that traumatic childhood experiences, such as physical abuse, can chemically alter how the brain reacts to stressful situations. And there are also psychiatrists and others who note that a child's temperament is likely shaped by a number of factors including their innate fortitude, the emotional support they receive from adults and the stress they endure in their daily lives.

"It's not [that] some children are born aggressive," says Karen Bierman, a psychologist at Pennsylvania State University. "But if you take children and place them in settings where there are high rates of conflict and threat and hostility, their bodies will react to living in that sort of environment."

That is not to say, however, that emotional reactions are inevitably hard-wired early in life. Bierman maintains that any child, given enough help at a young age, can learn how to rein in his or her own aggressive impulses.

"Johnny, abused by his dad, grows up to abuse his son. But breaking the cycle takes on new significance when Johnny, abused by his dad, can go out and get a gun."

On this, most violence prevention researchers can agree. But what is the right age to offer help? Intervene too early and some children may feel stigmatized; too late, children may shun the attention. In school-based programs, should only the most troubled youngsters be targeted or is it more useful to include whole classrooms? How important is counseling as opposed to simple instruction? Can any program work without the support of the family? And what combination of strategies will help the most children at the lowest cost?

Conflict Resolution

Bierman is now evaluating an elementary school–based program in rural Pennsylvania that provides conflict resolution training for all children starting in kindergarten. Parents of children who still exhibit behavioral problems in first grade are encouraged to enroll themselves in counseling classes while keeping their child in a program of weekly counseling, academic tutoring and social-skill-building "friendship groups." Counselors and tutors also make home visits in some cases. Children who fail to shake off aggression problems in their earliest years may continue to use the services as they advance through elementary school, but most of the children reportedly succeed early in overcoming hostile impulses.

The program, funded by three federal research grants, has brought an unprecedented level of calm to the classroom, Bierman says. But the federal support is only for the experiment, and it's unclear whether local taxpayers will be willing to eventually foot the bill for what are, admittedly, expensive counseling services. "Does the data really demonstrate that this is cost-effective in the long run? Will you, in fact, save money on more expensive services from special ed to probation?" No one yet knows, she says. It is still too early to tell.

> *"Victim Services offers classes in how to avoid confrontation and cope with the violence that touches [students'] lives."*

Unhealthy Children

Victim Services' Linda Lausell is willing to talk about costs—the costs of living dangerously. They are high, she says, and children pay the price. Across the nation, health statistics show increasing levels of youth depression, suicide and, as the East New York survey shows, post-traumatic stress syndrome.

As program director for an agency that made its name serving crime victims and battered women, it's not surprising that Lausell's theories on violence prevention dwell on the corrosive effects of trauma and fear. Children who live in fear of being hurt or killed, she argues, are the ones most likely to lash out themselves.

It's an old theory, she admits. Johnny, abused by his dad, grows up to abuse his son. But breaking the cycle takes on new significance when Johnny, abused by his dad, can go out and get a gun.

"We keep seeing this over and over again," Lausell says. "Often there is a whole history of victimization, starting in the home, coupled with what's going on in the community, coupled with what's going on in school.

"They end up trying to cope with victimization the best way they know how, trying to regain the power that's been lost and trying to defend against the fear. They do that by identifying with the aggressor and trying to hurt before they get hurt.". . .

Success in Conflict Resolution

New York City is also home to one of the country's original and most well respected school-based conflict resolution programs, the 10-year-old Resolving Conflicts Creatively Program, which offers teachers throughout the city a comprehensive antiviolence curriculum for classroom use. It has received widespread and much-deserved attention in the media for its success developing peer training, coping and leadership skills for students growing up in urban neighborhoods. The Victim Services program in East New York, however, has set out to take antiviolence work to another level by going beyond the classroom, into counseling and community organizing.

In both of East New York's junior high schools—IS 302 and IS 292—Victim Services offers classes in how to avoid confrontation and cope with the violence that touches their lives. They also have full-time adult counselors staffing a "safe harbor" room in each school. Students are encouraged to use these rooms in their free time and are told they can visit any time if there is a crisis.

Finally, counselors at IS 302 have begun to convince students to help out with a community-wide antiviolence campaign coordinated by New York City's Department of Health and United Community Centers. Students have chosen which posters would be most appropriate for their classmates and, in November 1995, helped bring out an estimated 75 kids to a Friday night candlelight vigil. Community organizing, Lausell says, is a critical part of helping kids move firmly away from the temptation of violence. "Speaking out against something, becoming active in a movement, is very healing and therapeutic," she says. "This is not just patching them up so that we make better cripples out of them. They have something to contribute toward change."

Solid Schooling

Intermediate School 292 was built in the 1960s, before short hallways and long banks of windows were considered a security liability. The low glass panes, all too vulnerable to young fists, drive Principal Levi Brisbane crazy. "You don't build buildings like this anymore," he grouses. But Victor Hall likes the windows and the courtyard below. A trim 39-year-old with an imposing Vandyke and a penchant for dark blue blazers, Hall could be confused for a principal, were it not for his flashy ties and sympathy for day-dreamers. He admits it: "I like to look at the trees."

> *"In every school there is an undercurrent of gossip . . . misconstruing innocent phrases, breaking up old alliances and creating new ones sometimes bent on physical revenge."*

Hall can afford the pleasure. As the school's "safe harbor" room counselor, he is associated with class games and lunchtime recess. It is Principal Brisbane who has to worry about safely shepherding more than 1,000 kids through class each day.

According to other staff members, Brisbane inherited a school in chaos in 1990. Guidance counselors talk about days in the late 1980s when groups of students would gang up against each other, declaring allegiance depending on which side of Pennsylvania Avenue they happened to live. High school students from nearby Maxwell and Thomas Jefferson High Schools would stubbornly hang out in front of the school. Weapons like knives, box cutters and razor blades surfaced intermittently and, at a particularly low point, one student was caught with a gun. Both kids and teachers alike chafed under the traditional academic regime of the former principal.

Brisbane divided students and staff into four easier-to-manage mini-schools, loosely tailored to the students' career ambitions. Working with a community task force, he stepped up security, issuing school identification cards, instituting random once-a-week metal detector inspections and working with the local police to keep the area around the school clear. But he says it has been the Victim Services program . . . that has provided the school with a much needed steam-release valve.

Teaching Reasonable Thought

"I've seen students here get into a fight because they were bumped. I tell them, you wouldn't be able to ride the subways in New York if you had a combative attitude toward everyone who bumped you—you'd be fighting all the way." He chuckles. "How does a child react? You have to train them."

This is one of Hall's jobs. He backs up a core group of staff and teachers trained in conflict resolution who spot growing feuds early and make students sit down and talk out their differences. By early November 1995, reports Guidance Counselor Mary Ann Greene, her office alone had held 120 mediation sessions. Students training to be peer mediation counselors meet in an after-school club called "Generation NeXt."

After three months on the job here, Hall is enjoying the attentions of candid and occasionally worshipful youngsters. It's a long way from his previous three years working at two different high schools in Manhattan and the South Bronx. There, he said, many students had built emotional walls around themselves that required Herculean strength to scale. While this is not as true of junior high school students, he says many are slipping away from adult influence. That, Hall says, is because adults frequently make the mistake of dismissing young people's problems as trivial.

He Said, She Said

Take the common enough predicament of "He said, she said" conflicts. In every school there is an undercurrent of gossip that roils the hallways, misconstruing innocent phrases, breaking up old alliances and creating new ones sometimes bent on physical revenge. Violence counselors, Halls says, don't ignore it.

"When you hear it through the grapevine, things change," explains Aisha, a student hanging out in the safe room one recent afternoon. "They'll be like, 'I don't like Aisha's attitude.'

"Then it will be, 'She said she don't like Aisha's attitude and she wants to fight her.'

"Then it will pass down, 'She don't like Aisha's attitude, she wants to fight her, and, yea, she said that she'll beat her up.'

"And by the time it gets to you, it will be 'She don't like Aisha's attitude, she says she wants to fight her, she'll beat her up, and she'll take her any time, any place.' That's how it usually is, and in my experience, I know. I was recently involved in gossip and it almost got us all in big trouble."

The big trouble was a classroom brawl that could have landed Aisha and her friends on the suspension list. Instead, administrators took mercy and

> *"It's a question of getting enough energy focused on preventing violence and building support structures for young people."*

funneled the crowd into Hall's safe harbor room. He took one look at the situation, particularly at Aisha, who is a natural leader, and started the "Trendsetters Club." Now Aisha and her friends—presciently placed in the junior high's fourth floor Law and Government mini-school—are running an anti-gossip campaign.

"Now on the fourth floor it's a big thing," Aisha insists. "Everybody's saying, I don't want to hear the gossip. Really! On our floor, you still see everybody running around the lunchroom, but you don't see fights. It's helped a lot."

Masks of Youth

In the back of Room 312, an old art room stocked with high-energy games like Nerf hoop and table hockey, a poem called "The Mask" is taped above Hall's desk. It begins: "The mask hides all my fears / The mask covers all my tears / The mask keeps people from seeing / the torment which is my being."

Although many of the kids he sees leap into the room ready to tease and laugh, Hall's biggest job is dealing with masks. Steadily, throughout the day, more somber kids arrive, heading back to Hall's desk where he has created a private corner behind a stack of old bookcases.

Around noon on a raw mid-November day, Leo arrives, his face screwed up in anger. He waits pensively as Hall sets up a couple of other kids with a game of ring-toss and then takes him to the back for a quiet conference. When Hall stops to deal with shouting in the hallway, Leo's head pops up from behind the bookcases. His expression, for a moment simply curious, tightens up again as he spies Nathaniel sitting across the room. The boy had called Leo a jerk 10 minutes earlier.

Leo walks over and stands above Nathaniel.

"I'm in your face," he says.

Nathaniel, more than a head taller, stands up.

"No. I'm in your face."

Hall quickly strides over. With one glare he stops the fight, cold. Leo shirks back to the corner, his expression stony. "Jerk," Nathaniel reaffirms, turning back to the table.

Discussing Options

An articulate eighth grader with a strict upbringing by his grandmother, Nathaniel complains he has to deal with too many "ignorant" kids like Leo in this school. They travel in crowds and dominate the cafeteria, he says, intimidating those who simply want to eat their lunch. When it's pointed out that he did not need to call Leo a "jerk" to his face, Nathaniel replies, "It's better to fight with your mouth than your hands."

His table hockey partner, a little sprite of a sixth-grade girl, interrupts. "I wouldn't have stood up to him. I would have walked away."

"One of these days you're going to have to stand up and defend yourself," Nathaniel fires back.

Counseling kids this age requires a soft sell. Hall has to traverse a thicket of differing values and needs.

He has set aside Tuesdays and Thursdays for the school's youngest students, the sixth graders. They are still impressionable, he feels, and he has made it his mission to get to know each one of them in hopes of creating allies for the next two years. His work among seventh and eighth graders relies more on temptation (an open playroom stocked with games, devoid of teachers) and salvation (he can save an accused child from suspension). Happy students get his bemused but distracted attention. The distraught get long private conferences and, in the most serious cases, a closed door session with the room to themselves.

Is It Working?

One thing is obvious watching the comings and goings in the safe harbor room. It is often filled with students ducking away from the gaze of their more aggressive peers in the hallways. The question is inevitable: Is Hall reaching those kids with the greatest potential to become violent, or just those students seeking to avoid them?

Hall answers that two ways. First of all, the teachers and administrators gladly make a practice of sending the school's agitators his way. He estimates that helping deeply troubled children takes up more than half of his time. So yes, he says, many of the children with the greatest potential for violence do come his way.

As to whether he can influence them, he looks back to his childhood and who reached him. Raised on Kelly Street in the South Bronx, he was steeped in a culture of violence. At 11, he says, he watched as a man standing less than a yard from him crumpled under bullet fire. "Our heroes were the guys out there doing it. If you were in the street that we played on, those were the guys who had the status. I have seen people get shot. I have seen people get stabbed."

Hall adds that he also had a strong family that held him close and, he says, saved him from a sorry fate. Many of his students are not so lucky, he says, so he does not emphasize the family connection. Instead he trusts his own connection and that of other adults and students will make a difference. It's a question of getting enough energy focused on preventing violence and building support structures for young people.

When Hall tells kids about his own violent past, they often ask how he managed to end up here, teaching.

"Were you in jail?" one child guessed. No, he tells him.

"Were you arrested?" the child guesses again. No, Hall says. He says he must occasionally remind children that prison stays are not the only way of escaping from a violent neighborhood alive.

Trying to Reduce Youth Violence

No matter what the results of the NYU study, scheduled for completion in 1998, the real measure of Victim Services' success will lie in the youth violence statistics, says Roger Hayes, director of the city Health Department's Injury Prevention Program.

"One of the criticisms has been, do we really know if this stuff works? There has certainly been a lot of strong anecdotal data from people in schools saying that it's really changed the environment of the schools. It's reduced fighting in the lunchroom and the hallways. But the big question still remains: Does it reduce more serious violence?

"Kids will tell you in surveys and conversations that they're more afraid going to and from school than while they are actually in school," he observes. "Hopefully, if we can build on this, from the school into the community, we can gradually have some effect."

An antiviolence public health army is going to have to be built one person at a time, says Hall. He tells his charges that he kept himself out of trouble as a teenager because he deliberately chose one road over another. "I wanted to go to school. I wanted to do well in school. I just made different choices than everybody else was making." And then, he says, he sits and waits until the children start telling their own stories. Hall explains to them that anger or sadness or whatever they feel is OK. But there are better ways than fighting to work it off.

"It always comes down to listening to their other choices," Hall says. "What choices, besides the violent ones, could they have made? We try to help them see that violence is not the way to get by. . . . Maybe in your neighborhood it's how everybody is doing it, but it's not the only way."

A Grassroots Peace Movement Is Reducing Youth Violence

by John Brown Childs

About the author: *John Brown Childs, a professor of sociology at the University of California, Santa Cruz, is the author of* Transcommunality: Roots of Social Justice in an Age of Crisis. *He has been involved in organizing youth peace summits as a member of the board of directors of Barrios Unidos, a group of activists working for youth peace.*

America is at war. It is a bloody war. It is not overseas, but right here at home on our streets. The casualties are youth who are dying and being injured by the hundreds of thousands, and their families, loved ones, and friends who face constant waves of pain and loss. In Los Angeles County alone, 7,388 young people were killed in street violence between 1979 and 1994. Since 1988 the leading cause of death for teen-age males is by gun. Nationwide every day, 135,000 children carry guns to school. Juvenile arrest for murder increased by 127.9 percent between 1984 and 1993. In the midst of the violence thousands are being imprisoned. By the year 2010, at current rates, there will be more people in prison than are enrolled in college. But the increase in imprisonment and the building of prisons shows no signs of slowing down the violence. The Justice Department estimates that youth violence and crime will increase over the next 10 years. The limitations of prisons are clear, even to those who run them—85 percent of the 157 prison wardens surveyed in 1993 by Senator Paul Simon's subcommittee on the Constitution rejected the popular crime fighting solutions of "more prisons" as ineffective. As Nane Alexjandrez of the National Coalition of Barrios Unidos says, "What kind of society allows so many of its youth to die and be maimed without doing something constructive?" Clearly other ways must be found to more constructively bring peace to the streets.

Excerpted from John Brown Childs, "Peace in the Streets," *Z Magazine*, November 1996. Reprinted by permission of the author.

Moving Peace

Those ways are being developed through a major nationwide Youth Peace Movement emerging from the barrios, ghettos, and reservations. The Youth Peace Movement, consisting of a wide range of community-based groups led by dedicated activists, many of them with direct experience on the street, is aiming to end violence through constructive developments instead of repressive force.

Rather than waging a "war on crime" that brings more police and prisons, peace activists are painstakingly creating a multidimensional structure of interwoven personal/social/cultural/educational/economic supports that pull youth away from violence and toward constructive peace. I have identified some 3,100 community-based peace organizations nationwide, and this is just the tip of the iceberg. . . .

> *"The Youth Peace Movement . . . is aiming to end violence through constructive developments instead of repressive force."*

This peace movement is of significance not only for its efforts to end the violence, but also because its work has direct ramifications for political strength and community social/cultural rebirth.

An important aspect of the overall strategy for many peace activists is to emphasize personal responsibility and the development of positive community-focused values for youth. Unlike many well-meaning but out-of-touch liberals who point only to the impact of the economic system as the cause for violence, the streetwise peace activists assert that youth must take responsibility for the development and inculcation of community-based values. As Khalid Shah, director of Stop the Violence–Institute the Peace (STV-ITP) says in an interview with Robert Wright (*Unity LA*), "Now people have no regard for life, no regard for gender, no regard for anything and it's like the principles and everything are gone. . . . Now it's about, I'm not even going to get my clothes dirty. I'm just going to shoot you." Consequently, emphasizes Shah, "We have to redefine what our values are." Simultaneously, in contrast to conservative emphasis on ruthless individualism, the peace activists also recognize that in harsh environments, youth need various kinds of constructive support if their taking of personal responsibility is to succeed. Trying to "pull yourself up by your own bootstraps" when others are shooting at you requires the sustenance of broad community social/cultural/economic structures that can support and inspire those struggling to escape the cold hold of the vice of violence.

Trust and Support

Providing community support structures is based on the understanding and belief in the ultimate positive potential of youth no matter how hard-edged they have been. As Luis Rodriguez, Chicago-based activist and author of *La Vida*

Loca: Always Running, Gang Days in LA, emphasized at the two 1996 peace summits sponsored by the National Coalition of Barrios Unidos in Santa Cruz and Washington, D.C., the transformational capabilities inherent in youth are wrongly denied by those in media and government who judge them as incorrigibles. Like most of these peace activists, Rodriguez, who came out of the environment of violence and retribution, understands their untapped potential. "I tell you," he says, "that you have the creativity, the potential. I've been where you are, I know you can do it."

Peace activists understand that to tap and nurture such potential also requires a strong economic foundation in the inner cities and on the reservations. Some of that, say many peace activists, should come from the government. As Blanca Martinez of Nuestro Centro said at the Santa Cruz Barrios Unidos Summit, "We need more education, we need more programs. They are pumping our tax dollars into more prisons, more juvenile systems, more court systems. Hey, let's give back to the barrios, it's our money anyway, because we worked for it. It's our kids, it's our tears, our blood, our sweat. This is about empowering the community." But, while recognizing a potentially positive partnership role for government, the Youth Peace Movement offers a grassroots approach, rather than a top-down bureaucratic model that characterized much of the war on poverty in the 1960s. Today, the strategies and methods are being developed within and from the communities. Any partnership with progressive government will have to entail mutual respect and a recognition that the impetus and knowledge to save the communities is to be found inside them, rather than solely in the hands of outside "experts" and federal program directors.

Youth Leadership

Although much of the initial pathways for the peace movement are being charted by veterans of the street, it is youth who are providing both the mass element and the next generation of leadership. For example, at the 1996 Washington, D.C., National Coalition of Barrios Unidos Peace Summit easily 75 percent of those present were people under 21. It was these young women and men who spoke with such fervor, conviction, and experience about the pain of loss

"Providing community support structures is based on the understanding and belief in the ultimate positive potential of youth no matter how hard-edged they have been."

through violence, about moving toward peace rather than retribution. Importantly, a large proportion of these youth are already heads of Barrios Unidos chapters or are playing important roles in this organization. Similarly, Mike Barrero's Institute for Violence Reduction emphasizes the leadership role of youth, as do the Black Community Awareness Development Organization, Stop the Violence–Institute the Peace, Young Voices, and many others.

The peace movement leaders, from elders to youth, also are developing a unique approach to violence that emphasizes the need to develop negotiations for truces, cease-fires, and peace settlements among warring street organizations. As Nane Alexjandrez points out, the "gangs are not going to be wished away." Nor are police "crackdowns" stopping them. The historic peace between Crips and Bloods in Los Angeles is the cornerstone of this diplomacy/peace-making approach. But such peace negotiations are taking place around the country. Not all succeed. Not all last. Some are sabotaged. Revelations in the *San Jose Mercury-News* about the CIA's direct involvement in the crack co-caine epidemic that destroyed so much community infrastructure demonstrate yet another way in which elements of official society work against constructive grassroots efforts in the cities. Nonetheless, the nationwide peace efforts continue. When connected to the other social/economic/cultural dimensions of the peace movement, there is solid indication that the negotiation approach can bear fruit. For example, in Santa Cruz Juvenile Hall, Barrios Unidos workers Albino Garcia and Elizabeth Ayala have effectively worked to bring together hostile factions in productive ways, despite predictions that such an effort would fail. Similar efforts are taking place in Long Beach, Pittsburgh, Chicago, Albuquerque, and Boston.

Building Alliance

Peace activists see cooperation among different communities as essential. As Jitu Sidiki of the Black Community Awareness Development Organization stated at the Santa Cruz summit, "solidarity with Barrios Unidos" and with Latinos in general is necessary because "what Barrios Unidos is doing also affects what happens in African-American communities as well." Similarly, Khalid Shah and Henry Stuckey of Stop the Violence–Institute the Peace are developing a working relationship with Barrios Unidos. As Khalid Shah says, "We don't worry about your religion, your color, or how much money you make. But we have one common goal and that is the issue of violence that is killing us all. So, if we can come together on that issue and make leadership accountable, then we can get some things done."

> *"The Youth Peace Movement . . . works against the usual forms of racial 'divide-and-rule' that historically drives apart those who have so much in common."*

It is within this alliance-building context that Barrios Unidos recently hosted visiting delegations from youth focused organizations from several African nations; the Pueblo Laguna Native American nation that is wrestling with increasing youth alienation and gang membership; and Khalid Shah and Henry Stuckey. In Phoenix, Barrios Unidos activist Rudy Buchanan, whose family roots are in both the African and Mexican American communities, and who has lost two sons to gang and police violence, is working tirelessly to create inter-racial bridges. Such alliance orientations are common among many youth peace activists. Overall, the Youth Peace Movement is creating a "rainbow alliance" from the ground up.

This alliance building is an important example of what I call "transcommunality." Transcommunal cooperation does not require that communities and organizations give up their own agendas and concerns. Rather than being a "melting pot approach," transcommunality depends for its success on cooperating groups having solid roots in their own communities, cultures, and outlooks. In this type of alliance building, the Youth Peace Movement offers a crucial development that works against the usual forms of racial "divide-and-rule" that historically drives apart those who have so much in common. . . .

Time for a Renaissance

In sum, the Youth Peace Movement organizational foundations now being created effectively position us for the creation of a 21st Century Community Renaissance/Renacimiento de la Communidad. This renaissance will contain some elements that were common to previous approaches such as the New Deal during the Great Depression and the War on Poverty. But it will differ from them because it originates from the grassroots, and so is being fundamentally shaped by the concerns, the knowledge, and the outlooks of those who experience the frontlines of poverty and violence. Grassroots organizations will maintain their autonomy and objectives, but will avoid being isolated into weak racial/ethnic compartments, as they develop overall strategies of constructive interaction among themselves and with other diverse zones of society.

Organized Youth Activities Can Prevent Violence

by Bob Herbert

About the author: *Bob Herbert is a syndicated columnist for the* New York Times *and a former NBC News reporter.*

Marisa Vural, a 16-year-old high school student, told the police commissioner in 1996 that it is easier in many New York neighborhoods for a child to get a gun than a library card.

The comment was not meant as an attack on the [former] commissioner, William Bratton, who has done a remarkable job combating crime in the past couple of years. It was an expression of the frustration of young people who have to cope with the fear of violent crime, and who do not have nearly enough organized, constructive activities to absorb their energies, enrich their lives and keep them out of trouble.

Violence Is Too Easy

Ms. Vural and Bratton were participants in a forum on the prevention of youth violence that was co-sponsored by the Harvard School of Public Health and the Metropolitan Life Insurance Company. While there has been a significant decrease in violent crime nationally, there continues to be a steady increase in criminal violence committed by juveniles.

For example, the rate of known homicide offenders aged 14 to 17 has climbed from 16.2 per 100,000 youngsters in 1990 to 19.1 in 1994. One in nine youngsters in a national survey said they had cut class or stayed away from school because of a fear of crime.

Tom Brokaw, who hosted a panel at the forum, asked a teen-ager how easy it would be to get a gun if he had $100. The teen saw no need to spend that much money. He said he could give a 10-year-old $40 and feel assured that the youngster would return in 20 minutes "with a loaded .22."

Reprinted from Bob Herbert, "In America: Trouble After School," *Liberal Opinion Week*, March 18, 1996, by permission of *The New York Times*. Copyright © 1996 by The New York Times Company.

Organized Youth Activities Are Needed

Hugh Price, president of the National Urban League, noted (at his own forum) that the rate of violent juvenile crime has doubled in the last decade and is likely to double again in the next. Price is stressing the need for a vast expansion of organized youth activities that are supervised by responsible adults.

"These programs are not a substitute for prosecuting really bad actors," Price said. "But they are a complementary strategy for preventing young adolescents from becoming bad actors."

Prevention, despite the canards from certain conservative quarters, is not a dirty word. The National Center for Juvenile Justice released a study in the fall of 1995 showing that the peak hours for juvenile crime are between 3 and 6 p.m., the period immediately after school. If adults saw to it that youngsters were constructively engaged in that period, crime would go down. Instead, for a variety of reasons, including relentless budget cuts, we are giving youngsters less and less to do after school.

"Most urban school systems are too strapped financially to provide the rich array of extracurricular activities that they offered a mere generation ago," said Price. Other recreational and cultural programs have vanished, or are in such dire shape financially they reach only a small percentage of the youngsters who need them.

So the kids find things to do on their own. They do not all get into trouble by any means, but many find themselves sliding down the dangerous slope of drugs, sex, gangs and hard-core criminal activity.

Stop Abandoning Kids

Marisa Vural said the girls she knows who have joined gangs did so because they wanted protection, some form of family life, and love—all of which are supposed to be provided in abundance by responsible adults. What has happened to enormous numbers of inner-city kids is that they have been abandoned on virtually all fronts by adults who should be caring for them. That includes, in too many cases, their parents, politicians and school officials who won't even insist that they have textbooks, much less extracurricular activities, and a general public that has no real interest in them at all.

Brokaw asked if any of the six youngsters who participated in the forum had been hurt in a violent encounter. All raised their hands. He asked how many had lost friends to violence. All raised their hands. He asked how many had experienced a situation in which they thought they would die, and all raised their hands.

Price, of course, is on to something. Organized and properly supervised activities for kids is an investment in a safer future for everyone. But it is just one step back from the appalling near-total abandonment of responsibility for inner-city kids by adults across the spectrum.

Giving Teachers More Control Can Reduce Youth Violence

by Stephen Goode

About the author: *Stephen Goode is a staff writer for* Insight, *a weekly news-magazine.*

His message is clear—and harsh. "American classrooms these days too often are combat zones where teachers perform under combat conditions," says C. Stephen Wallis. "Before we can improve our schools, we are going to have to make them safe." Wallis, an assistant principal at Howard High School in Howard County, Md., speaks frequently to parents and teachers and at think tanks such as Washington's Heritage Foundation about the disorder he finds pandemic in America's public schools. "We now accept behavior we would not have tolerated only a few years ago," says Wallis. Many students regularly carry guns, knives and other weapons. Drug and alcohol abuse are rampant. "Every day we steal from students' time that should be devoted to their instruction [because public schools] lack the order necessary for learning."

School Statistics

The statistics that Wallis and others cite from a number of sources support their dark prognosis:

- The National League of Cities reports that school violence in 1995 resulted in student deaths or injuries in 41 percent of American cities with populations of 100,000 or more.
- An estimated 900 teachers are threatened each hour of the school day with bodily harm, and almost 40 teachers are actually attacked.
- Nearly 40 percent of public-school students consider their schools unsafe.

From coast to coast, in elementary schools and high schools, students and teachers are touched by violence in one form or another. At Florence Nightingale

Middle School in Los Angeles, first-year principal Marylou Amato held meetings with students and parents in October 1995 after a 3-year-old girl was murdered near the school and her 2-year-old brother wounded. In Tavares, Fla., groups of volunteer parents patrol school hallways since a 13-year-old was shot to death. The school offers a hotline through which students can report violence anonymously.

Teachers Get Tough

What to do? School administrators are hiring more security personnel and installing metal detectors at entrances. But more importantly, teachers' unions are urging schools to adopt strict behavior codes—and enforce them. In some places, teachers have taken disruptive students to court and persuaded judges to fine the students and their families as well as have the students expelled from school.

In the fall of 1995, for example, the American Federation of Teachers, or AFT, began a nationwide campaign for what the 875,000-member union calls "commonsense change." It wants school districts to develop explicit codes of student conduct. "Unless you have order . . . not much learning will go on," says AFT President Albert Shanker.

In September 1995, teachers in Florida asked a state senate committee to give them the right to expel disruptive students without the elaborate process and administrative paperwork necessary in most districts. In St. Louis, a task force investigating violence in the city's schools suggested that assaults on teachers be regarded as an automatic felony, similar to assaults on police officers. The Seattle public-school system has adopted a "zero-tolerance" approach to violence, as has the whole state of West Virginia. Students who attack teachers or bring weapons to school in these jurisdictions are expelled automatically.

A New Attitude

What all this amounts to, says Wallis, is a new attitude toward discipline, once frowned upon as abusive and restrictive. More and more educators are viewing discipline "as a kindness on the part of teachers, a necessary part of growing up, as necessary to personal growth," says Wallis.

For many teachers, however, the most aggravating aspect of school violence and disruption is that they get little or no support from school administrators who "fear lawsuits from irate parents" more than they care about teachers, says Deborah Sanville, a teacher of government at Hayfield High School in Fairfax County, Va.

> *"In St. Louis, a task force investigating violence in the city's schools suggested that assaults on teachers be regarded as an automatic felony."*

Sanville made education history in 1995 when she took a disruptive student to court—and won a ruling that banished the student from the school for a full

year and fined him $100. The student, loud-mouthed in class and verbally abu-
sive toward Sanville, had raised an arm to strike her when a male faculty member stepped between them and received the blow.

Sanville regards the court's decision as a victory for teachers—who have been
ordered by courts to accept abusive students in the past far more often than
they've been relieved of them. "I pressed charges immediately," she says. "I
told the school that day [that she was going to take the issue to court regardless
of what school officials wanted]. It was behavior that was illegal. It was behavior that would not be tolerated at a mall. Why should it be tolerated in school?"

The court order also called for the student to enroll in an anger-therapy program. Indeed, even tough-sounding educators such as Wallis do not want expelled students stranded without the possibility of guidance and genuine help.
Wallis argues the need for "transitional schools [that] aren't a joke," where the
behavior of incorrigible students can be monitored by professionals.

> *"Court decisions favoring teachers who are victims of violence may be the most effective—and immediate—way to deal with the problem."*

The Job Corps and the National Guard offer other alternatives for problem kids, adds Wallis, who favors hiring retired military personnel to staff public schools in one-to-one tutorial programs, for example. "The U.S. armed forces are a superb re-
serve of talent with science and technology training ideal for kids," he says.

But the recent successful court decisions favoring teachers who are victims of
violence may be the most effective—and immediate—way to deal with the
problem. It satisfies teachers' concerns that disruptive students be dealt with seriously and not ignored, says Sanville. And it has the advantage of bypassing
pusillanimous school administrators and, if successful, gets at students where
they hurt by fining them and their families.

Sanville has advice for teachers who want to sue violent students: "Do it immediately and follow through and don't let school administration hinder your
efforts." Teachers' unions in Chicago, New York and Miami now urge teachers
to sue when a student's behavior becomes intolerable. Word gets out among
students about successful court cases, says Sanville, who notes that Hayfield
students were impressed by the amount of media coverage her own case received.

The biggest award thus far in court cases involving violent students has gone
to Fran Cook of Alexandria, Ky., a Spanish teacher who won $25,000 in puni-
tive damages in 1995 and $8,500 in emotional damages. The jury stated on the
record that the student in question "exceeded the bounds of common decency"
not only for his classroom behavior but also when he left a note after he graduated urging other students to talk "about different methods of murder" in
Cook's classes.

There are other signs of change. In New York City, the United Federation of Teachers reported that the number of instances of physical attack on teachers and staff was down 23 percent in 1994 compared with 1993. The union attributes the change to the extensive support it now provides teachers, including those suing students.

In Atlanta, a recent survey showed the number of firearms confiscated by school officials was down by more than half from the previous year and that assault and battery and criminal trespass were down by 35 percent. School police attributed the decline to the presence of more metal detectors in the schools. All was not rosy, however. The same survey found illegal drug use up by 17 percent.

But almost everyone agrees with the motto adopted in one form or another by school districts as diverse as Ventura County, Calif., and Baltimore: "The First Line of Defense Is the Home." Wallis proposes that schools have parents sign a "parent contract." Parents would acknowledge "full responsibility for support of the school" by promising that their children will come to school "daily and punctually and that they are academically and behaviorally ready to learn."

Wallis says he is nostalgic for "the lost quality of civility" on the part of students. People are too quick to say schools only reflect the society they're in, he says. "Schools should be the one place where the parameters are so that that is not true. They should be places that create an atmosphere conducive to achievement."

Outreach Programs Can Reduce Youth Violence

by Robert Coles

About the author: *Robert Coles, a professor of psychiatry and medical humanities at Harvard Medical School, won a Pulitzer Prize in 1973 for his five-volume Children of Crisis series. He is also a contributing editor for the* New Republic *and a columnist for the* New Oxford Review.

In recent years I've become much connected to some black ministers in Boston, as well as to some youth workers who are white and black—all of whom are trying to connect with youngsters who have dropped out of school, who are gang members, and who more than flirt with law-breaking (violence, drug dealing) as a way of life. My youngest son, now only recently out of college, was the one who first helped me meet such young people—he had done volunteer work with them: taught in a program aimed at school dropouts, at children dismissed from the public schools as "unmanageable," as "violent," as "severely disturbed." I had become quite worried about my son, not the boys and girls he was getting to know: What could he, a mere college student, do to be of help to such stubbornly disinterested students, almost all of them black—and not least, I have to add, what might happen to him as he ventured into neighborhoods regarded as beyond the pale, alas, by so many people in the Boston metropolitan region?

The Need to Educate

My son came back to his dormitory, and to our home, with stories of fear and danger, sometimes, but also of sadness and frustration: How to work with youths defiantly uninterested in education? He would try exhortation, not often to any effect. He would try intense efforts at engagement, personal and intellectual, not often to any effect. He would try a kind of crude pragmatism, or a more elevated version of espoused practicality—not often to any effect. These boys and girls shrugged their shoulders, turned their faces away, as he recited moral truisms and educational pieties, as he tried to establish working involvements or alliances, as he spoke of the economic and social possibilities that literacy and diplomas can offer young people. Finally, in desperation, he tried to put aside for a while his urgently felt need to tutor, to educate children much in need of learning, and instead sought some, any common ground: things to discuss and, even more important, things to do that would keep him somehow in touch with "them" (what he realized those boys and girls had become to him, a collective "other," alien, frustratingly hard to figure, never mind reach and influence).

> *"Particular youth workers, particular ministers or teachers, particular volunteers . . . have reached some of those children by putting themselves 'out there,' 'on the line.'"*

I still remember my son Michael's accounts of what he called "progress"— some conversations with youths as he played basketball with them, as he taught them hockey in a rink. They had inquired about his life—his interests and hobbies. He had told them what he was doing—his activities, his course of study. He had managed to go further, mention what he hoped to be doing in the future—a career in medicine. One of the boys, at age 10 a "runner" for a bigtime drug dealer, asked how one becomes a doctor. Mike responded with information in a matter-of-fact way—even as the two of them shot baskets. A week later, the boy was interested enough to bring the subject up, ask more questions while all the time insisting that school, any kind of school, was simply not for him. Two months later, though, Michael had shown this boy a hospital, introduced him to some doctors and nurses, explained to him how various clinics work—their purposes, the kinds of people who come to them. Gradually, the boy began to turn toward schooling, as Michael presented it to him—a book they looked at together, some newspapers and magazines they jointly read. Finally, Michael volunteered to do some explicit tutoring in English and math, and the offer was accepted, though with hesitation. A later summary description by my son went like this: "It took three months of being challenged, tested, doubted, put in my place, before we could even begin to work together academically."

Parish Outreach

A year later I became involved with a group of black ministers in Boston, who in their own manner are taking on struggles similar to those Michael has been waging. These black men are determined to try to reclaim the streets of their parishes—and to do so are willing to go many extra miles: middle of the night outreach efforts with gang members; educational, medical, and legal assistance programs that are church-based, but include home visits; a public posture that mirrors the private conviction that one has to find a credible means of initial engagement with young people who are significantly "outside" a society's institutional life (its schools, its organized athletic and social activities, its businesses), and, too, connect with such individuals morally as well as intellectually or legally or medically. Put differently, these youths may well be in trouble with the law (or headed that way); they may have medical problems, drug and alcohol problems; they may be school dropouts already, or well down that road—but until they learn to talk with some of us who want to work with them, *and* listen to us, hear what we are saying and trying to accomplish (and why), there is scant hope they will be persuaded to change their ways, the direction of their lives.

Slowly we have realized that our best hope with these gang members, these school dropouts, is to walk the streets, work with those youth workers who are doing just that—taking a chance (taking the risk) of informal neighborhood conversation and encounters, in stores, on playgrounds, in homes. Each of the ministers has described what amounts to a kind of conversion, a time when he realized that the pulpit, the church school, the conventional programs and activities simply were of no avail—these children often slept by day, lived (gabbed and fought and "dealed") by night. Particular youth workers, particular ministers or teachers, particular volunteers, such as my son, have reached some of those children by putting themselves "out there," "on the line": a departure from the established routines and customs of a city's institutional life.

Valuable Experiences

This summer [1994], 30 years after the Freedom Schools of the Mississippi Freedom Summer, we hope to establish street academies on that model—places where young people might assemble to talk, to listen, to learn, and, yes, to teach. My son has kept telling me, reminding himself, how much he has come to know, courtesy of his young athletic colleagues, his informants, his regular acquaintances, if not, eventually, friends. Their assumptions, their values and expectations, are important to understand for those of

> *"These are children much in need of moral and civic education."*

us who hope to persuade them of the advantages and virtues of another life. An especially knowing youth worker, Jim McGillvary, made the same point as he prepared to introduce me to some gang members one early evening: "Try to get them talking to you, ask them questions that will send them the signal that you're interested in them." Yes, I thought, easier to say than to do—even as I was quaking in my (teacher's, doctor's, white man's, suburban) boots. But no matter the barriers, Jim was there to start us out, and soon enough I was hearing (the two of us white men were hearing) 12- and 13- and 14-year-old black youths give accounts of their ongoing lives, and their sense of what lay ahead: not all that much! Underneath all that street jive, that sullen braggadocio, that "hey, man, what's your deal" mix of cool and insolence, was another story, waiting to be told, entrusted: I'm a decade old, and I may not last another decade, and so I'm scared out of my mind, but I see no way out, and I'm not sure what to do, where to go, whom to believe.

Trying to Make a Difference

These are children much in need of moral and civic education, yet adrift and scared, eager to find family and protection in a gang. Will all the well-meaning efforts at gun control, at condom distribution, at "violence prevention" reach such youths, make a difference in their lives? They are already at a remove from all that, from our schools, even. In some schools, of course, habitual truancy is a fact of daily life—and not an occasion for concern, for an attempt at outreach. "I try to make the cash I can, and I hope I stick around, that's what I try to do"—those words a response to this question of mine: "What do you hope to do when you get older?" An 11-year-old gang member, drug dealer, school dropout letting me in on things—but a month later he did say that "maybe" he'd be on the lookout for a better deal, if he saw one. He wasn't quite ready, I knew, to have that kind of vision (there are "better deals" around him, *I know!*), but we hope that our "freedom schools," our "street academies" will be available for children like him—informal places where he and others can meet with some ministers and teachers and college students and medical students and law students willing to be there, to hang around, to offer their interested selves as a "line," a moral connection, to our world, which some of those kids (as I've heard them do so commonly) call "that other place," meaning where all of us, black and white, rich and poor, try to live lawfully and with some reasonable hope in our lives.

Church-Based Programs Can Reduce Youth Violence

by Jean Sindab

About the author: *Jean Sindab directs the U.S. National Council of Churches' Environmental and Economic Justice Desk and cochairs The Things That Make for Peace, an antiviolence network of churches.*

It was a shining moment—for the church, for racial solidarity, for living out a Christian witness. It occurred during the closing worship of the Congress on Urban Ministry, an event that brought together 800 pastors, lay people, and gang members (another term is street youth) to discuss urban problems of economic and environmental justice, gang violence, homelessness and racism.

It had been a long week, generating the kind of excitement and controversy such social justice issues tend to elicit at church meetings. Not everyone—pastors from 27 cities and seven foreign countries—felt so comfortable with the 25 gang members who attended: they were new to the mix. But it was important to our network that they be invited to tell their own story and issue their own challenge to the churches.

Being a Friend

Odies, one of the street youth, went for a walk and met and befriended a homeless man, inviting him back to the hotel for a meal. Odies had been in the session on homelessness and violence. Perhaps it was the stories he heard there that drew him to his new friend and made him want to help him.

The hotel management, however, was not so inclined. They were willing to let in the cleaned-up homeless to tell their stories, but not this unkempt, dirty fellow. So in spite of Odies's explanations and entreaties, they ordered the man out.

Odies got upset and insisted that the man had a right to stay as his guest. So the hotel called security, and then Odies got really upset. Security then called the police to ask them to remove Odies and his new friend. Odies did not take

Reprinted from Jean Sindab, "Youthful Peacemaking," *One World*, July 1994, by permission of the World Council of Churches Publications Office, Geneva, Switzerland.

kindly to that and became more agitated. And Odies is very big and very black. He personifies the fear of America today on issues of crime and violence.

Four squad cars responded to the hotel's call. Now Odies was mad and frustrated and more than a little confused. He understood in his previous encounters with the police that he may have been involved in some wrongdoing.

But here he was simply trying to feed a hungry homeless man. What was the crime here? And he a legitimate participant of a church meeting at that! The police pulled their clubs and stepped towards Odies. His intended act of kindness had generated a full-blown crisis.

The Police Back Off

In another part of the hotel the closing worship was in full swing. We were giving praises for the blessings of the week. Someone rushed to alert the convenor, David Fencheck, that a major confrontation was taking place in the lobby. He rushed into the lobby just in time to see the police moving towards Odies with raised clubs.

And then the moment happened. David, a middle-aged white man who probably had not been that much at ease with the gang members in the first place, put himself between Odies and the police and announced in an unwavering voice: "You will have to go through me to get to him. And if you touch either one of us, 500 people will be in this lobby in five seconds."

The police backed off. The homeless man slipped out in the ensuing melee, probably feeling that one meal was not worth all this. Left standing in the lobby face-to-face was Odies, the gangbanger, and David, the intervener.

Solidarity

For both it was a transforming moment. The conference came alive in the person of David. He brought a whole new meaning to the phrase "standing in solidarity with the oppressed". He now knows in a powerful way what that means, what it calls for from us as a people of faith.

"Our major objectives have given rise to our name: we are about 'the things that make for peace,' working to end racism, sexism and economic injustice."

For Odies, perhaps the first time in his life, he saw someone he regarded as a power figure step into a new place as a fellow-struggler. But most important, he witnessed the churches' commitment to support youth as they attempt to change their lives.

David made real the promise of those that sit around a new table in the ecumenical movement: a network called The Things That Make for Peace. This network emerged from the churches' commitment to follow up on the Urban Peace and Justice Summit (the Gang Summit) of April 1993, which brought together 160 gang leaders and church observers in Kansas City.

The three-day meeting witnessed a truce between some of the most notorious gang leaders in urban America. The religious community participated as observers, and Benjamin Chavis, vice-president of the US National Council of Churches (NCC), and I were selected as co-chairs of the observers. Leading church people such as Jim Wallis, editor of *Sojourners*, and Yvonne Delk, moderator of the WCC's [World Council of Churches] Programme to Combat Racism (PCR) Working Group, were on the advisory committee leading up to the event.

Church Involvement

The churches' involvement came after a WCC/NCC delegation visit to Los Angeles after the 1992 riots. In a meeting with gang leaders, the delegation asked what they could do to help. The youth responded: "You can help lead us to the Lord. . . . We have some habits that only God can cure." This search for spirituality was reflected at the summit as gang members from different faiths worshipped together in a black Baptist church pastored by Mac Charles Jones, a member of the WCC Central Committee.

"In many cities churches, community development corporations and government agencies are involving themselves in job creation and training."

After the summit church representatives met briefly to discuss follow-up. Between April and November 1994 we helped with fund-raising, facilitating dialogue to keep the truce agreement moving forwards, and mobilising denominations to get involved. In November 1993 we convened our first official meeting. Many of the NCC member churches, together with representatives from World Vision, and Roman Catholic and evangelical activists sat together at the table. We decided to focus on the same five themes as the summit: peace, unity, economic development, police brutality and women.

Since that time we have had several meetings. Our major objectives have given rise to our name: we are about "the things that make for peace", working to end racism, sexism and economic injustice. We have chosen five US cities on which to focus our energies: Boston, Kansas City, Minneapolis, Los Angeles and Santa Cruz, California.

They were chosen because pastors living in these cities were amongst the top leadership of the summit. In each city we work with pastors who have established an anti-violence ministry focused on youth. We also have a network of street youth connected to us.

Telling Their Stories

The network has three major tasks. The first is to provide forums and create opportunities for young folk to tell their stories to other young people and to churches. We have a standing policy that youths must be at all our meetings when we are discussing their issues.

In January 1994 the NCC submitted an application to the national service "Americorps" to secure support to hire youths to work with local councils of churches in 12 cities throughout the country, including our designated five. If approved, their voices will become an important part of this local ministry.

Jim Wallis produced a special *Sojourners* issue on urban violence and youth (August 1993), emphasising the Boston "Ten-Point Coalition"—a proposal for citywide church mobilisation put together by churches working in Boston's inner-city neighborhoods.

In February 1994 the NCC sent a CBS television team to Boston to film five days of the churches' gang-related work around the coalition. This resulted in a one-hour pro-

> *"[The pastors] walk the streets of pain, they go into the drug houses, they are in the courts, the schools, the hospitals and the funeral homes."*

gramme on church anti-violence work called "Love Them One by One", which was shown throughout the US. This programme helped bring national attention to the project, which is focused on reclaiming youth and the entire community.

Activities and Invitations

We have generated other media stories about the network. We also secured a planning grant for the work in Kansas City to raise the visibility of youth work. In March 1994 two youths addressed an NCC committee that is producing a curriculum on violence for the churches. In April 1994 the Congress on Urban Ministry held a three-day workshop conducted by youth on how the churches could become involved in anti-violence activities in co-operation with local youths.

We have encouraged invitations for youths from churches and other social justice organisations. In May 1994 talks were held with White House staff to discuss the network's activities. The network co-chair addressed the board of the Children's Defence Fund, which is also working on an anti-violence initiative.

In June 1994 the network is being hosted by Harvard Divinity School, whose dean, Robert Thieman, has taken an interest in our work. In July 1994 a national organisation is inviting members to a panel on violence and environment with US Vice-President Al Gore. In September 1994 we are planning a meeting in Washington with leading members of Congress and staff members in the White House. We have also set up meetings between the youths and foundations.

Economic Alternatives

The network's second task is to establish alternative economic opportunities. At the gang summit and all subsequent encounters with street youth and those who work with them, the emphasis has been on creating economic alternatives to the underground drug economy which drives so much of the crime and violence in urban America.

We have put together economic development technical assistance teams that are travelling to each of the five target cities to discuss with community development experts the specifics of generating entrepreneurship, jobs and training opportunities for youth.

In all five cities pastors and youths are involved in economic development activities, producing T-shirts and tie-dye clothing, silk-screening posters, renovating housing, providing security services, purchasing and renovating old houses, establishing apprenticeships, producing "cross-colour" clothing, starting up businesses in beauty culture and child and elderly people's care, and working in urban gardens to sell to local markets.

One of the most promising opportunities lies in the field of environmental clean-up. We are working with churches that are providing jobs and training in this area. In Chicago, Bethel New Life, a Lutheran-based community development corporation, has hired over 60 people to work in their recycling plant. In New York city, Columbia University is initiating a programme for youths to remove lead from old buildings. Lead poisoning is a leading cause of illness in inner-city communities. The removal of asbestos can also create training and job opportunities.

Involving Youth

In many cities churches, community development corporations and government agencies are involving themselves in job creation and training in the environmental field. As the cities seek to attract investment, environmentally degraded land serves as a disincentive. Huge sums of money are required to make the land suitable for new investment projects.

Unskilled or semi-skilled street youths are a good target constituency for environmental clean-up work for several reasons. For a start, street youths have a strong need to give something to their community. They accept responsibility for some of the problems there and believe that cleaning up vacant lots, planting gardens and flower boxes, and renovating old houses are ways in which they can contribute.

Secondly, there are decent, living wages to be made in this field. Most young people involved in drug-dealing want to leave because of the pain it causes the community and the tremendous danger in which it places them. At the summit young people repeatedly stated that "we should not have to risk our lives to make a living". At the same time, working in fast-food places is not an alternative many with responsibilities can afford.

Thirdly, the urban environment has become a dumping ground for toxins mainly because of the lack of information about the danger to health they pose. Working in this area would raise consciousness around environmental issues. It could also alert residents to the notion of what "sustainable development" actually means. Businesses are beginning to negotiate investing in urban areas if local environmental regulations are relaxed. The involvement of youths could prevent this.

Street Ministries

The network's third task is to secure additional church support for local anti-violence initiatives. The issue of crime and violence is creating fear and anger throughout the US. Lack of jobs and urban investment and racism exacerbate this situation. At base, our urban communities are facing a spiritual crisis that churches must address. Moreover, because of the gravity of the situation, the churches must be willing to assume new forms of organisation to meet new needs and challenges.

The pastors involved in our network have established street ministries. They walk the streets of pain, they go into the drug houses, they are in the courts, the schools, the hospitals and the funeral homes. They are teaching and preaching. They are reaching out, bringing in, breaking stereotypical perceptions of the church, attending to needs and, most of all, giving love

"The pastors in the network are using the gospel and love to save our youths."

and assurance. They are holding up a people's gospel, emphasising love and redemption.

Kansas City is one example. After the summit several of the gang leaders went to co-hosts Mac Charles Jones and Sam Mann and asked for their support. They wanted to continue the peace process in the city and bring in more young people. The result is a church-based youth group called Break and Build—break down the walls between the gangs, between the races, sexes and classes, and build a new society.

The group has been working together across gang lines. With NCC support they are negotiating a huge grant to set up self-reliant programmes in the summit's five main areas. They have pulled together a coalition of churches, judges, and foundation, municipal and non-governmental organisation staff that together will make up five working groups on education, women, economic development, criminal justice and peace.

Challenges for Peace

Their biggest challenge at the moment is to entice more churches to join their efforts. At present pastors of the largest United Methodist and Presbyterian churches are involved. But we do not have enough additional churches joining the initiative.

The pastors in the network are using the gospel and love to save our youths. This is not a two-hours-a-week, but a 24-hours-a-day, seven-days-a-week ministry, bringing these young people back from the fringes of society where they have been pushed. The pastors deal with the young people's tremendous personal and family problems and responsibilities. They guide them in trusting God's love to give them the strength to stay on the path of transformation.

These young people are just discovering the power of God in their lives. As one young man said: "It is really hard when you are trying to turn your life around. But I believe God saved me for a specific purpose, so I have a mission to accomplish."

Can we help these young people in their mission? I believe so. It won't be easy, but we have no other choice. They are our future. We have to bring in more church partners, mobilise more local congregations to be involved.

We have to be as strong as David, the intervener, and be willing to stand with our young people in the tough places of life, to be their advocates and friends, to confront the powers and principalities on their behalf.

Because of David, Odies can continue, fortified on his path towards transformation. We need more shining moments like this, more moments when we stand with the oppressed as a witness to God's love. This is what our faith and our belief in Jesus Christ our saviour should be about: being doers of the word, not just sayers. This is indeed doing the things that make for peace.

Chapter 4

Should Violent Youths Receive Harsh Punishment?

Harsh Punishment for Violent Youths: An Overview

by Fox Butterfield

About the author: *Fox Butterfield, a* New York Times *correspondent, is the author of* All God's Children: The Bosket Family and the American Tradition of Violence.

In the most drastic changes to the juvenile justice system since the founding of the first family court a century ago, almost all 50 states have overhauled their laws between 1994 and 1996, allowing more youths to be tried as adults and scrapping longtime protections like the confidentiality of juvenile court proceedings.

The thrust of the new laws is to get more juveniles into the adult criminal justice system, where they will presumably serve longer sentences under more punitive conditions.

Proponents of the changes say that getting tough with teen-agers is the only way to stop the epidemic of juvenile crime. Over the past decade, for example, arrest rates for homicides committed by 14- to 17-year-olds have more than tripled. And with the number of teen-agers projected to increase by 20 percent over the next decade, many criminologists expect a new surge in crime.

Tough Measures Increase

"The thinking behind the juvenile court, that everything be done in the best interest of the child, is from a bygone era," said Patricia L. West, director of the Virginia Department of Juvenile Justice, which was created by the State Legislature in April, 1996.

While the original juvenile court, established in Chicago in 1899, was intended to deal with miscreants who might throw a rock through a shopkeeper's window, "now we have juveniles committing violent repeat crimes no one ever anticipated," Ms. West said.

So Virginia has adjusted its philosophy, she said, making issues of public safety and victims' rights as important as protecting the interest of the child. Among the changes in Virginia's new law, which parallels those adopted recently in many other states, are provisions requiring any child 14 or older who is charged with murder to be tried as an adult.

> *"Proponents of . . . getting tough with teen-agers [say it] is the only way to stop the epidemic of juvenile crime."*

The law also gives prosecutors and judges greatly expanded authority to transfer other juveniles into adult courts for crimes including armed robbery and burglary. And, in a sharp departure from a century of practices intended to protect youths, juvenile court proceedings in felony cases will be open to the public, juveniles will be fingerprinted, and their records will no longer be expunged.

In New York, Gov. George E. Pataki is pushing to increase the minimum sentences for many juvenile offenders, to transfer all 16-year-olds in detention centers run by the State Division for Youth to adult prisons and to sharply increase sentences for youths convicted of a second felony.

Eliminating Childhood

Critics say politicians and others clamoring for these measures are endangering children and are unaware of the consequences.

We are stepping down a very grim path toward eliminating childhood, said Lisa Greer, an official of the Los Angeles County Public Defender's Office who is a member of a state task force studying ways to overhaul the juvenile justice system in California. Several bills that would at least double or triple the number of young people who could be tried as adults are before the California Legislature.

Howard Snyder, director of systems research for the National Center for Juvenile Justice in Pittsburgh, said, "The interesting thing is that these people yelling to put more kids into the adult system seem to be forgetting that they have been yelling that the adult prison system is a failure and is letting too many criminals out."

Barry Krisberg, president of the National Council on Crime and Delinquency in San Francisco, said, "What we are really frightened about is guns, but instead of launching a war against guns we are launching a war against kids."

What is disturbing, he said, is that the public is trying to lower the age of adulthood rather than see what is happening as a failure of society.

Because the changes in juvenile laws are happening so fast, with some states altering their statutes almost every year, there are no national data on the total number of juveniles tried and incarcerated as adults, Mr. Snyder said.

Adult Prisons May Be Ineffective for Juveniles

But a study of juvenile offenders tried in adult courts in Florida found that those sentenced to adult prisons reverted to a life of crime more quickly after they were released, and committed more crimes and more serious crimes, than those in juvenile institutions.

"Over all, the results suggest that transfer in Florida has had little deterrent value," wrote the authors, who include Donna Bishop and Charles Frazier, professors at the University of Florida. Nor, the authors concluded, has trying juveniles in adult courts "produced any incapacitative benefits that enhance public safety."

The study's findings are similar to those of a report that compared the records of 15- and 16-year-olds charged with robbery and burglary from Newark and Paterson, N.J., and Brooklyn and Queens. Under state law, the teen-agers in New Jersey were treated as juveniles while those in New York were treated as adults.

The survey found that offenders in both states were incarcerated for equal amounts of time, so that the juvenile court system was no more lenient than the adult courts, said Prof. Jeffrey Fagan, the author of the study and director of the Center for Violence Research and Prevention at the Columbia University School of Public Health.

More important, Professor Fagan said, he also found that the youths sentenced as juveniles in New Jersey were significantly less likely to be re-arrested than those sentenced as adults in New York.

One reason being incarcerated in adult prisons may lead to worse outcomes, the professor suggested, is that youthful offenders suffer "contagion effects" from being housed with older, more hardened criminals. Another reason is that adult prisons tend to have fewer services, like psychological counseling or job training.

"Critics say politicians and others clamoring for [harsh juvenile crime] measures are endangering children and are unaware of the consequences."

Professor Fagan believes that incarcerating juveniles in adult prisons has another drawback: the dangers to the young people confined.

On April 25, 1996, for example, a 17-year-old black youth, Damico Watkins, who was serving a 7-to-25-year sentence for acting as the lookout in a botched robbery of a pizza shop, was stabbed to death in an Ohio adult prison near Columbus by members of a white supremacist group.

His mother, Kimberly Watkins, has filed a $100 million wrongful death lawsuit against the prison, charging that the guards did not do enough to protect her son.

Too Young for the Law?

A case that both proponents of the tough new laws and their critics agree may be a turning point in the debate is that of the 6-year-old boy charged with attempted murder in April 1996 in Richmond, Calif., after being accused of dumping a neighbor's newborn baby out of its bassinet and beating it nearly to death. If the infant dies, the 6-year-old could be charged with murder.

The incident is fraught with significance, said Mr. Krisberg of the National Council on Crime and Delinquency, because under English common law children under the age of 7 could not be charged with the commission of a crime, and those from 7 to 14 were protected by a "presumption of infancy," a belief that they were too young to have a criminal intent.

American reformers in the 19th century tried a series of experiments to make the treatment of juveniles more humane, first by creating "houses of refuge" to separate youthful delinquents from adult prisoners, and later by establishing an independent juvenile court system.

> *"Legislators are rushing to make sure juveniles receive the maximum punishment, turning the juvenile court system upside down."*

The first juvenile court, created by the social worker Jane Addams, was designed to be a civil rather than a criminal court, and the accused were to be defined less by their offenses than by their youth. Children were thought to be still susceptible to rehabilitation, and the judges were to act informally, serving like doctors, to dispense the right treatment for the offender rather than punishment.

Now legislators are rushing to make sure juveniles receive the maximum punishment, turning the juvenile court system upside down.

"I'm not interested in legislating out childhood, said Gil Garcetti, the Los Angeles County District Attorney, who backs a bill that would automatically transfer juveniles to adult court for serious crimes. "My concern is that juvenile crime has been rising unacceptably fast, and kids learn they can get away with it because there is no real punishment for the first few crimes."

Kids Get Adult Treatment

Perhaps the most sweeping changes were instituted in Florida in 1994. Prosecutors now have the authority to try juveniles as young as 14 as adults, and delinquents with three previous convictions are automatically tried as adults.

Moreover, judges have the authority to confine high-risk juveniles in temporary detention centers indefinitely until a place becomes available in a regular secure institution.

One result is that Florida is sending more juveniles to adult courts than all the other states combined, some 7,000 cases in 1995, said Henry George White, executive director of the Florida Juvenile Justice Advisory Board.

But at the same time, Mr. White said, some of the temporary detention centers are at 200 percent of capacity, and the state is forced to let more young people out sooner, with less treatment, than the law intended.

"At a cost of $93 a day," Mr. White said, "it would be cheaper just to put a kid in a hotel or send him to Harvard for a year."

Juvenile Justice Needs to Be Tougher

by Ed Koch

About the author: *Ed Koch, former mayor of New York City, appears as the judge on television's* The People's Court.

Too often, in New York and other jurisdictions, the law treats juvenile criminals as delinquent children, while they act more like feral animals. Juveniles seem to view the lack of restraints as a license to attack the elderly, the infirm, and other children who are not able to defend themselves.

Each year juveniles are committing more crimes than ever before. According to Department of Justice statistics, the number of juveniles arrested for murder increased 104 percent nationwide from 1970–1992. Since 1980, juvenile gang killings, the fastest growing murder circumstance, have increased 371 percent.

The System Is Too Easy

Judges and prosecutors are unable to take appropriate action to stanch this bloody flow because we have created unreasonable legal cushions for juveniles who commit serious crimes. In our zeal to protect the privacy of young thugs who in many cases will grow up to be older thugs, we've established a system where convicted juvenile criminals can't be identified to the public. Wouldn't you like to know if the kid down the block is a convicted arsonist? Or a sex offender? In New York, teenagers cannot be fingerprinted and photographed for certain felonies, including possession of a loaded gun or shooting someone resulting in physical injury. Why not?

Family Court prosecutors in New York are not permitted to get arrest and search warrants when a juvenile is involved—even if the prosecutor knows that a murder weapon is in the juvenile's home. Believe it or not, there is no legal mechanism available to get a search warrant and seize that murder weapon in the state of New York.

When juveniles convicted in family courts graduate to the adult courts, dis-

Reprinted from Ed Koch, "Get Control of Juvenile Terrorists," *The American Enterprise,* May/June 1995, by permission of *The American Enterprise*, a Washington, D.C.–based magazine of politics, business, and culture.

trict attorneys and judges are often not allowed access to their full criminal history because juvenile records are placed off limits by confidentiality restrictions. Courts are sometimes told individuals are first-time offenders when they are nothing of the kind. Nationally, the recidivism rate for teenage offenders runs as high as 75 percent. There will be no controlling this until full juvenile records are made available to courts for purposes of imposing the appropriate punishment on chronic offenders.

Inadequate Laws

Juveniles engage in crime because there is no respect for law or authority, and little expectation of arrest or punishment. Our state legislators fail to recognize that the crimes committed by these "little rascals" have gone way beyond pickpocketing, slashing tires, and drinking beer in public. The laws created to handle those misdemeanors are simply not adequate to deal with the serious felonies that juveniles are now committing.

In New York, for example, the maximum juvenile sentence for serious crimes like shooting someone, gang robbery, and burglary is 18 months. For the most heinous felonies like murder and rape, juvenile sentences range from three to five years, with the maximum rarely applied.

> *"We have created unreasonable legal cushions for juveniles who commit serious crimes."*

All of England was horrified when two 10-year-olds kidnapped and murdered a toddler. Prime Minister John Major summed up the feelings of most responsible people when he said, "I feel strongly that society needs to condemn a little more and understand a little less." Regrettably, that common sense response is rarely found in our state legislatures.

Recently in New Jersey, seven-year-old twin boys were arrested for breaking into a church, their third burglary in two weeks. Previously, according to press reports, they burglarized and ransacked a school, causing $30,000 worth of damage, and broke into a private house. After their most recent arrest they were again turned over to their mother, a recovering drug addict. The state Division of Youth and Family Services will "now send a caretaker to check on the boys to make sure they are home and out of trouble," according to a story in the local New Jersey newspaper.

Don't Look Away

Why was nothing done after the first burglary? And even if it made some kind of sense on the first occasion, it surely makes no sense to leave those children in the custody of their mother now. Without intervention, experience shows us that their rap sheets will grow and grow.

Aside from toughening the laws for handling juvenile crimes, what can we do to try and get youngsters off the criminal path? It is almost universally agreed that public schools for a whole host of reasons are not teaching morality. One proposal that I believe Congress should explore, and perhaps install on a test basis in Washington, D.C., is a scouting operation for children starting at age five that would be available from 3 to 6 p.m.

The second proposal, designed for those 17 and older, is a Civilian Conservation Corps designed to teach young people job skills, provide them with drug treatment if they need it, and assist them with getting their general equivalency diplomas. After serving two years in such a corps, those who entered with criminal records could be eligible for an executive pardon if they remained drug free and avoided run-ins with the law for a three-year period.

To cope with today's explosion of juvenile crime we must be very tough— tough on the criminals, and tough on ourselves. We should no longer view heinous behavior as a phase that a child will outgrow. Serious juvenile delinquency is now part of our culture, and we need urgent measures to punish and rehabilitate young people who are violating the rights of others.

Violent Youths Should Be Punished as Adults

by Robert L. Sexton

About the author: *Robert L. Sexton is a professor of economics at Pepperdine University in Malibu, California.*

A vast majority of states in the United States do not gain jurisdiction over young offenders in criminal courts until they reach the age of 18. As a result, the law has little control over juvenile crime and there is much recidivism. This situation could be ameliorated without the use of additional scarce resources by redefining the age at which offenders are treated as adults to, say 16, or lower yet if it is politically feasible. According to Larry J. Siegel and Joseph Senna, numerous authorities in the field believe that most youths over the age of 14 can be held accountable for their own actions. . . .

The Growing Juvenile Crime Problem

A recent report from the U.S. Department of Justice highlights the alarming increase in juvenile crime from 1988–1992—aggravated assault cases were up 80%; homicides increased 55%; robberies went up 52% and forcible rape cases rose by 27%. In 1990, more than a third of all murders in the United States were committed by individuals under the age of 21. Among 18-year-olds the homicide rate doubled between 1985 and 1992. During that same period the rate for 16-year-olds increased 138 percent while homicidal rates for adults declined by 20 percent. Thus, most of the increase in homicides from 1985–1992 was due to a surge in killings by the young. The rates of juvenile crime differ markedly between different ethnic groups, but the principles here discussed would apply equally to juvenile offenders irrespective of ethnic background.

Overall, the American juvenile crime rate is rising. According to Uniform Crime Reports, juvenile arrests were up 11 percent from 1993–1994. Even more disturbing is the fact that while 15- and 16-year-olds make up only a small proportion of our population, they commit a large percentage of all violent crime.

Excerpted from Robert L. Sexton, "Tackling Juvenile Crime," *Journal of Social, Political, and Economic Studies*, vol. 21, no. 2, Summer 1996, pp. 191–97. Reprinted by permission of The Council for Social and Economic Studies.

There are presently 40 million children now under the age of ten, and projections show the number of teenagers increasing by almost 25% by the year 2005. If the current trend continues, violent crimes will reach horrific levels.

The fact that teenagers are committing more violent acts at an earlier age is undoubtedly responsible for the rising growth in the nation's violent-crime rate. And the age cohort responsible for much of the recent youth violence is the smallest it has been in recent years. But what can effectively be done about juvenile crime when federal and state governments are under severe budgetary constraints?

Lowering the Age Requirement on Adult Courts

The influence of drugs, drug money, gang-related incidents and the ease of acquiring a lethal weapon are all contributing factors to the juvenile crime problem. In the past, we have tried two approaches to reducing the inordinate amount of crime: increasing the budget for law enforcement and imposing more stringent statutes and stiffer penalties on those apprehended. However, one particularly effective way to increase the sentence or fine for juvenile offenses that has not been considered seriously is to reduce the age requirement for adult courts.

According to a 1989 U.S. Department of Justice Report, *The Juvenile Courts' Response to Violent Crimes,* only 5 percent of juveniles are tried in the federal system as adults. Lowering the age requirement to, say, 15 or 16 years of age for "adult" courts might be an effective strategy for all cases. The cost to society of a trial is the same regardless of the age of the criminal, and it is no secret that juvenile courts are considerably more lenient than adult courts. In light of the persistent recidivism among juvenile criminals, it makes sense that if tried as adults they could be given longer sentences and required to spend time in state prisons rather than in juvenile detention centers.

One serious problem in dealing with young offenders is the lack of data regarding serious crimes committed before the age of 18. Under current laws in most states, felonies and misdemeanors committed by minors are not made public. Hence, many apparent first-time offenders appearing in adult courts have in fact committed many serious crimes as juveniles, but the evidence is not available. If offending youths of 16 years and above were tried as adults, their criminal records would be disclosed at an earlier age.

> *"Numerous authorities in the field believe that most youths over the age of 14 can be held accountable for their own actions."*

This is important because past criminal records have a lot to do with current sentencing. Another advantage of having greater access to juvenile criminal records is that prosecutors can increase the probability of convicting the right person.

The Bureau of Justice Statistics has estimated that 38 percent of inmates incarcerated for murder in a state prison in 1986 had a prior juvenile conviction. The same study found that 54 percent of state prisoners convicted of robbery as adults had a juvenile record.

Access to Criminal Records

There is also a need to maintain an up-to-date computerized record of criminal history data that is reliable and accurate so that judges can detain dangerous suspects before trial. Lacking this information, serious criminals are too often released pending trial and put back on the streets where they commit fresh crimes while awaiting trial for their previous offense.

Access to the crime records of youthful repeat offenders at an earlier age, and the threat of spending more time in prison, rather than less time in a juvenile detention center, would have a significant deterrent effect and would protect innocent citizens from much violent juvenile crime. Since the vast majority of states do not grant adult jurisdiction over young offenders in criminal courts until the age of 18, it is not surprising that criminal activity is so prevalent among the young, since they pay such a low "price" for it.

> *"While 15- and 16-year-olds make up only a small proportion of our population, they commit a large percentage of all violent crime."*

Some might be concerned that first-time juvenile offenders might be prosecuted to the full extent of the law in adult courts, spend time in state prisons and consequently turn into hardened criminals. However, this is not a compelling argument, since most juvenile crime is committed by repeat juvenile offenders and sentencing for first time juvenile offenders, even if tried in adult courts, would not be the same as that for repeat offenders. It is true that it would be possible to lower the juvenile crime rate by enforcing existing laws more rigorously, but this is unlikely to happen because of the high cost of additional police equipment and a larger police force, and a simple adjustment of the age at which youths may be tried as adults would achieve massive benefits at virtually no additional cost.

Juvenile Courts

The critics of harsher punishments for juveniles may ask, "Why are we attacking the juvenile court? Do we really believe that the adult courts will produce better results? Or that youths coming out of the state penitentiary are more likely to become model citizens than kids coming out of a juvenile institution?" We need to look at the facts:

Firstly, the number of juveniles waived to adult courts is relatively small, and until the adult court age is lowered (at the very least for repeat juvenile offenders) we will not accurately know the impact that adult courts would have on crime rates. However, the fact is that research appears to confirm that waivers of youths into adult courts for serious offenses increase the certainty of punishment. A study by Donna Martin Hamparian (1987) found that 91% of the waived youths were convicted.

Secondly, the most serious or intractable juveniles are not currently always those who are waived to adult courts. An analysis of Florida juveniles that were waived to adult courts revealed that "very few of the juveniles were dangerous or repeat offenders." Rather most were charged with property offenses. These findings are consistent with those of M.A. Bortner, who found that remanded juveniles were not typically dangerous or retractable. Consequently, it sometimes appears, as in the Florida case, that adult courts are lenient on juveniles when these have been arrested for non-violent crimes. It may be assumed that they would be more severe with those arrested for violent crimes, especially if they already have a serious crime record.

Thirdly is the fact that most juvenile crime is committed by "chronic offenders." According to Marvin Wolfgang's well-known study of Philadelphia youths, chronic juvenile offenders committed 65–75 percent of serious crimes. Furthermore, the hardcore juvenile offenders committed most of the crimes and were rarely punished. He found that only 14 percent of the first five arrests resulted in punishment. And those few who were imprisoned committed fewer and less serious crimes after their release. This study casts serious doubt on the juvenile justice system's ability to rehabilitate chronic offenders.

> *"It is not surprising that criminal activity is so prevalent among the young, since they pay such a low 'price' for it."*

And chronic offenders appear to be the serious problem. In 1988, A.J. Beck, S.A. Kline, and L. Greenfield, in a Bureau of Justice Statistics study that focused on state-operated juvenile facilities, found that almost 43% of the juveniles detained had been arrested more than five times and more than 20 percent had been arrested more than ten times. Again the conclusion from this study confirms that the arrest and juvenile court experience did little to deter repeat offenders. A 1990 study found that youths who spent 14 months in a California Youth Authority institution had a rearrest rate of 70 percent. All of these studies cast serious doubt on the juvenile justice system's ability to rehabilitate chronic offenders.

Don't Let Repeat Offenders Get Away

The juvenile justice system has their counterpart to adult court plea bargaining. Department of Justice statistics reveal that only 60 percent of all children arrested by the police are actually referred to juvenile courts. The others are either warned, parents are notified or they are referred to social service programs.

If we are to make any progress towards controlling violent juvenile crime, court records on juveniles must be opened. Repeat juvenile offenders should know that the authorities have access to past records and will use that information when handing down their sentences. After all, don't taxpayers have a right to know what they're getting for $85,000 a year—the cost of keeping a juvenile offender in a secure facility in the state of New York?

The average cost per year for adult prisoners is $28,000. Most would probably agree that in order to keep repeat juvenile offenders off the streets we need to open juvenile court records, enforce strict laws and apply firm uniform sentencing provisions. This will have two effects. One, keep chronic juvenile offenders in prison for longer periods of time and two, deter others from pursuing careers as criminals. . . .

Cost-Controlled Solutions

For the most part, politicians have ignored strategies that would minimize enforcement costs in the "war against juvenile crime." Since these costs are substantial there is a clear economic advantage in favor of introducing a lower adult court age limit rather than far more costly and less well targeted increases in police budgets. And the explosion in teenage violence by many of those less than 18 years of age might lead to a political acceptance of an adult court age limit of 16 years or younger for juvenile offenders.

Of course, it would be naive to exclusively blame the juvenile justice system for the increases in violent juvenile crime. And any solution to the problem will have to also address issues such as education and family values. Educational vouchers, especially in the inner cities where they are needed the most might be an effective first step. A voucher program could give rise to alternative high school programs that include vocational training. It is time that we look for some fresh, cost-controlled solutions to handling the growth in juvenile crime.

Authorities Should Have Increased Access to the Records of Violent Youths

by James Wootton

About the author: *James Wootton is the president of Safe Streets Coalition, an organization that works to remove violent criminals from the streets and to prevent at-risk youth from becoming involved in criminal activities.*

Violent teenage criminals are increasingly vicious. John DiIulio, Professor of Politics and Public Affairs at Princeton University, says that "the difference between the juvenile criminals of the 1950s and those of the 1970s and early 1980s was the difference between the Sharks and the Jets of West Side Story and the Bloods and the Crips. It is not inconceivable that the demographic surge of the next ten years will bring with it young criminals who make the Bloods and the Crips look tame."

The Rising Tide of Juvenile Violence

According to the Council on Crime in America, a bipartisan commission chaired by former Attorney General Griffin Bell and former White House Drug Policy Director William J. Bennett, crimes committed by males ages 14 to 17 will increase by 23 percent between 1995 and 2005. Because of the deterioration of family life, and also because of their easy access to guns, these juveniles are likely to commit more vicious crimes than their predecessors, targeting strangers as well as known enemies. Louis Freeh, Director of the Federal Bureau of Investigation, believes that continuation of current trends in juvenile crime "portends future crime and violence at nearly unprecedented levels." Recent reports of juvenile crime dropping are of little comfort in light of the coming demographic surge of juveniles in their crime-prone years from dysfunctional families.

Excerpted from James Wootton's testimony before the Subcommittee on Youth Violence, Committee on the Judiciary, U.S. Senate, April 16, 1997.

Growing numbers of young people, often from these dysfunctional families, are committing murder, rape, robbery, kidnapping, and other violent acts. As Professor John DiIulio and others argue, these emotionally damaged young people, growing up without faith, fathers, or families, often are the products of sexual or physical abuse. They live in an aimless and violent present; have no sense of the past and no hope for the future; and act, often ruthlessly, to gratify whatever urges or desires drive them at the moment. They commit unspeakably brutal crimes against other people, and their lack of remorse is shocking. They are what Professor DiIulio and others call urban "superpredators." They are the ultimate urban nightmare, and their numbers are growing. The number of juveniles arrested for violent crimes has increased nearly 60 percent over the last ten years. . . .

> *"Growing numbers of young people . . . are committing murder, rape, robbery, kidnapping, and other violent acts."*

Young people ages 12 to 17 are the most frequent victims of violent crime. They are raped, robbed, or assaulted at five times the rate of adults 35 years old or older. In 1992, one juvenile in 13 was the victim of violent crime, up 23 percent from 1987. Also in 1992, 23 percent of the victims of the 6.6 million violent crimes committed in the United States were juveniles; the juvenile victimization rate was 74.2 cases per 1,000 juveniles, compared to 13.9 cases per 1,000 adults 35 years old or older. Overall, the sad fact is that crime has seriously affected teenagers' lives, especially those who live in neighborhoods seriously hurt by crime, drugs and gangs. The effects are insidious and long-standing. Teenagers protect themselves by carrying weapons, skipping school, changing their routes to and from classes, changing friends or letting their grades slip. For many young Americans, the carefree days of adolescence are a nostalgic fantasy.

Even more shocking than the sheer volume of violent juvenile crime is the brutality of the crime committed for trivial motives—a pair of sneakers, a jacket, a real or imagined insult, a momentary cheap thrill. For example:

- A 59-year-old man out on a morning stroll in Lake Tahoe was fatally shot four times by teenagers "looking for someone to scare." The police say the four teenagers—just 15 and 16 years old—were "thrill shooting."
- A 12-year-old and two other youths were charged with kidnapping a 57-year-old man and taking a joy ride in his Toyota. As the man pleaded for his life, the juveniles shot him to death.
- A 14-year-old boy was murdered while trying to reclaim a $2,500 stereo system he had received from his grandfather. Five juveniles, ranging in age from 15 through 17 years, were charged with the crime.

Seasoned big-city homicide detectives have a hard time coming to grips with the horror of these kinds of cases: The crimes are senseless, the motives banal, and the perpetrators all so young. These shocking incidents—which occur in

America's suburbs as well as its inner cities—are creating a growing consensus among the American people: They have had enough. Lenient sentencing based strictly on age is no longer acceptable for crimes of this magnitude.

Loss of Public Confidence

Polls show that Americans are unhappy with the system as it is: 49 percent believe rehabilitation programs for juveniles are not successful, 52 percent believe the punishments juveniles receive should be the same as those given adults, and 83 percent think juveniles who commit two or more crimes should receive the same sentencing as adults. A 1995 Gallup poll found that 72 percent of Americans also advocate the death penalty for juveniles who commit murder, as opposed to 24 percent in 1957.

Teenagers themselves take a hard stance on how their peers should be treated if they commit violent crimes. Over 93 percent believe that those accused of murder or rape should be tried as adults. Moreover, they do not believe these offenders should receive special consideration because of their age. This is consistent with broad public, judicial, and law enforcement sentiment, which generally has favored holding juveniles more accountable for their criminal actions in recent years.

The juvenile justice system that prevails in many states today does juvenile criminals no favors by being lenient. According to a 1985 Rand Corporation study, "waiting for chronic offenders to build a record of many arrests and minor dispositions only compounds the problems that must be dealt with later."

Failure to Target Serious Habitual Offenders

In many states, the greatest single weakness of the effort to combat juvenile crime is a simple failure to target the most dangerous young offenders. This weakness arises from a reluctance on the part of juvenile justice officials to admit that there is a point at which a delinquent youth becomes such a threat to the community that he or she must be held accountable and incarcerated. Under the current system, the seriously violent juvenile can become invisible by being mixed in with the general population of non-violent and non-habitual juvenile offenders.

> *"The juvenile justice system that prevails in many states today does juvenile criminals no favors by being lenient."*

Overwhelmingly, most urban young people who get arrested for a crime get arrested only once; seldom are they a serious or long-term threat to the safety of other citizens. Put another way, not all juvenile delinquents are alike, and very few are serious habitual offenders (SHO). The official failure to discriminate between minor offenders and hard-core criminal youth undermines the effectiveness of the entire system.

The most active juvenile delinquents also are the most dangerous. Often invisible to the officials who preside over the system, they are painfully visible to the victims they assault, rob, and kill. The official failure to develop credible control measures to suppress habitual juvenile offenders also sows the seeds of racial prejudice. With the rise of juvenile crime, an increasingly angry and insecure public tends to look upon all juveniles, particularly black male teenagers, as threats to the community. Most juvenile offenders, however, are not: 58 percent of young black males never have any contact with the police; and of the other 42 percent, an overwhelming majority do not go on to become SHOs. It is therefore vital that state and local officials, as well as taxpayers, begin to think and act differently toward the occasional juvenile delinquent. The SHO, on the other hand, is a career criminal in the making.

> *"The greatest single weakness of the effort to combat juvenile crime is a simple failure to target the most dangerous young offenders."*

The Information Gap

Chronic offenders usually can be identified solely on the basis of their juvenile records. This evidence, however, normally does not accumulate until after the youth's 16th birthday, and a failure to make that information available through the FBI slows the process. If additional factors describing the youth's school performance and home situation are included, the age at which youthful chronic offenders can be identified and an intervention mounted may be moved up several years.

In reality, these young criminals are shunted in and out of state and local agencies who are supposed to be running the system but who often seem to lack a collective awareness of the kind of young people they are processing. Too often, they are oblivious to the repeated and increasingly serious nature of the behavior of these young criminals. This official failure to share information can occur for many reasons: because it is not required by state law, because of bureaucratic inertia or lack of imagination, or even because of simple negligence. It is a key weakness in the current system. Most of the juvenile codes in the United States contain statutory language indicating that the juvenile judge should consider police reports, field interview reports, citations, social history information (such as data on school, family, and work), drug involvement information, motor vehicle operation information, associates' history, offense digests, and victimization data. Only rarely, however, is this information used or shared among youth service agencies; it often is not even made available to the presiding judge. . . .

A Program That Works

The Serious Habitual Offender Comprehensive Action Program (SHOCAP) system has been employed successfully in over 150 communities in the United

States and Canada, including Oxnard, California; Colorado Springs, Colorado; Tallahassee, Florida; Prince William County, Virginia; and Tampa, Florida (Hillsborough County Sheriff's Office). SHOCAP works in these communities because it provides accurate, documented support to police in tactical operations focused on their most active criminals. SHOCAP enables law enforcement officials to give direction to police in the field so that they can use their patrol activities to prevent and suppress the criminal activities of SHOs. Through computers and information sharing, SHOCAP provides field forces with comprehensive information on a serious habitual offender's criminal activities beyond beat or shift boundaries. The system works because a computerized case file—either on-line in a police cruiser or accessible by police dispatchers—can be punched up by the police within seconds. . . .

Perhaps the most dramatic example of SHOCAP's effectiveness is Oxnard, California. Despite having one of the lowest police-to-population ratios in the country, over a three-year period in the 1980s, Oxnard experienced a 38 percent reduction in violent crime and a 60 percent drop in the murder rate. It did this by targeting and successfully incarcerating a greater number of SHOs than were targeted and incarcerated in jurisdictions not using SHOCAP. Recognizing that most crime is committed by a small minority of felons, Oxnard officials used SHOCAP to remove 30 of these hard-core juvenile offenders from the streets. . . .

Expungement Laws Are No Longer Appropriate

Expungement laws hearken back to a simpler past. The practice "was designed to deal with delinquents who stole hubcaps, not those who mug old ladies," notes sociologist Rita Kramer in *At a Tender Age: Violent Youth and Juvenile Justice.* Gargantuan increases in violent juvenile crime noted above underscore the point. Today's juvenile offenders are generally distinguishable from their adult criminal counterparts only by their age—an arbitrary factor indeed.

"Chronic offenders usually can be identified solely on the basis of their juvenile records."

The philosophy underlying expungement legislation can be traced to what is known as the Chicago School of Criminology, which, during the 1920s and 1930s, championed environmental explanations of criminality. The Chicago School (the term refers to a broad-based intellectual movement that started at the University of Chicago) rejected traditional criminological theories that focused on issues of individual morality and volition and concentrated instead on factors external to the individual. This new model viewed America as a "criminogenic" society in which ghettos and slums taught the people who lived there how to become criminal by giving them deviant cultural values.

This environmental model reached its high-water mark in the early 1960s with Robert K. Merton's "strain theory," which posited that America's sup-posed obsession with ambition and success led to crime and deviance. Strain theory viewed delinquency as arising from the frustration felt by individuals who were unable to achieve culturally defined goals because they were denied the institutionalized means of doing so.

In the 1960s—the decade during which most expungement statutes currently in force were written—expungement advocates espoused what is known as the "labeling" or "social reaction" model. The labeling perspective is based on the premise that the very act of labeling those who are apprehended as "different" creates deviants who are different only because they have been "tagged" with the deviant label.

As criminologist Frank Tannenbaum, a prominent labeling-perspective theo-rist, argued in his 1983 book *Crime and the Community,* "The process of mak-ing the criminal . . . is a process of tagging, defining, identifying, segregating, describing, emphasizing, making conscious and self-conscious; it becomes a way of stimulating, suggesting, emphasizing, and evoking the very traits that are complained of." Hence, the only way to rehabilitate juvenile delinquents is to send them into adulthood with this label detached.

Profile of a Serious Habitual Offender

In every community, there is the potential for only 2 percent of the juvenile offender population to be responsible for up to 60% of the violent juvenile crime. These serious repeat offenders, who all too often eventually become adult career criminals, bleed the life out of the community, endangering public safety and undermining eco-nomic stability.

> *"Almost without exception, the adult career criminal was a serious habitual offender as a juvenile."*

In general, only 25 to 35 juveniles in every 100,000 members of the population will engage in criminal activity that matches the serious habitual offender pattern. Based on criteria de-veloped by the Reagan team at the Department of Justice, this means that 0.03 percent to 0.04 percent of all juveniles between 14 and 17 years old will be SHOs. At the same time, for each SHO, four other juveniles are at risk of be-coming SHOs themselves.

Data collected and analyzed by the Reagan Administration team at the U.S. Department of Justice in the 1980s presents a graphic portrait of the serious, ha-bitual offender. The typical SHO is male, aged 15 years and six months old; he has been arrested 11 to 14 times, exclusive of status offenses, and five times for felonies. He comes from a dysfunctional family, and in 46 percent of cases, at least one of his parents has an arrest history. He has received long-term and continuing social services from as many as six different community service agencies, including family, youth, mental health, social services, school, juvenile, or police authorities, and continues to drain these resources for years before he is finally incarcerated as a career criminal.

The typical SHO's family history follows a classic pattern of social pathologies: 53 percent of his siblings have a history of arrest, and in 59 percent of these cases there is no father figure in the home. The absence of a father is particularly destructive for boys; only 2 percent of SHOs are female. Furthermore, 68 percent of these offenders have committed crimes of violence, 15 percent have a history of committing sex crimes, and 51 percent have a reported missing or runaway record. If a broken family characterized by physical or sexual abuse is an early indicator of criminal behavior, then virtually all of these serious habitual offenders fit this category. . . .

> *"It is imperative that the defendant's sentence account for his criminal history from the date of birth up."*

Cutting Short a Criminal Career

For law-abiding citizens, the career criminal is Public Enemy Number One. By using modern information technology and case management, as embodied in Serious Habitual Offender Comprehensive Action Programs, law enforcement officers and local government officials can target and track society's most dangerous criminals. Almost without exception, the adult career criminal was a serious habitual offender as a juvenile. Once again, this is a very small minority of the population: 94 percent of the juveniles arrested for a criminal offense are never arrested again; 4 percent are arrested on a regular basis, while only 2 percent are arrested repeatedly and go on to become serious habitual offenders and career criminals. Career criminals exhibit common patterns of behavior, as well as a relationship between age and criminal behavior. Unfortunately, however, today's juvenile justice and adult criminal justice systems are not adequately linked.

Since both the volume and intensity of juvenile crime have increased and are likely to escalate in the future, it is no longer feasible to wait until these career criminals reach adulthood to protect society from their actions. There are stages in the life of the typical career criminal. By channeling resources on the basis of a comprehensive case management system, SHOCAP can play a crucial role in stifling a criminal career at each stage. State and local officials therefore should adopt a SHOCAP program and try some juvenile offenders 18 years old and under as adults.

Stages of Development

In the first stage of criminal development, as amply documented by Patrick Fagan, these serious habitual offenders come from abusive, broken or neglectful homes. Looking backward through the SHOCAP telescope, local law enforcement and criminal justice officials can trace the pattern of abuse and neglect that often results in a delinquent and criminal lifestyle. Based on the SHOCAP criteria and amplified by indices of negative social conditions identified by the Heritage Foundation, state and local officials can design an early intervention strategy for those juveniles who are at risk of becoming serious habitual offenders and career criminals. Such a strategy can focus community resources, including private sector charitable, social, and religious institutions, on potential and active SHOs and stop their criminal careers before they gain momentum.

> *"Expungement and juvenile record secrecy are actually an astonishingly counterproductive policy that benefits only young criminals."*

In the second stage of the criminal's development, from 13 to 18 years of age, the SHOCAP process helps judges and other state and local criminal justice officials answer a critical question: Is the offender, based on his record, likely to respond to intensive intervention by social service agencies, or is he in fact a youthful career criminal who cannot be rehabilitated and should be locked up? State corrections officials simply do not know how to rehabilitate some violent young criminals who pose such a clear danger to society. They must be separated from the community and controlled. SHOCAP can help state and local judges and other responsible officials determine who among a larger class of young offenders are the incorrigibles.

From the vantage point of public safety, the best that state and local officials can do with the incorrigible SHO when the crime is serious is try him as an adult, sentence him as an adult, and require him to serve at least 85% of his sentence, as required by truth-in-sentencing laws which are called for by recent federal legislation and enacted in 25 states now eligible for federal assistance. This would mean that a 15-year-old serious habitual offender who is given 20 years for second degree murder would serve at least 17 years before being released at age 32.

Thus, the serious offender would have spent his highest crime years locked up, unable to create more victims.

Keep Their Records

During the third stage of a criminal's career, from 18 to 30 years of age, SHOCAP gives state and local criminal justice officials complete criminal histories of career offenders at the time they are arrested. The police, prosecutors, and judges know instantly that they are dealing with a SHO and not a petty or first-time offender. Currently, however, an adult criminal's previous juvenile records are not available to the system in most jurisdictions. As a result, 18-year-olds with lengthy records of serious and violent crime frequently are treated as first-time offenders.

But current expungement statutes rarely make such a distinction, choosing instead to delete a teenager's criminal record upon reaching majority (or sooner), regardless of whether it consists of a one-time arrest for public urination or numerous convictions for assault, burglary, or rape. As the number of offenses increases, the underlying delinquency becomes more troublesome, and it is likely that anti-social pattern will continue throughout a criminal's adult years.

Given that adult criminality is often predicated upon juvenile delinquency, it follows that criminals have the most to gain, and that society the most to lose, from any expungement scheme that allows individuals to start with a "clean slate"—or, more appropriately, a cleaned slate upon reaching majority. That expungement is being challenged both intellectually and politically indicates that the costs may have finally become too much to bear.

Consider the Child's History

That's one of the major points in *United States v. Davis,* a 1995 case involving a convicted felon's due process challenge to the United States Sentencing Guidelines' directive to consider juvenile convictions in calculating a defendant's prior criminal history. Writing for the court, Judge William J. Bauer of the Seventh Circuit Court of Appeals powerfully stated: "It is imperative that the defendant's sentence account for his criminal history from the date of birth up to and including the moment of sentencing. The consideration of the defendant's juvenile record is essential, because it is clear that the 'magic age' of eighteen, seventeen, or sixteen, whatever it may be in a specific state, cannot wipe out all previous contacts with the law. The pubescent transgressions . . . help the sentencing judge to determine whether the defendant has simply taken one wrong turn from the straight and narrow or is a criminal recidivist."

Supporters say confidentiality of juvenile records is an enlightened practice that merely forgives youthful transgressions. But expungement and juvenile record secrecy are actually an astonishingly counterproductive policy that benefits only young criminals. The practice prevents society from acting on the simple fact that those who have committed crimes in the past are likely to commit crimes in the future and hence should be treated differently from true first-time offenders.

Harsh Punishment Will Not Help Violent Youths

by Lane Nelson

About the author: *Lane Nelson is a staff writer for the* Angolite, *a prison news magazine published by the Louisiana State Penitentiary in Angola, Louisiana.*

The little girl walked up to the repairman who sat in his truck taking a break. She looked into his eyes while holding the heavy pistol in her two small hands. Without saying a word she pulled the trigger and blew his face off, then turned around and walked away without blinking. She was 13 years old, and pregnant. "The way she did the shooting was nothing less than a hit," Wisconsin prosecutor Lovell Johnson told a jury in the closing arguments of little one's trial. "She did it quickly. She did it quietly. She did it slowly." The jury found her guilty of first degree murder. The girl, whose name was withheld because of her age, committed the murder on instruction from adult drug dealer Danny "Crazy" Conner, who had mistakenly suspected the repairman for a police undercover agent.

A cold-blooded murder committed by one so young creates fodder for politicians and frightens the public. In turn, hysteria swirls: "They commit an adult crime, give them adult time!" On the campaign trail, Republican presidential candidate Bob Dole calls for tougher measures to deal with juvenile criminals, complaining that "many of the rules affecting juveniles were designed when the worst offenses committed by teenagers included joyriding and truancy." But throughout history a few teens have always committed horrendous crimes. Take, for example, 12-year-old Hannah Ocuish, who in 1786 attacked and killed a 6-year-old girl. Ocuish was hanged for her crime. In 1944, 14-year-old George Stinney killed two young girls. Like Ocuish, Stinney was put to death. The list goes on, but the fact is violent juveniles have always been around, and they always will be. . . .

Punishing Children Like Adults

In 1995 the right-wing magazine *American Enterprise* called for harsher punishments for children. "There is no alternative to building more prisons," they

Reprinted, with permission, from Lane Nelson, "Kids Are Different," *The Angolite*, July/August 1996.

said, and presented a Gallup poll about juveniles who commit serious crimes. One question asked how juvenile delinquents should be treated. Seventy-nine percent of those asked said the same as adults; only 19 percent said with more lenience.

> *"Most juveniles who are transferred to adult court for prosecution end up going to prison, and for nonviolent crimes."*

"If a teenager commits a crime as an adult, he should be prosecuted as an adult," President Bill Clinton said on the 1996 reelection trail. Not to be outdone, Dole reminded voters that while in the Senate he introduced legislation allowing 13-year-olds to be prosecuted in adult court, and had moved to lower the age of execution from 18 to 16 in federal proceedings.

Tyris Wilkerson was arrested for burglary in Louisiana at the age of eight. The following year he was arrested for sexual battery. A year later, when he was ten years old, he and three other boys committed a forcible rape. Authorities placed Wilkerson on one-year probation. At age eleven, police arrested him for firing a gun in city limits, and a month later he was picked up for aggravated assault, possession of a stolen vehicle and possession of a sawed-off shotgun. Authorities prosecuted him in juvenile court, and he received a two-year sentence to Tallulah Christian Acres group home—a privately run juvenile facility. Eleven months later he was released, and shortly afterwards picked up for traffic violations. Two months later, in September 1995, 14-year-old habitually violent criminal Tyris Wilkerson was arrested for killing a 40-year-old man during an armed robbery. Police claimed the youngster had committed two other armed robberies just prior to the killing, in which the victims were shot but not killed.

A Waiver Law

Wilkerson became the first juvenile prosecuted in Baton Rouge under a new waiver law that allows transferring children as young as 14 to adult court, and to adult prisons. A jury found him guilty of second degree murder and he received the mandatory juvenile life sentence, which means he will be released when he turns 31. While a juvenile life sentence is mandatory for a 14-year-old murderer convicted in either juvenile or adult court, 15-, 16- and 17-year-olds can only receive a juvenile life sentence if they are convicted in juvenile court. If convicted of murder in adult court, they receive the adult sentence—life without parole.

Designed to remove young predators from society for the safety of the community, the waiver law is aimed at violent kids like Wilkerson, said state Senator Jay Dardenne (R-Baton Rouge). Dardenne was a leading supporter of the 1994 waiver bill. The same year 24 other states passed laws making it easier to try children as adults. Twenty-two states followed Louisiana's lead and set the minimum age for adult prosecution of serious violent crimes at age 14. In Montana 12-year-olds can be sent to adult court, and in Vermont the minimum age is 10.

In Florida, a 1994 law equips prosecutors with the authority to prosecute a 14-year-old as an adult if he or she is a repeat offender or has committed a first degree felony.

"We will put you in jail. We will put you in prison. The free ride is over," Palm Beach County state attorney Barry Kriescher told a group of inmates in a juvenile prison. "This is your last chance. I'm telling you, y'all better take me seriously because I'm taking you seriously." Between 1994 and 1996, reported *CNN*, Kriescher has nearly doubled the number of children under 18 who have been prosecuted in adult criminal court. Stephanie Powell was 14 when he tried her for capital murder. She is now serving 20 years in a state prison.

Something Is Not Working

The General Accounting Office (GAO), the investigative arm of Congress, released a 1995 study showing most juveniles who are transferred to adult court for prosecution end up going to prison, and for nonviolent crimes. Thirty-four percent of the transferred cases involved crimes against people, and 45 percent involved property. Another 12 percent involved drug crimes, and 9 percent involved public disorder offenses. The tactic is not working as intended.

> *"Incarcerating juveniles in adult prisons has very little to do with rehabilitation and prevention."*

In November 1995, Florida had more than 600 youngsters under 18 in adult prisons. A U.S. Justice Department study found that sentencing juveniles to Florida's adult system not only had no deterrent effect, but the kids sent to adult prison "committed more new crimes and more serious new crimes than similar kids sent to the juvenile system." Even Kriescher admitted the harsh reality: "If 60% of the children are re-offending, then that proves [putting children in adult prisons] doesn't work. But the question is, what do you substitute for that?"

Northeastern University surveyed 540 police chiefs. Most said the best way to reduce juvenile crime and violence is to invest in programs that help children get a good start in life. Only 14 percent favored prosecuting juveniles as adults. "[T]he preventive programs," Buffalo Police Chief Gil Kerlikowske said, "are getting lost.". . .

Kids Are Not Adults

"It looks tough but is shortsighted," Michael E. Saucier told the U.S. Congress in March 1994. Saucier is the national chairperson for the Coalition for Juvenile Justice. He believes that incarcerating juveniles in adult prisons has very little to do with rehabilitation and prevention. "Juveniles in adult institutions are five times more likely to be sexually assaulted, twice as likely to be beaten by staff, and 50 percent more likely to be attacked with a weapon than youths in a juvenile facility."

Professor David M. Altshculer, John Hopkins Institute, agrees with Saucier. In his article, "Tough and Smart Juvenile Incarceration" (*St. Louis University Law Review,* 1994), he explains that while prosecuting juveniles in adult court has dramatically climbed since the 1980s, it has shown no gainful deterrent effect. Altshculer noted that "the problem is proponents of any of the get-tough measures . . . tend to focus almost exclusively on punishment and retributive goals, often to the exclusion of offender treatment, rehabilitation, and advocacy. The point is that evidence supporting a specific deterrent effect of incarceration on offenders is altogether lacking."

> *"Juveniles who were institutionalized had a much higher recidivism rate (46%) than those who were not (14%)."*

In 1989 the South Carolina Department of Youth Services released a comprehensive study that traced 39,250 males with juvenile police records from 1964 to 1971. The study found that juveniles who were institutionalized had a much higher recidivism rate (46%) than those who were not (14%).

"Crack cocaine, guns and teenagers have come into my court too many times," said Louisiana district court Judge Ross Foote in 1994 when sentencing 17-year-old Dwaine Young for murder. "I've sent too many of them away." Young was convicted of shooting a 30-year-old man in the chest during a crack deal. "Facing teenagers with life imprisonment doesn't get any easier," Foote told *Associated Press.* Young received the mandatory adult life sentence without parole.

A Baton Rouge jury recently expressed concern over sentencing Damien Riley to spend the rest of his life in prison. At 15, Riley shot and killed a comic-book store owner during a robbery. Tried as an adult, the evidence was more than enough to convict him of second degree murder. But in an unusual move the jury attached a note to their verdict. The note read: "We, the jury, would like to ask that if it is in the judge's power, this young man be given any consideration allowed by the law during sentencing." The judge explained to the troubled jurors that second degree murder carries a mandatory life sentence without parole, and that he was unable to afford Riley any leniency.

Louisiana's juvenile life law should be expanded to cover 15- and 16-year-olds like Riley. It protects society by locking up a child predator during his crime-prone years, while allowing for a second chance. At age 31 he will still be able to make something of his life when released. With the right educational opportunities during his incarceration, and the right attitude, he will have a fair chance to make it.

Helpless Youth

Toby Dupre arrived at [the penitentiary in] Angola in 1995, a boy in a man's world. His demeanor is polite and open, hiding the bouts of deep depression he suffers. Right now Dupre is desperately trying to grow patches of hair on his face to look older. He wants to fit in; he wants to survive. He was arrested at the age of 16 for his involvement in a 1994 robbery/murder of a ShopRight clerk in Houma, Louisiana. After the prosecutor's office transferred his case to adult court, a jury found him guilty of accessory to second degree murder. He was sentenced to spend the rest of his life in prison. Dupre didn't get the benefit of a juvenile life term with the prospect of a second chance down the road.

"I worry about being here," he told the *Angolite,* "because of all the stories I've heard about this place and because of how young I am. I don't know how the older prisoners are going to treat me." The day he arrived in prison he was assigned to a one-man cell in the Clinical Services Unit (CSU), partly due to his battle with depression, mostly due to his youth. CSU is a more restrictive environment than the general prison population. For now that suits Dupre just fine.

Along with Dupre are 13 other kids in CSU who have come to Angola over the past 18 months. All were arrested at the ages of 15 or 16 and, except for two, are serving life terms or sentences long enough to keep them here until they die. "We've been getting a lot of kids in here lately," said Angola prisoner Checo Yancy, an inmate counsel who serves CSU. "It's my opinion they are being transferred out of the parish jails as soon as they are convicted. The reason for that is these kids are a problem for the sheriffs to protect. They may have been predators on the street, but when they come to jail or prison they become possible prey."

> *"Kids are a problem for the sheriffs to protect. They may have been predators on the street, but when they come to jail or prison they become possible prey."*

Yancy is working with prison officials to get some of the kids into the prison population—the ones he feels can make it. "If they can get into the mainstream of prison life," said Yancy, "then they can avail themselves of educational opportunities and positive programs the inmate clubs have." Because of an increasing influx of kids being sent to Angola, Yancy foresees another problem. "Angola is going to run out of places to keep these kids until they grow older and bigger," he said. "There is only one physically big kid at CSU right now. The rest are just little children. But you have to keep in mind some have been convicted of very serious crimes."

Difficult Cases

Toby Dupre's case raises questions about sending children away for life. Born in Terrebonne Parish, Louisiana, he moved with his family to Mississippi at the age of 14. His dad is a welder and licensed minister, his mother an office worker. He has a younger brother 14, a sister 16 and another sister 21. None have been in trouble with the law. His family supports him by visiting as much as possible and sending him money each month.

He says he experimented with alcohol and marijuana in the 4th grade, but never graduated to hard drugs. He dropped out of school when he was 16. "I witnessed something that happened in school and some kids threatened to kill me," he said. "I was afraid so I quit going to school." Dupre has always had mental and emotional problems, and was teased by other kids while growing up.

Asked what he would do differently, he said: "I wouldn't do drugs. To me drugs seemed to be the answer to my problems and I was accepted in that circle of friends. But now I know better. All my problems were still there when the drugs wore off." He also said with watery eyes, "I would treat my parents differently, show real love to them. I realize now they were trying to teach me the right way."

Three people were involved in the crime: Dupre, James Herbert, 17, and Chris Ellender, 30. According to news accounts, Herbert walked into the

> *"The threat of twenty years in prison has no deterrent impact for a youngster who thinks summer vacation lasts forever."*

ShopRight, pulled a gun and shot to death the clerk, a 55-year-old woman, and snatched the money from the register. Dupre and Ellender sat in the car during the crime. Police arrested the trio a short time later. Under threat of the death penalty, Herbert pleaded guilty to first degree murder, agreeing to testify against the other two. He told the jury all three planned the robbery. Dupre and Ellender denied it, saying they did not know Herbert was going into the store to rob it. The jury believed Herbert and now all three sit in Angola serving natural life sentences.

The system dealt Dupre a harsh blow. He is a first offender who seems to have fallen in with the wrong people and put himself in the wrong place at the wrong time. Now his life is over before it ever began. . . .

Most Youths Can Be Saved

"Unless something is done soon, some of today's newborns will become tomorrow's super predators—merciless criminals capable of committing the most vicious of acts for the most trivial of reasons," Republican presidential candidate Bob Dole said recently. In trying to make political capital out of public fear, a common tactic these days, he calls for new get-tough measures to combat juvenile violence. In addition to stiffer sentencing and making more juvenile offenders eligible for servitude in adult prisons, he advocates that juvenile arrest records be made public and stick with delinquents forever, like adult arrest records. Permanently branding all children arrested for any offense "criminal" for life, damaging future employment and educational opportunities, regardless of whether the child grows out of what is often temporary misbehavior, is a bizarre notion that has nothing to do with prevention and a lot to do with Draconian styles of punishment. . . .

With Dole and other get-tough advocates, the problem is how they see the problem. Seizing on sensational exceptions, they draw sweeping conclusions from anecdotal evidence. The truth is, as study after study has shown, only a few kids are lost forever. Most troubled youth can be salvaged. . . .

Sweeping get-tough "feel good" policies do not work. . . . What they do accomplish is to squander scarce resources that could be put to better use. Enhancing drug-abuse and vo-tech [vocational-technical] programs for at-risk and troubled youth, for example. Cracking down on truancy, as New York City has done. Focusing juvenile anti-crime police efforts in specific urban areas, rather than fritter away money and effort on broad-brush ineffective tactics. Above all, widespread community and parental concern . . . needs to be stepped up.

Kids are different. They do not think like adults. The average child doesn't have the tools to control impulsive behavior. When he learns, as he learns, he matures into a responsible adult. Just as significant, kids do not understand time as adults do. They live in the now. The threat of twenty years in prison has no deterrent impact for a youngster who thinks summer vacation lasts forever.

Until society learns to restructure itself by resurrecting the nuclear family and eliminating poverty, child abuse and neglect, perhaps it should turn away from those who urge destroying children in the name of safety and reexamine the tried and true way of transforming young males into productive citizens: education by parents, teachers, counselors—the entire community. The best early indicator of career criminality is skipping school and hanging out on the street. Education is the antidote, the key that opens dreams and keeps hope alive.

Violent Youths Should Not Be Tried as Adults

by James A. Gondles Jr.

About the author: *James A. Gondles Jr. is a contributor to* Corrections Today.

Congress, the president, our governors and our state legislators have embarked on a sobering approach to juvenile justice. Recently, state and federal legislation has been passed which allows prosecutors to determine where a juvenile is tried—in juvenile or adult court. That's wrong. The American scales of justice should be equal or at least we should constantly strive to make them so. A judge, and not the prosecutor, should make the decision on which court a juvenile goes to. The prosecutor's job is to present the state's or public's case against a juvenile so accused. To allow the prosecutor to determine which court a juvenile goes to also would determine where the juvenile would serve time, if convicted. It is, in my opinion, a flawed and quite unbalanced approach to fairness.

I believe that in violent offenses such as rape, felonious assault or murder, juveniles can be tried as adults, if a judge so determines, and can serve time in adult institutions. Most adult corrections directors and wardens do not want juveniles in their systems. These juveniles are special needs offenders. As Reginald Wilkinson, American Correctional Association (ACA) president and the Ohio director says, their systems are capable of incarcerating, treating and meeting the needs of juveniles. And in some cases, the juveniles belong in those systems. But trying 9-, 10- and 11-year-olds as adults is wrong.

Still Children

Kids today may be maturing physically earlier than before, but mentally they still require teaching, training, loving, skill-building and learning through years of maturity. Bodies may be growing faster, but no child is born with morals, with judgment, or with remorse; they learn these and other emotions and controls.

Excerpted from James A. Gondles Jr., "Kids Are Kids, Not Adults," *Corrections Today,* June 1997. Reprinted by permission of the American Correctional Association.

Juvenile records are subject to public scrutiny now in many places. Why? So the public can be protected, so the public's right to know and the press' right to know is exercised, we're told. So the end result is that a 12-, 13- or 14-year-old will live with his or her juvenile mistakes throughout life. In most cases, people stop committing crimes in their late 30s or 40s, sometimes after that. I believe our criminal justice system can continue to protect our citizens without attaching the "scarlet letter" to kids for life.

I believe that not only should the Office of Juvenile Justice and Delinquency Prevention (OJJDP) be continued, but that it should be the highest of priorities for increased funding. OJJDP has made a positive impact on how we view, treat and work with juveniles. And while I didn't always like the requirements placed on me when I was a sheriff, I believe OJJDP's mandates have been protective of juveniles' rights and generally on the right course.

Nurture Children

Kids are our future. Kids who are abused, neglected and unloved have very little chance to "go the right way." They can't walk away from lives of crime—they don't know about programs, alternatives and services available to them unless an adult becomes involved. A child is nearly at a dead-end if he or she suffers at the hands of adults, whether it's parents' or others'.

"[Children] can't walk away from lives of crime—they don't know about programs, alternatives and services available to them unless an adult becomes involved."

The call for a national "crackdown on juvenile offenders" and the fear of a "new generation of super predators" is, I believe, an overreaction to one of our weakest emotions—fear.

Are there juveniles who belong in institutions in order for society to be protected? Of course. Should some of them serve substantial sentences? Of course. Some may even require continued institutionalization because they are beyond treatment or help. I hope critics to my opinion will not charge me with coddling, softness and the other adjectives often used for those who hold opinions like these on children. I hope those who agree with me on most of what I've written won't shout, "Hooray for Jim; he sees it our way."

Empathy

What I would like everyone to do is to close their eyes, sit in a quiet place and remember their childhoods. Reflect on them, think about them, meditate about them. Were you happy most of the time; did your parent or parents tell you that you were loved; did they show it? Did you have teachers, coaches, counselors, clergy, relatives or friends who set examples for you? Did adults make a difference in your life? Think about the possibility of virtually nothing but negatives blocking you at every step you took as a child.

183

Think about your own kids, grandchildren, nieces, nephews or friends' children. Don't they make you laugh? Don't they make you smile? Aren't they bringing joy, purpose and meaning to your lives? Don't you want them to be happy, to do well in life and to lead moral lives of sharing, caring and giving like you do? Think about your son or daughter "messing up" and landing in the juvenile justice system. How would you like them to be sentenced to adult court, adult prisons, with public juvenile records and less protection of their rights?

Finding the Right Focus

Today it is so easy to criticize, to tear down, second guess and propose quick-fix solutions. The debate will rage on about why we got where we are today with our kids. Is it family values, too much sex and violence in television and the media, too much leisure time, too much money to spend? Is it not enough spiritual faith, a breakdown in discipline, inadequate schools, a welfare state? Is it parents too busy to spend time with kids, more neglect, child abuse and drug and alcohol use?

We may not even have discovered what we've failed to do. Whatever the reason, more kids use guns, alcohol, drugs and do other things that we as a nation are uncomfortable seeing our kids do.

But it troubles me deeply that our focus is on juvenile justice and not juvenile education. It's about trials and not about schools or discipline. It's about punishment and not about mentoring. It's about dropping mandates and not about day care. No, I can't understand it and I don't agree with it. We will never, in my view, solve our problems on the back end with punishments. We will solve our problems only when we are united with a higher purpose of doing better on the front end with day care, preschool, schools, churches, other institutions and yes, families.

Society Should Focus on Prevention, Not Punishment

by John Allen

About the author: *John Allen writes for the* National Catholic Reporter.

One evening in summer 1996, 16-year-old Asha Sidhu and her boyfriend were saying good night. Feeling awkward in front of Asha's younger brother and sister, they received permission from Asha's mom, Amber, to sit in their car a couple of blocks away.

Shortly after, a member of the San Diego Police Department pulled up. In an earlier era, the officer might have shone a flashlight in the car and waved the kids home, but not this time: It was after 10 p.m., and Asha was in violation of San Diego's new curfew ordinance. The officer arrested her on the spot.

"I didn't know where my daughter was for hours," said Amber. "I was panic-stricken." To make matters worse, the family had gone rock-climbing the day before, leaving Asha's fingertips roughened. While in custody, the police accused her of using acid to remove her prints, and subjected her to interrogation about various crimes. Asha, an honors student, was eventually released, but her mother still seethes over the incident. "Why couldn't the officer have just brought her home and asked me what was going on?" she asked.

Getting Tough

The answer lies, at least partly, in the get-tough approach to teenagers that has swept America in the past decade. A national mood of concern about youth crime, coupled with demographic projections showing a boom in the teenage population, have given rise to a host of measures designed to crack down on kids. Consider these signs of the times:
- Cities are dusting off existing youth curfew ordinances or writing new ones at breakneck speed. Indeed, the lust for action is sometimes so overwhelming that elected officials don't even bother to check the statute books to see what's already there. One New Jersey city council has passed a curfew ordi-

Reprinted from John Allen, "U.S. Teens Face Rash of Get-Tough Actions as Nation's Fear Grows," *National Catholic Reporter*, January 10, 1997, by permission of the *National Catholic Reporter*.

nance three times, each time forgetting about its previous vote.

- Increasingly, states are treating juvenile offenders as adults, and the federal government is also getting in on the act. The 1994 Crime Bill expanded federal authority to prosecute juveniles as adults despite research showing that placing juveniles in the hands of the adult system actually makes them more likely to commit serious crimes later.
- Youth boot camps are growing in popularity. Florida leads the nation with six fully operational sites. The camps emphasize military-style discipline and a punitive approach to misbehavior.
- Zero-tolerance policing is being practiced in many communities, a program in which police do not tolerate even minor infractions by teenagers (such as having a radio up too loud). The result in some inner-city neighborhoods is nearly constant police supervision.

> *"The average adult believes juveniles commit 43 percent of violent crimes, when the actual figure is just 13 percent."*

- In perhaps the most extreme example of this get-tough trend, several states, including Alabama, Tennessee, Mississippi and California, have considered legislation authorizing paddling as a response to juvenile crime.

The California ordinance, which passed two Assembly committees before narrowly losing on the floor, would have required the paddling to be administered by a parent in front of a judge, with the bailiff ready to step in should the parent prove insufficiently energetic.

Taken together, these measures express America's growing fear of its own children. A 1994 Gallup Poll revealed that the average adult believes juveniles commit 43 percent of violent crimes, when the actual figure is just 13 percent.

Politically Appealing

Given this national alarm, it's no surprise that get-tough measures enjoy political appeal. Youth advocates are worried about their long-term consequences, however, not just for those teens caught up in a juvenile justice system now more interested in punishment than rehabilitation, but also for the vast majority of non-offending adolescents whose real needs are ignored by a law-and-order emphasis.

Despite concerns about the dangers of a punitive approach, no one disputes that youth crime is a serious problem. "During a six-year period from 1985 to 1991, the rate of homicide committed by 13- and 14-year-old boys was up 157 percent; the rate of homicide committed by 15-year-old boys was up 212 percent," said Jack Levin, director of the program for the study of violence and conflict at Northeastern University. "These statistics tell us that something's wrong."

The National Center for Injury Prevention and Control in Atlanta reports that arrest rates for homicide among youth 14–17 years of age increased 41 percent between 1989 and 1994, compared to a decline of 25 percent for adults during the same period.

Making these figures all the more alarming for advocates of a crackdown on youth violence is the projected spike in the teenage population over the next 15 years. The number of 14- to 17-year-olds in America is expected to rise from 14.6 million in 1995 to 17.4 million by 2010, a 19 percent increase, according to Census Bureau data.

Preventing Superpredators

This trend has prompted speculation about a future in which hordes of "superpredator" teenagers fill hospitals and morgues with their victims, an apocalyptic scenario that has generated strong popular support for get-tough approaches. In one telling development, the Democratic speaker of the New York State Assembly, Sheldon Silver, recently reversed his long-standing opposition to punitive measures for kids. In fact, Silver has gone even farther than his Republican critics in insisting that every juvenile offender, no matter how trivial the crime nor how understandable the motives, must receive some "taste of punishment."

Supporters of this approach point to the most recent statistics, which suggest a downturn in juvenile crime. From 1993 to 1995, juvenile homicides fell 10 percent nationally. Dr. Deborah Prothrow-Stith of the Harvard school of public health agrees that the most recent news is encouraging, pointing to Boston, which has not had a single juvenile homicide in 1996. Just three years ago, it had 16. Advocates of curfews, paddling and the like see in these numbers a vindication of the deterrent value of swift and sure punishment.

A Little Guidance

Others, however, are not so sure. "A lot of the get-tough stuff works, but not for the reason that people think," Levin said. "It's not that they're so tough, not that they're punitive, it's that they supervise youngsters. For the first time, we're actually paying attention to what teenagers do. We're giving them a little guidance, supervision, control. . . . For the first time in 20 years, we're giving them direction for their lives, providing them with role models," he said.

"Teenagers today lack the stability that only strong adult role models can provide."

Levin's analysis points to the force many observers see as the root of teen crime: the withdrawal of adults, especially parents, from the lives of children. "Teenagers today lack the stability that only strong adult role models can provide," said Fr. Michael Scully, pastor of St. Joseph's Parish In Hays, Kan., and author of several books on youth ministry. "Adults have to take an interest."

Levin agrees. "For 20 to 25 years, we have permitted our teenagers to raise themselves," he said, citing that 57 percent of children lack full-time adult supervision. A lack of concern on the part of the adult population, Levin argues, and not anything inherently evil about this generation of teenagers, has produced such high youth crime numbers.

By the same logic, the get-tough approach works because it signals a return of interest, albeit driven by fear, on the part of adults in what's going on in the lives of their teenagers. "For 15 years, thousands of people in Boston have been working on violence prevention. In general, the community has made a serious commitment to dealing with the problem and it's paying off," said Prothrow-Stith. "This is what's helping, not stricter punishment."

> *"Kids are going to make mistakes, but we must never desert them."*

The Future Is Bleak

Although any decline in youth crime is good news, observers such as Levin and Prothrow-Stith worry that if the crackdown mentality gets the credit for it, Americans may come to believe that the problems of the young can be solved by a few good, swift kicks, rather than the longer-term, hard work of rearing them well. Such a belief could bode ill on many fronts.

For one thing, in the present climate, the future is bleak for those relatively few youngsters who do engage in serious crime. Given that most of these kids are in the inner city, a law-and-order approach inevitably means more incarceration for the poor and minorities. It is now possible for a young person to enter the prison system as a child and never come out.

"The get-tough attitude is going to mean that some individuals will be under the supervision of the government from the cradle to the grave," said Kenneth Adams, a professor of criminology at Sam Houston State University. "That should worry us." Fr. Scully agreed, saying, "Kids are going to make mistakes, but we must never desert them."

Restricting Liberties

For the vast majority of teens who do not engage in serious misconduct (according to one statistic, only 0.5 percent of young people commit violent crimes), the get-tough wave means widespread restrictions on their civil liberties. Curfews are one example. "The police already have the ability to arrest teenagers involved in real crime. The curfew adds nothing more than the obligation to arrest the innocent as well," said Jordan Budd, staff counsel for the American Civil Liberties Union Foundation of San Diego and Imperial Counties.

In another instance, the Supreme Court has authorized random drug-testing of students in public schools, overturning an earlier standard that had required individualized suspicion before such tests could be administered. In effect, the court held that it's reasonable to suspect all teenagers of drug use. The cumulative effect of such moves, observers say, is to convince youth that they are second-class citizens, making them even less likely to develop a stake in adult society and less likely to respect its institutions.

According to some experts, the greatest danger of the crackdown mentality is that it obscures America's vision of what is really needed to help kids: time, energy and resources. "The get-tough approach is an indication that we've lost our way, that we don't know what to do," said John Roberto, director of the Center for Ministry Development in Naugatuck, Conn. "We should focus on the work that needs to be done to build the assets of young people."

Roberto, whose youth ministry programs serve over 100 dioceses across the country, said, "The blame-the-kids approach resorts to slogans and quick fixes. The real answer—building communities—is long-term hard work."

Church Efforts Succeed

The irony, Roberto points out, is that plenty of well-known strategies exist to address the problem. He pointed to a study by the Center for Applied Research in the Apostolate, which confirmed the success of several programs designed to nurture healthy young people. It's not like we don't know what works. What we need is the will to do it," he said.

"The greatest danger of the crackdown mentality is that it obscures America's vision of what is really needed to help kids."

Levin agreed that models do exist that point the way to a society willing to care for its children. He pointed to midnight basketball programs, gun buy-backs, toy gun buy-backs, active PTA/PTO organizations, peer mediation programs, programs in which college and university students serve as mentors, businesses creating summer jobs and community centers as measures with a track record of success.

Like Roberto, Levin sees will, not ideas, as the problem. "We have to reach our youngsters before they become criminals," he said. "We have to spend time with our kids and re-establish the credibility of our institutions—our families, our churches, our businesses, our universities, our schools. That's what we really have to do."

Challenges for All

Rebuilding that credibility is both an individual and a social challenge. Programs such as those called for by Roberto and Levin will cost money, and given the anti-tax mantra adopted by both Republicans and Democrats in the 1996 election, generating support will be difficult. Even more important, however, is that adults sacrifice time as well as dollars. "Teenagers need adults to be involved in their lives," said Fr. Scully. "We need to figure out where teenagers are coming from," he says, "and only sustained involvement can make that happen."

"Teens need time and energy from adults. We've pigeonholed it to the professionals, but everybody has a role to play," said Roberto. He also argues that the church must be a voice crying in the law-and-order wilderness. "The church has to take up this call and act more thoroughly. We can be a voice for young people. If we took up the call for young people, we could make a sizable difference," he said.

As long as America relies on law enforcement to deal with its kids, however, the more fundamental issues remain on the back burner. "In Dallas recently, they conducted a curfew sweep, and for 25 percent of the kids they could not locate a parent," Adams said. How, he asks, will "get tough" help solve that problem?

Blame Is Easy

For a society unwilling to invest the resources necessary to get at root causes, punitive measures may offer some comfort. "People feel insecure economically, and so there's resistance to dealing with delinquency through measures that require an investment, such as education, after-school programs and the like. In this climate of thought, it's a helpful belief to say 'It's their fault,'" said Professor Steven Kleinberg, a sociologist at Rice University.

The national discussion about youth crime seems to take a "blame the kids" stance for granted. The terms of the debate boil down to what hour the curfew should be set (President Bill Clinton favors 8 p.m.), and how many more jail cells to build. However understandable, Prothrow-Stith sees this approach as dangerous. "It's like trying to prevent lung cancer with better chemotherapy, or new surgery techniques," she said. "It can't be done. The severity of punishment we mete out isn't the issue. We have to get to kids before the problem develops."

For Levin, it's another analogy that troubles him as he surveys the adolescent landscape. "Building prisons to fight crime," he said, "is like building cemeteries to fight disease." Unless America rethinks its approach to youth issues, observers such as Levin fear, we may need plenty of both.

Bibliography

Books

Ram Ahuja	*Youth and Crime.* Jaipur, India: Rawat Publications, 1996.
Huub Angenent	*Background Factors of Juvenile Delinquency.* New York: Lang, 1996.
William Ayers	*A Kind and Just Parent: The Children of Juvenile Court.* Boston: Beacon, 1997.
Janet Bode	*Hard Time: A Real Life Look at Juvenile Crime and Violence.* New York: HarperCollins, 1996.
Gwyneth Boswell	*Young and Dangerous.* Brookfield, VT: Avebury, 1996.
Wanda L. Brown	*Stopping the Violence, Creating Safe Passages for Youth.* Sacramento, CA: Assembly Publications Office, 1995.
Jeffrey A. Butts	*Waiting for Justice.* Pittsburgh: National Center for Juvenile Justice, 1996.
Meda Chesney-Lind	*Girls, Delinquency, and Juvenile Justice.* Belmont, CA: West/Wadsworth, 1998.
Shirley Dicks	*Young Blood: Juvenile Justice and the Death Penalty.* Amherst, NY: Prometheus Books, 1995.
Anthony N. Doob	*Youth Crime and Youth Justice System in Canada.* Toronto: University of Toronto, 1995.
Clifford K. Dorne	*American Juvenile Justice.* San Francisco: Austin & Winfield, 1995.
Janet Dutrey and Linda Lantieri	*Peacing Our Schools.* Boston: Beacon, 1996.
Brenda Geiger	*Family, Justice, and Delinquency.* Westport, CT: Greenwood, 1995.
Henry A. Giroux	*Fugitive Cultures: Race, Violence, and Youth.* New York: Routledge, 1996.
Susan Guarino-Ghezzi	*Balancing Juvenile Justice.* New Brunswick, NJ: Transaction, 1996.
Vernon T. Harlan	*Youth Street Gangs: Breaking the Gangs Cycle in Urban America.* San Francisco: Austin & Winfield, 1997.
John Hubner	*Somebody Else's Children.* New York: Crown, 1996.
Edward Humes	*No Matter How Loud I Shout.* New York: Simon & Schuster, 1996.
Bruce M. Kirk	*Negative Images: A Simple Matter of Black and White?* Brookfield, VT: Avebury, 1996.

Cheryl Lee Maxson	*Responding to Troubled Youth*. New York: Oxford University Press, 1997.
Anne McGillivray	*Governing Childhood*. Brookfield, VT: Dartmouth, 1997.
Peter Reinharz	*Killer Kids, Bad Law*. New York: Barricade Books, 1996.
William B. Sanders	*Gangbangs and Drive-bys: Grounded Culture and Juvenile Gang Violence*. New York: Aldine de Gruyter, 1994.
Judy Sheindlin	*Don't Pee on My Leg and Tell Me It's Raining*. New York: HarperCollins, 1996.
Donald J. Shoemaker	*International Handbook on Juvenile Justice*. Westport, CT: Greenwood, 1996.
Andrea D. Shorter	*Out of Sight, Out of Mind*. San Francisco: Center on Juvenile & Criminal Justice, 1996.
Simon I. Singer	*Recriminalizing Delinquency*. New York: Cambridge University Press, 1996.
Ved Varma	*Violence in Children and Adolescents*. Bristol, PA: Jessica Kingsley, 1997.

Periodicals

James C. Backstrom	"Solving the Juvenile Crime Crisis: A Prosecutor's Perspective," *Juvenile Justice Update*, December/January 1997. Available from Civic Research Institute, Inc., 4490 U.S. Route 27, PO Box 585, Kingston, NJ 08528.
Susan Baily	"Adolescents Who Murder," *Journal of Adolescence*, February 1996.
Donna Bishop et al.	"The Transfer of Juveniles to Criminal Court: Does It Make a Difference?" *Crime & Delinquency*, January 1996.
Linda Bowles	"Crime and Culpability," *Washington Times*, May 25, 1996. Available from 3600 New York Ave. NE, Washington, DC 20002.
Philip Brasfield	"Eulogy for a Boy Next Door," *Other Side*, January/February 1995. Available from 300 W. Apsley, Philadelphia, PA 19144.
Rebecca Carr	"A Debate over Punishment and Prevention," *Congressional Quarterly Weekly Report*, October 5, 1996. Available from 1414 22nd St. NW, Washington, DC 20037.
Marshall Croddy	"Violence Redux," *Social Education*, September 1997. Available from National Council for the Social Studies, 3501 Neward St. NW, Washington, DC 20016.
Mark Curriden	"Hard Times for Bad Kids," *ABA Journal*, February 1995.
Chandra Czape	"And When She Was Bad . . . ," *American Legion Magazine*, January 1997. Available from 700 N. Pennsylvania St., PO Box 1055, Indianapolis, IN 46206.
Paula Dempsey	"Race in the Hood: Conflict and Violence Among Urban Youth," *Library Journal*, August 1997. Available at 1-800-677-6694.
Dale Eisler	"A Season of Deaths," *Maclean's*, September 8, 1997.
Christopher J. Farley and James Willwerth	"Dead Teen Walking," *Time*, January 19, 1998.

Bibliography

Grant Farred	"Menace II Society: No Way Out for the Boys in the Hood," *Michigan Quarterly Review*, Summer 1996. Available from University of Michigan, 915 E. Washington St., Ann Arbor, MI 48109-1070.
Mark Fraser	"Aggressive Behavior in Childhood and Early Adolescence," *Social Work*, July 1996.
Pam Frederick	"Cell's Angels," *City Limits*, February 1997.
Evan Gahr	"Towns Turn Teens into Pumpkins," *Insight*, February 3, 1997. Available from PO Box 581367, Minneapolis, MN 55458-1367.
Henry A. Giroux	"Beating Up on Kids," *Z Magazine*, July/August 1996.
Carey Goldberg	"Brutal Case Illustrates Trend of Guns' Replacing Toys," *New York Times*, August 3, 1996.
Jan Hoffman	"An Infant's Death, an Ancient 'Why?' " *New York Times*, December 22, 1996.
John Hundly	"In the Line of Fire: Youth, Guns, and Violence in Urban America," *Journal of Adolescence*, December 1996.
John Krakauer	"Loving Them to Death," *Outside*, October 1995. Available from PO Box 59384, Boulder, CO 80322-9384.
Mike Males and Faye Docuyanan	"Giving Up on the Young," *Progressive*, February 1996.
Elizabeth Mehren	"As Bad as They Wanna Be," *Los Angeles Times*, May 17, 1996. Available from PO Box 7032, Torrance, CA 90504.
Janet Reno	"Taking America Back for Our Children," *Crime & Delinquency*, January 1998.
Henry J. Reske	"When Detention Fails," *ABA Journal*, April 1996.
Dennis Romero	"Target: Parents," *Los Angeles Times*, March 21, 1995.
Hanna Rosin	"Tupac Is Everywhere," *New York,* June 2, 1997.
Martin Schreiber	"Juvenile Crime in the 1990s," *Japan Quarterly*, April–June, 1997.
Bruce Shapiro	"Behind the Bell Curve," *Nation,* January 6, 1997.
Daniel Sneider	"When Does a Child Become Responsible for Violent Acts?" *Christian Science Monitor*, May 17, 1996.
Jim Wallis	"With Unconditional Love," *Sojourners*, September/October 1997.
Woody West	"A Slap on the Wrist for 'Naughty' Kids," *Insight*, August 19, 1996.
Gurney Williams III	"Doing Time for Junior's Crime," *American Legion Magazine*, January 1997.
Gordon Witkin	"Swift and Certain Punishment," *U.S. News & World Report*, December 29, 1997.
Eduard Wynne	"Youth Disorder," *World & I*, February 1997. Available from 3400 New York Ave. NE, Washington, DC 20002.

Organizations to Contact

The editors have compiled the following list of organizations concerned with the issues debated in this book. The descriptions are derived from materials provided by the organizations. All have publications or information available for interested readers. The list was compiled on the date of publication of the present volume; the information provided here may change. Be aware that many organizations take several weeks or longer to respond to inquiries, so allow as much time as possible.

ABA Juvenile Justice Center
740 15th St. NW, 10th Fl.
Washington, DC 20005-1009
(202) 662-1506
fax: (202) 662-1501
web address: http://www.abanet.org/crimjust/juvjust

An organization of the American Bar Association, the Juvenile Justice Center disseminates information on juvenile justice systems across the country. The center provides leadership to state and local practitioners, bar associations, judges, youth workers, correctional agency staff, and policy makers. Its publications include the book *Checklist for Use in Juvenile Delinquency Proceedings,* the report *America's Children at Risk,* and the quarterly *Criminal Justice Magazine.*

Campaign for an Effective Crime Policy (CECP)
918 F St. NW, Suite 501
Washington, DC 20004
(202) 628-1903
fax: (202) 628-1091
e-mail: carter@crimepolicy.com
web address: http://www.sproject.com/home.htm

CECP's purpose is to promote information, ideas, discussion, and debate about criminal justice policy and to advocate alternative sentencing policies. The campaign's core document, available to the public, is the book *A Call for Rational Debate on Crime and Punishment.*

Coalition to Stop Gun Violence (CSGV)
1000 16th St. NW, Suite 603
Washington, DC 20002
(202) 530-0340
fax: (202) 530-0331
e-mail: noguns@aol.com
web address: http://www.gunfree.org

Formerly the National Coalition to Ban Handguns, CSGV lobbies at the local, state, and federal levels to ban the sale of handguns and assault weapons to individuals. It also litigates cases against firearms makers. Its publications include various informational sheets on gun violence and the papers "Overrated: The NRA's Role in the 1994 Elections" and "The Unspoken Tragedy: Firearm Suicide in the United States."

National Association of Juvenile Correctional Agencies (NAJCA)
55 Albin Rd.
Bow, NH 03304-3703
(603) 224-9749
fax: (603) 226-4020

NAJCA promotes research and legislation to improve the juvenile justice system. It opposes the death penalty for juveniles and the placement of juvenile offenders in adult prisons. NAJCA publishes the quarterly newsletter *NAJCA News.*

National Center on Institutions and Alternatives (NCIA)
3125 Mt. Vernon Ave.
Alexandria, VA 22305
(703) 684-0307
fax: (703) 684-6037
e-mail: ncia@igc.apc.org
web address: http://www.ncianet.org/ncia

NCIA works to reduce the number of people institutionalized in prisons and mental hospitals. It favors the least restrictive forms of detention for juvenile offenders, and it opposes sentencing juveniles as adults and executing juvenile murderers. NCIA publishes the monthly *Augustus: A Journal of Progressive Human Services,* the book *Juvenile Decarceration: The Politics of Correctional Reform,* and the booklet *Scared Straight: Second Look.*

National Council on Crime and Delinquency (NCCD)
685 Market St., Suite 620
San Francisco, CA 94105
(415) 896-6223
fax: (415) 896-5109
e-mail: pianica@aol.com
web address: http://www.nccd.com

NCCD comprises corrections specialists and others interested in the juvenile justice system and the prevention of crime and delinquency. It advocates community-based treatment programs rather than imprisonment for delinquent youths. It opposes placing minors in adult jails and executing those who have committed capital offenses before age eighteen. It publishes the quarterlies *Crime and Delinquency* and the *Journal of Research in Crime and Delinquency* as well as policy papers, including the *Juvenile Justice Policy Statement* and *Unlocking Juvenile Corrections: Evaluating the Massachusetts Department of Youth Services.*

National Crime Prevention Council (NCPC)
1700 K St. NW, 2nd Fl.
Washington, DC 20006-3817
(202) 466-6272
fax: (202) 296-1356
e-mail: tcc@ncpc.org
web address: http://www.ncpc.org/

NCPC provides training and technical assistance to groups and individuals interested in crime prevention. It advocates job training and recreation programs as means to reduce youth crime and violence. The council, which sponsors the Take a Bite Out of Crime campaign, publishes the book *Preventing Violence: Program Ideas and Examples,* the booklet *Violence, Youth, and a Way Out,* and the newsletter *Catalyst,* which is published ten times a year.

National Criminal Justice Association (NCJA)
444 N. Capitol St. NW, Suite 618
Washington, DC 20001
(202) 624-1440
fax: (202) 508-3859
e-mail: ncja@sso.org
web address: http://sso.org/ncja.htm

NCJA is an association of state and local police chiefs, judges, attorneys, and other criminal justice officials that seeks to improve the administration of state criminal and juvenile justice programs. It publishes the monthly newsletter *Justice Bulletin.*

National Institute of Justice (NIJ)
PO Box 6000
Rockville, MD 20850
(800) 851-3420
e-mail: askncjrs@ncjrs.aspensys.com
web address: http://www.ojp.usdoj.gov/nij/

NIJ is a research and development agency that documents crime and its control. It publishes and distributes its information through the National Criminal Justice Reference Service, an international clearinghouse that provides information and research about criminal justice. Its publications include the research briefs *Gang Crime and Law Enforcement Recordkeeping* and *Street Gang Crime in Chicago.*

National Legal Aid and Defender Association
1625 K St. NW, Suite 910
Washington, DC 20006
(202) 452-0620
fax: (202) 872-1031
e-mail: info@nlada.org
web address: http://www.nlada.org

The association provides information, technical support, and management assistance to local organizations that provide legal services for the poor. It publishes the *Capital Report* bimonthly and *Cornerstone* five times a year.

National Organization for Victim Assistance (NOVA)
1757 Park Rd. NW
Washington, DC 20010
(202) 232-6682, (800) TRY-NOVA
fax: (202) 462-2255
e-mail: NOVA@try-nova.org

NOVA serves as a national forum for victim advocacy by assisting victims of crime, providing education and technical assistance to those who assist victims, and serving as a membership organization for those who support the victims movement. NOVA publishes the monthly *NOVA Newsletter.*

Office of Juvenile Justice and Delinquency Prevention (OJJDP)
633 Indiana Ave. NW
Washington, DC 20531
(202) 307-0751

As the primary federal agency charged with monitoring and improving the juvenile justice system, OJJDP develops and funds programs to advance juvenile justice. Among its goals are the prevention and control of illegal drug use and serious juvenile crime. Through its National Youth Gang Clearinghouse, OJJDP investigates and focuses public attention on the problem of youth gangs. The office publishes the *OJJDP Juvenile Justice Bulletin* periodically.

VERA Institute of Justice
377 Broadway
New York, NY 10013
(212) 334-1300
fax: (212) 941-9407
web address: http://www.vera.org

VERA works with government and local communities to develop solutions to urgent problems in New York City and around the world. VERA's criminal justice and social reform initiatives have included bail reform, community policing, substance abuse treatment, urban economic development, jury reform, job training for people with developmental disabilities, and the prevention of adolescent violence. VERA maintains the Louis Schweitzer Library, a resource for those interested in criminal justice and social reform, and publishes the *Catalog of Selected Publications of the Louis Schweitzer Library.*

Victims of Crime and Leniency (VOCAL)
PO Box 4449
Montgomery, AL 36103
(334) 262-7197, (800) 239-3219
fax: (334) 262-7121

VOCAL is an organization of crime victims who seek to ensure that their rights are recognized and protected. Members believe that the U.S. justice system goes to great lengths to protect the rights of criminals while discounting those of victims. VOCAL publishes the quarterly newsletter *VOCAL Voice.*

Youth Crime Watch of America (YCWA)
9300 S. Dadeland Blvd., Suite 100
Miami, FL 33156
(305) 670-2409
fax: (305) 670-3805
e-mail: ycwa@ycwa.org
web address: http://www.ycwa.org

YCWA is dedicated to establishing Youth Crime Watch programs across the United States. It strives to give youths the tools and guidance necessary to actively reduce crime and drug use in their schools and communities. YCWA publications include a variety of resources on beginning new Youth Crime Watch programs as well as the book *Talking to Youth About Crime Prevention,* the workbook *Community Based Youth Crime Watch Program Handbook,* and the motivational video *A Call for Young Heroes.*

Youth Policy Institute (YPI)
1333 Green Ct.
Washington, DC 20005-4103
(202) 638-2144
fax: (202) 638-2325
e-mail: corpsnet@mnsinc.com

YPI monitors federal policies concerning youths and families and provides information on these policies to interested organizations and individuals. The institute believes most incidents of youth violence result from youths' watching violence on television and in movies. It also believes that schools and communities should try to solve the problem of youth violence. YPI publishes the monthly magazines *American Family* and *Youth Policy* and the triannual journal *Future Choices.*

Index

Adams, Kenneth, 188, 190
Adolescent Wellness Program, 53
African Americans, 21, 56, 62, 90
  and illegitimacy rate, 78, 79
  incarceration of, 66
  and murder rate, 63
  and poverty, 64
  and stereotypes, 169
  and suicide rate, 50
  and weapons at school, 44
Aid to Families with Dependent Children
  (AFDC), 106
Alabama, 79
alcohol. *See* drugs/alcohol
Alexjandrez, Nane, 131, 134
Allen, George F., 18
Allen, John, 185
Alpert, Geoffrey, 18
Altschuler, David M., 178
American Bar Association's Center on
  Children and the Law, 111
American Civil Liberties Union (ACLU),
  106, 108, 109, 188
American Correctional Association (ACA),
  182
American Enterprise, 175
American Enterprise Institute, 79, 110
American Federation of Teachers (AFT),
  139
American Psychological Association's
  Commission on Violence and Youth, 94,
  102
American Society of Criminology, 60
Al-Amin, Abu Qadir, 31
arrest rates, 57, 119, 121
  of African Americans/minorities, 56, 62
  increase in, 50-51, 161
    for youth-perpetrated homicide, 54, 55-
      56, 154, 186-87
  of one-time offenders, 28-29, 58
  see also juvenile justice system; youth
    violence
Artz, Sibylle, 34
Associated Press, 178

Atlantic Monthly, 60
Australia, 61
Ayala, Elizabeth, 134

Baltimore, 141
  City School District, 46
Bandow, Douglas, 111
Barclay School (Baltimore), 101, 103
Bastian, L.D., 44
Beck, A.J., 164
Bennett, William, 61, 79-80, 166
Berke, Richard, 18
Best Parent Is Both Parents, The (Levy),
  78
Bierman, Karen, 124, 125
Black Community Awareness
  Development Organization, 134
Blumstein, Alfred, 60
Bortner, M.A., 164
Boston, 142, 148, 187, 188
  Police Department, 53
  Ten-Point Coalition, 149
  Violence Prevention Project, 52
Boston University, 110
Boys & Girls Clubs, 52
Brady law, 53
Braithwaite, John, 85
Brisbane, Levi, 126
Brokaw, Tom, 136, 137
Brown, David E., 108
Brownfeld, Allan C., 78
Bureau of Alcohol, Tobacco and Firearms
  (BATF), 53
Butterfield, Fox, 154

California, 31, 88, 141, 170, 185
  arrest of minorities in, 62, 63
  and sentencing law, 65-66
  and trial of youths as adults, 28, 155
  Youth Authority, 68, 164
  see also Los Angeles; Santa Cruz
Canada, 61, 92, 170
Catalano, Richard, 73, 74
Cato Institute, 111

causes of crime, 27, 73
  availability of firearms, 24, 29, 136, 162
    as cause of increased violence, 30, 49,
      51-52, 167
    indirect, 62, 75
  cultural pressures, 34, 35
  dysfunctional family, 171, 172
  lack of community, 81-82, 90
  peer pressure, 36, 72
  see also parental neglect; poverty
Center for Applied Research, 189
Center for Ministry Development, 189
Center for Research on Aggression, 99
Center for Violence Research and
  Prevention, 156
Center on Juvenile and Criminal Justice, 31
Centers for Disease Control and Prevention
  (CDC), 44, 75, 104, 123
  Youth Risk Behavior Survey (YRBS), 41,
    42, 43, 48
Centerwall, B.S., 92
Chicago, 22, 56, 99, 119, 140
  community development in, 150
  and juvenile-perpetrated homicides, 51
  as place of first juvenile court, 154
  School of Criminology, 170
child abuse, 23-24, 99, 101, 125
  and child pornography, 80
  and domestic violence, 102
  and incarceration of children, 66
  see also children
children, 167, 181
  deprived of childhood, 96-97, 98, 155,
    167
  and need for attention/guidance, 71, 182
  and need for understanding, 31, 102, 183-
    84
  as victims of violence, 20-21, 22, 25, 75,
    87
    by adults, 50, 52
    under five years old, 139
    by peers, 19
  as witnesses to violence, 95, 96
    psychological effects of, 97-98, 100-
      101, 103-104
    in war zones, 100, 102-103
  see also child abuse; families/parents;
    schools
Children's Defense Fund (CDF), 49, 97,
  149
Children's Rights Council, 78, 79
Childs, John Brown, 131
Chisholm, Patricia, 33
Chronicle of Higher Education, 94
CIA (Central Intelligence Agency), 134

Clemons, Charles, 98
Clinton, Bill, 66, 80, 176, 190
  administration, 61, 80
Coalition for Juvenile Justice, 177
Cogswell, Catherine, 37
Coles, Robert, 142
Colorado, 27, 99, 115, 116, 170
  Department of Corrections, 118
Congressional Office of Technology
  Assessment, 73
Congress on Urban Ministry, 146, 149
Cornell University, 100
Corrado, Ray, 34, 35
Council on Crime in America, 63, 166
crime, 55
  declining, 66
  property, 51, 55, 67
  spread of, 17-18
  see also youth violence
Crime and the Community (Tannenbaum),
  171
Crime Bill of 1994, 186
Crime, Shame, and Reintegration
  (Braithwaite), 85
Crohnkhite, Clyde, 29, 30
Cuomo, Mario, 18
curfew, 106, 185, 187, 190
  ineffectiveness of, 109-10
  as restriction of liberty, 108, 188

Dallao, Mary, 115
Davidson, Howard, 111
DeJong, W., 41
Delattre, Edwin, 110
Delk, Yvonne, 148
Detroit, 17, 51, 56, 90
DiIulio, John, 60, 87, 109, 166
  on young as superpredators, 107, 167
Dole, Bob, 175, 176, 180
Donegan, Craig, 106
drive-by shooting, 20, 67
Drug Free Act, 46
drugs/alcohol, 71, 138, 179-80
  and children as dealers, 143
  economy of, 149, 162
  testing, in schools, 188
Dryfoos, G., 71

Edelman, Marian Wright, 97
Eisenhower, Dwight, 76
Elliott, Delbert, 72
England, 93, 102, 159
Erikson Institute for Advanced Study in
  Child Development, 100
Eron, Leonard, 92, 102

Fagan, Jeffrey, 156
Fagan, Patrick, 172
families/parents, 83, 141, 164, 166-67, 184
  as building blocks of society, 82
  and illegitimacy, 78, 79
  legal responsibility of, 110-11
  need involvement with children, 103,
    111-12
  need stability, 181
    for prevention of crime, 84-86, 90
  see also parental neglect
Al-Farabi, Ishag, 98
FBI (Federal Bureau of Investigation), 27,
  60, 87, 166, 169
  on arrest rates, 119
  Supplementary Homicide Reports
    (SHRs), 58
  Uniform Crime Reports (UCRs), 56, 161
fear of violence, 65, 66, 96, 98
  created by media/politicians, 49
  and demand for anticrime measures, 17
  and overreaction of police, 147
  punitive approach encouraged by, 186
  see also gangs; media; schools
Feder, Don, 75
Feld, Barry, 112
Fencheck, David, 147, 152
Fenley, Mary Ann, 123
Filner, Judy, 112
First Amendment, 94
First Freedom Coalition, 110
Florida, 156, 164, 170, 177
  Juvenile Justice Advisory Board, 157
  killing of tourists in, 65
  and violence in schools, 139, 140
Fox, James Alan, 59, 60, 87, 90
Freedom Schools, 144
Freeh, Louis, 60, 166
Freenfield, L., 164
Freud, Anna, 102
Friday, Jennifer C., 40
Fuller, Donald, 32

Gallup poll, 168, 176, 186
Gallup Poll Monthly, 60
gangs, 71, 87-90, 99, 137, 142
  increasing viciousness of, 165
  peace between, 134
  perceived as safe by kids, 101, 137, 145
  and perpetuation of violence, 87-90
  and racial identities, 89
  see also outreach programs
Garbarino, James, 100, 103
Garcia, Albino, 134
General Accounting Office (GAO), 177

George Washington School of Medicine,
  24
Georgia, 79
Gillespie, Nick, 119
Goldstein, Arnold, 100
Gondles, James, Jr., 182
Goode, Stephen, 138
Gore, Al, 149
Gould, Stephen Jay, 59
Great Depression, 62, 76, 135
Greenwood, Peter, 109, 111, 114, 120
  exaggerated comments of, 63
  on widespread nature of crime, 27
Greer, Lisa, 155
Greiner, Laura Ross, 99
Grief Assistance Program, 95, 97
Gun Free School Zones Act, 46, 48

Hacker, Nina George, 87
Hall, Victor, 126, 127, 128, 129, 130
Harris, Lou, 45
Harvard University, 70, 73, 187
  Divinity School, 149
  School of Public Health, 52, 107, 136
Hasty, Ron, 103
Hawkins, David, 73, 74
Hayes, Roger, 130
Head Start programs, 97, 106
Hector, Ken, 111
Henderson, Randi, 95
Hendrix, Napoleon, 103
Henry-Jenkins, Wanda, 97
Hepburn, Mary A., 91
Herbert, Bob, 19, 136
Heritage Foundation, 90, 173
Higgins, Tom, 28, 29
Hirschi, Travis, 71
Horwitz, Allan Y., 84
Huesmann, L.R., 92,
Huffington, Arianna, 87
Huizinga, David, 72

illegitimacy. *See under* families/parents
immigrants, 114
International Association of Chiefs of
  Police, 88

Jackson, Jesse, 107
Jackson, William M., 23, 24
Japan, 61, 85
Jarjoura, G. Roger, 78
Job Corps, 140
Johanson, Sue, 35
Johns Hopkins University, 101
Johnson, Haynes, 17

Johnson, Lyndon, 90
Johnson, Ulric, 53
Jones, Mac Charles, 148, 151
Jordan, Jim, 53
Journal of Research in Crime and Delinquency, 78
Joyce Foundation, The, 41, 43
Juvenile Justice and Delinquency Prevention Act, 70
juvenile justice system, 21, 155, 157
    leniency of, 25, 158-59
        fails to target repeat offenders, 168-69
        is exaggerated, 67-68
        Serious Habitual Offender Comprehensive Action Program, 169-70, 172-73
        see also arrest rates; juveniles tried as adults; prisons
juveniles tried as adults, 25, 27-28, 49, 155-57, 175
    benefits of, 162, 164-65
        access to records, 163, 173-74
    drawbacks of, 155-57, 177-81, 182-83
        include high recidivism rate, 178
    as increasing trend, 176-77, 186
    public support for, 168, 176
    in small numbers, 161, 162
    see also prevention of youth violence

Kansas City, Missouri, 147, 148, 149, 151
Kaufman, Miriam, 38
Kelly, Sharon Prat, 25
Kennedy, Robert, 60
Klaas, Polly, 65
Kleinberg, Steven, 190
Kline, S.A., 164
Koch, Ed, 157
Kotlowitz, Alex, 75
Kramer, Rita, 170
Kriescher, Barry, 177
Krisberg, Barry, 65, 111, 113, 155, 157
    on immigrants, 114
    on parent education, 112
    on teen curfews, 108, 109-10

Landsberg, Gerald, 123
Lanier, Saidat and Talonda, 20, 21, 24, 25
Larkin, June, 38
Lauritsen, J.L., 42
Lausell, Linda, 125
L.A. Youth, 54
Levin, Jack, 89, 187, 189, 190
    on adult neglect, 188
    on teen homicide rate, 186
Levine, Bettianne, 26

Levy, David L., 78, 79
LH Research, 41, 43, 44
Loeber, Rolf, 72
Loose, Cindy, 20
Los Angeles, 51, 56, 139, 148
Los Angeles Times, 26, 61, 62, 63
    on demand for crackdown on youth, 119
    on future growth of youth crime, 60
Lotke, Eric R., 54
Louisiana, 79, 176, 178, 179

MacLellan, Carey, 38, 39
Maginnis, Robert, 89
Males, Mike, 59
Martinez, Blanca, 133
McNulty, Paul J., 110
media, 19, 49, 54, 64
    and exaggeration of youth violence, 62, 65-66, 68
        and assumptions, 57
        through inaccurate statistics, 67
        and stereotyping, 59-60, 61
    television networks
        ABC, 66, 93
        CBS, 75, 93, 149
        CNN, 177
        NBC, 17, 93
    violence portrayed by, 61, 62, 91, 94, 113
        can increase violent behavior, 92-93
    see also fear of violence
Medved, Michael, 61
Mendel, Richard A., 70
Merton, Robert K., 171
Metropolitan Life Insurance Company, 136
    survey, 43, 44
Minneapolis, 17, 148
Mismeasure of Man, The (Gould), 59
moral values
    decline in, 76-77, 80, 98
    need for education in, 145, 160
Mothering Teens: Understanding the Adolescent Years (Kaufman), 38
Moynihan, Daniel Patrick, 79
Mr. Smith Goes to Washington (film), 77
Murphy, Lloyd, 24
Murray, Charles, 63, 79

National Academy of Sciences Panel on the Understanding and Control of Violent Behavior, 102
National Adolescent School Health Survey, 43
National Association for Mediation in Education, 112
National Association of Children's

Hospitals, 24
National Center for Injury Prevention and
    Control, 186
National Center for Juvenile Justice, 137,
    155
National Coalition of Barrios Unidos, 131,
    133, 134
National Conference of Mayors, 108, 109
National Council of Churches (NCC), 148,
    149, 151
National Council on Crime and
    Delinquency, 108, 155, 157
National Crime Analysis Program, 18
National Crime Survey, 18, 45, 66
National Educational Goals Report, 42
National Governors Association (NGA),
    108
National Guard, 140
National Institute of Mental Health, 99
National League of Cities, 138
National School Safety Center, 88
National Urban League, 137
Nauer, Kim, 122
Nelson, Lane, 175
New Jersey, 159, 185-86
Newsweek, 60, 61, 89
New York, 17, 51, 56, 79, 122
    availability of guns in, 136
    Central Park jogger attack, 87
    community service programs in, 150
    crackdown on truancy in, 181
    leniency of youth justice system in, 158,
        159
    punitive policies in, 18, 155
    reduction of school violence in, 140, 141
    survey of schools in, 40, 44, 47, 123, 125
New York Times, 18
New York Times Magazine, 63
New York University (NYU), 123, 130
North Carolina, 119

Office of Juvenile Justice and Delinquency
    Prevention (OJJDP), 23, 74, 183
Oklahoma, 64
outreach programs, 142-45, 151-52
    church-based, 146-48, 151-52, 190
    and media attention, 149
    and community cooperation, 150, 189
    see also moral values; prevention of
        youth violence

parental neglect, 23, 38, 67, 71, 190
    and absence of other adult supervision,
        30, 86, 137
    and drug use, 99

and repeat offenders, 171, 172
    see also child abuse
parents. *See* families/parents
Pataki, George E., 155
Paulson, Jerome, 24
Pennsylvania, 95, 96
Pennsylvania State University, 124
Picciano, Vincent, 21
post-traumatic stress disorder, 100, 103,
    123, 125
poverty, 27, 62-63, 71-72
    ignored by government, 63-64
    is linked to violence, 59
    is not direct cause of violence, 30, 76, 78
prevention of youth violence, 24-25, 52-53,
    74, 123, 165
    after-school programs, 25, 76, 106, 137
    Civilian Conservative Corps, 160
    education of parents, 106, 112
    and need for solidarity with oppressed,
        152
    peace movement, 132-35
        interracial, 134-35
    and punishment, 107-108
        dangers of, 185-87
        ineffectiveness of, 184
    time is right for, 52-53
    unrealistic plans for, 76
    see also children; curfew;
        families/parents; outreach programs;
        rehabilitation; schools
Price, Hugh, 137
prisons, 66, 131, 175, 190
    and detention centers, 163
    high cost of, 157, 165
    failure of, 155
    as deterrent to youth, 178, 181
    young offenders in, 177, 179
    see also arrest rates; juvenile justice
        system
Priver, Laura, 28
Prothrow-Stith, Deborah, 52, 53, 107, 113,
    114, 187
    on danger of punitive approach, 190
    on reduction of juvenile crime, 187
Public Agenda, The, 17

Quayle, Dan, 80

racism, 151, 169
    and stereotypes, 147
Rand, Michael, 21
Rand Corporation, 27, 63, 109, 120, 168
Reader's Digest, 60
Reagan administration, 171

Index

rehabilitation
  as appropriate for majority of young
    offenders, 29-30, 31, 180-81
  boot camps, 121, 140, 186
  as unpopular concept, 32
  see also prevention of youth violence;
    Youth Offender System (YOS)
Reiss, Albert J., Jr., 102
Reno, Janet, 18, 78
Richters, John E., 99, 100
Riley, Richard, 19
Roberto, John, 189
Robins, Lee, 71
Rodriguez, Luis, 132, 133
Romer, Roy, 115

Sampson, R.J., 42
San Antonio, Texas, 110
San Jose Mercury-News, 134
Santa Cruz, California, 133, 134, 148
Sanville, Deborah, 139, 140
Satcher, David, 75
Saucier, Michael E., 177, 178
Schiraldi, Vincent, 31
schools, 36, 72, 114, 123
  and conflict resolution programs, 45, 112-
    13, 125-26
  counseling in, 126, 127-30
  and drop-outs, 142, 144, 180
  security measures in, 107
  and truancy, 111, 145, 181
  violence in, 19, 138-39
    fear of, 167
    and need for discipline, 140
    reduction in, 141
  weapons in, 40, 42, 44, 127, 131
    increasing numbers of, 23, 41
      among younger students, 43
    prevention of, 46-48
    reasons for, 45
Scully, Rev. Michael, 187, 188, 189
Sex, Power, and the Violent School Girl
  (Artz), 34
Sexton, Robert L., 161
Shah, Khalid, 132, 134
Shakur, Tupac, 35
Shalala, Donna, 80
Shanker, Albert, 139
Sheley, J.F., 42, 47
Sikiki, Jitu, 134
Simon, Paul, 131
Sindab, Jean, 146
Singapore, 67
Slaby, Ronald, 70, 73
Smith, Douglas A., 78

Snyder, Howard, 155
Sojourners magazine, 148, 149
Spellman, Mark, 123
Spitzer, Arthur, 109
State of America's Children, The
  (Children's Defense Fund), 97
St. Louis University Law Review, 178
Stop of the Violence—Institute the Peace
  (STV-ITP), 132, 133
Stuckey, Henry, 134
suicide, 50
Swanson, Richard, 115, 116, 118
Syracuse University, 99

Tannenbaum, Frank, 171
Taylor, M., 44
Teens Against Gang Violence, 52
Tenant, Forrest, 30
Texas, 63
Thieman, Robert, 149
Things That Make for Peace network, 147
Thomas, Pierre, 20
Thornberry, Terence P., 72
Time magazine, 59, 119
truancy. *See under* schools

United Federation of Teachers, 141
United States, 17, 46, 61, 169
  arrest rates in, 121
  Bureau of Justice Statistics, 21, 40, 63,
    163, 164
  Census Bureau, 62, 187
    report on poverty, 63
  Congress, 49, 149, 160, 177
  Department of Education, 19, 52
  Department of Health and Human
    Services, 80
  Department of Justice, 19, 42, 52, 80, 120
    on anticipated increase in youth
      violence, 131
    on arrest rate, 107, 158
    on gangs, 88
    and increase in juvenile crime, 161, 166
      when youths are tried as adults, 177
    and *Juvenile Courts' Response to
      Violent Crimes* report, 162
  homicide rate in, 18, 66
  imprisonment rates in, 68
  Sentencing Guidelines, 174
  violent TV programs in, 91, 92, 93, 94
United States v. Davis, 174
Unity LA, 132
University of California at Los Angeles
  (UCLA), 120, 121
University of Florida, 156

203

University of Maryland, 103
University of Michigan, 102
University of Minnesota, 112
University of South Carolina, 18
University of Southern California, 29, 32
Urban Peace and Justice Summit, 147
USA Weekend, 75
U.S. News & World Report, 57, 59, 62, 63

Viano, Emilio, 81
Victim Services Program, 126, 127, 130
violence among girls, 35, 37, 122, 175
  causes of, 38, 137
  detachment of, 39
  as imitation of boys, 89
  increase in, 33, 36
  relative rarity of, 34
  see also youth violence
Violence Prevention Curriculum for
  Adolescents, 112
Virginia, 18, 22, 24, 155, 170
  Department of Juvenile Justice, 154
Virk, Reena, killing of, 33-34, 36, 37, 38,
  39
Vural, Marisa, 136, 137

Walchak, David G., 88
Walinsky, Adam, 60
Wallen, Jacqueline, 103
Wallis, C. Stephen, 138, 139
Wallis, Jim, 148
Wall Street Journal, 17, 79
Washington, D.C., 65, 106, 109, 119, 133
  child homicide victims in, 20
  scouting operation, 160
  single-parent households in, 79
  Youth Trauma Services Team, 98, 101
Washington Metropolitan Police
  Department, 109

Washington Times, 88
Watkins, Larry, 97, 98, 101
weapons. *See under* schools
West, Cornel, 89
West, Patricia L., 154
West Virginia, 79, 139
Wilkinson, Reginald, 182
Williams, Alex, 23
Williams, Gertrude, 101, 102
Wilson, James Q., 60, 61, 120, 121
Wolfgang, Marvin, 121, 164
Wootton, James, 166
World Council of Churches (WCC), 148
World Health Organization, 61
World Health Statistics, 61
World Vision, 148
Wright, J.D., 42
Wright, Joseph, 22, 23, 25

Young Offenders Act, 34
Youth Offender System (YOS), 115, 116,
  117, 118
Youth Peace Movement, 132, 133, 135
youth-perpetrated homicide. *See under*
  arrest rates, increase in
Youth Trauma Services Team, 98, 101
youth violence, 18, 19, 21, 40
  brutality of, 22, 88
  decreasing, 49, 53
  exaggerated, 54
  increasing, 23, 24, 161
    among younger violators, 26-27, 88
  for trivial motives, 90, 167
  and future, 60, 162, 166, 187, 188
  history of, 154, 157, 175
  reduction in, 51
  see also arrest rates; gangs; media;
    prevention of youth violence; violence
    among girls